"With a sonic boom, *Love InshAllah* breaks through the tired sound bites and stereotypes that can drown out authentic voices of Muslim women. This refreshingly diverse collection of stories about heartbreak, happily-ever-afters, and everything in between affirms that no one—orthodox or progressive, gay or straight—is immune from the universal hunger to love and be loved." —NAFISA HAJI, award-winning author of *The Writing on My Forehead* and *The Sweetness of Tears*

"These are gorgeously powerful women who love men and women, fight and laugh, lie to themselves and hold back nothing. You'll fall for some and be frustrated by others . . . You will not be able to put down these stories of women risking themselves for love." —LAURY SILVERS, author of *A Soaring Minaret: Abu Bakr al-Wasiti and the Rise of Baghdadi Sufism*

"As the Sufis say, the quest for the beloved is ultimately the heart's longing to unite with God. Listen with an open heart as these Muslim women reveal their journeys into the divine mystery of love." —KAMRAN PASHA, author of *Mother of the Believers* and *Shadow of the Swords*

"*Love InshAllah* is the most moving and emotionally honest book I have read in a long time. These bold new voices share stories that are romantic in the very best sense of the word—by turns intimate, sexy, funny, and sad." —CLARE WINTERTON, Executive Director of the International Museum of Women

"Given the damage done by Muslim men, non-Muslim men, and non-Muslim women claiming the sexual lives of Muslim women as their political territory, these stories provide a desperately needed corrective." —Michael Muhammad Knight, author of *The Taqwacores*

"*Love InshAllah* is beau   captivating as the next, the writer   of the heart, inviting the reader in   d this book." *Generosity Plan*

"This illuminating anthology . . . should be appl . . . , not only for its rarity and timeliness but also for its ability to celebrate these utterly normal, healthy, messy, and all-too human discussions about love and

sexuality which for too long have been buried under a veil of shame, fear, and self-imposed censorship." —WAJAHAT ALI, author of *Domestic Crusaders*

"What makes the book special is its celebration of differences and the ultimate transcendence of love. It is this common experience that connects not just the writers, but also the readers, pulled in as we are to these resonant, human stories told with exceptional skill." —ASMA T. UDDIN, founder and editor-in-chief of *AltMuslimah.com*

"Deeply touching and intimate . . . a perfect book to upend the stereotypes of veiled and abused Muslim women, these tales are filled with hope and humor and life." —IRVING KARCHMAR, author of *Master of the Jinn: A Sufi Novel*

"How we understand what love and America look like is expanded and made more representative of this country we all share thanks to this collection." —ALIA MALEK, author of *A Country Called Amreeka*

"Meaningful, poignant, and powerful." —RABBI RACHEL BARENBLAT, author of *70 Faces: Torah Poems*

"*Love Inshallah* provides us a rare glimpse into the intimate lives of Muslim women from very different backgrounds. The stories show that although the roadmap may be unique, the destination is universal—to love and be loved for who we are." —MANAL OMAR, author of *Barefoot in Baghdad*

"This collection is challenging and provocative. You'll be surprised, even shocked at their stories and the honesty with which they lay open their joys, as well as their vulnerable and sometimes wounded hearts." —SHELINA JANMOHAMED, author of *Love in a Headscarf*

"This book is an irreverent, witty reality-check. The women in this book are not only fulfilling a mission close to my heart—telling their own stories as Muslim American women, shattering stereotypes, building bridges—but they are doing so in a way that will entertain you, shock you, and make you fall in love with them." —ZAHRA SURATWALA, author, editor and co-founder of the *I Speak for Myself* series

EDITED BY
Ayesha Mattu &
Nura Maznavi

Love,
InshAllah

The Secret Love Lives of
American Muslim Women

SOFT SKULL PRESS
AN IMPRINT OF COUNTERPOINT

Library of Congress Cataloging-in-Publication Data is available.

ISBN: 978-1-59376-428-9

Soft Skull Press
An imprint of COUNTERPOINT
1919 Fifth Street
Berkeley, CA 94710

www.softskull.com

Printed in the United States of America

Distributed by Publishers Group West

10 9 8 7 6 5 4 3

Contents

To all those searching for love

Introduction

Muslim women—we just can't seem to catch a break. We're oppressed, submissive, and forced into arranged marriages by big-bearded men.

Oh, and let's not forget—we're also all hiding explosives under our clothes.

The truth is—like most women—we're independent and opinionated. And the only things hiding under our clothes are hearts yearning for love.

Everyone seems to have an opinion about Muslim women, even those—*especially* those—who have never met one. As American Muslim women, we decided this was an opportunity to raise our voices and tell our own stories. And what better tales to tell than love stories, which have universal appeal?

The search for love—with a Muslim twist—is captured in the title of this book, *Love, InshAllah*. "InshAllah" (God willing) encompasses the idea that it is only through the will of God that we attain what we seek in life, and is used widely among Muslims, regardless of their level of religious practice.

The subtitle, *The Secret Love Lives of American Muslim Women*, generated more controversy than we anticipated. Some accused us of playing into an Orientalist fantasy about Muslim women, or of writing a salacious exposé of our faith community. Our intent was neither. We wanted to challenge the stereotypes of the wider American audience by presenting stories that are rarely heard, and, within the faith community, to create a space for Muslim women to share their lives honestly, across the full range of their experiences.

This book is not a theological treatise or a dating manual. It is a reflection of reality. We recognize that no book can fully capture all the voices and perspectives within the community, but we offer this as a beginning. We hope these stories start conversations within families and between communities about the similarities that bind us together, while recognizing and respecting the differences that enrich us.

We had only one criterion for women submitting stories to this book: that they self-identify as both American and Muslim. Some within our country doubt our Americanness by virtue of our faith. Some in our faith community gauge our Muslimness based on adherence to practice. The writers of *Love, InshAllah* present complex lives and identities that defy both of these assumptions.

We start with "Allahu Alim." Every important journey ends by profoundly changing the one who undertook it. These writers set out on a path to find something greater than themselves.

The writers in "*Alif*" narrate the firsts that shaped their ideas about romance, sex, and their sense of self.

In "International *Habibti*," women live out the fantasy of falling in love with a beautiful stranger while traveling in Argentina, Sri Lanka, France, Egypt—or rounding an unexpected corner in New York City.

Next comes "Third Time's the *Naseeb*," where three women find unexpected and lasting love the third time around.

We end with "You've Got *Ayat*," in which age-old rites of love, dating, and courtship collide with twenty-first-century social networking.

These twenty-five writers are the daughters of immigrant parents and of families whose roots in America go back for centuries.

They live in small towns and big cities across the country and reflect a broad range of religious perspectives, from orthodox to cultural to secular. As such, they reflect the depth, breadth, and diversity of the American experience. For every story included in this book, there are thousands more out there, each as unique as the woman behind it.

We hope you'll enjoy hearing from these women as much as we have.

Ayesha Mattu and Nura Maznavi
February 14, 2012, San Francisco

Allahu Alim:

In Search of the Beloved

Leap of Faith

Aisha C. Saeed

"You're getting *married?*" my friend Amy exclaimed upon hearing the reason for my call. "Just so I'm clear, you've known him *six weeks* and—you're getting married?"

I launched into my rehearsed response. "When it's the right person, you just know. Some people live together for years and get married only to realize they hardly knew each other. You can know someone for five minutes or five years, but when it comes to how much time is enough to be sure, it varies from person to person."

"So when, exactly, in these six weeks did you fall in love with him?"

"Well . . . " I said, thrown off. I expected her skepticism, but I had not anticipated this question.

"Aisha, you do love him, don't you?" she asked, caution creeping into her voice.

"I'm not going to lie to you," I finally said. "I know I want to spend my life with him, so obviously I like him very much . . .

and, well, I don't know if I love him the way you might be asking me . . . but I know I will over time."

I heard nothing but static on the other line as Amy digested this information. "Let me get this straight," she finally said. "You don't love him. But you are marrying him."

"Well, yes," I said, understanding exactly how this might sound to her. "We met once and we've talked a lot—we've found so much we have in common and . . . "

"*Once!*" she squealed. "You met him once?!" Suddenly, her voice lowered to a near whisper. "Aisha, I've known you since tenth grade. I'm one of your best friends, and you know you can count on me. If you're being forced into this, you can tell me. I can help you."

I understood Amy's concerns. Had I not been raised in the Pakistani culture, in which brief courtships were perfectly appropriate—in fact, the rule rather than the exception—perhaps I, too, would be offering assistance to someone like me and helping her plot an escape. But this was not the case. Even though I was entering a semiarranged marriage, the prospect felt neither constricting nor stifling. Instead, I was happy, and excited for the future to come. But I had not always felt this way.

Reading *Pride and Prejudice* and discussing it with my fellow students in high school English class, I was struck by their reflections on what they clearly perceived to be a bygone era. For me, whispers of available suitors, and lavish wedding parties where girls of marriageable age with carefully applied makeup and gold jewelry hoped to catch the eye of a potential suitor or his mother, were not a thing of the past, but the present I lived and breathed. It was how my parents expected I would find my future husband; it's simply how it was done, though my own thoughts about the process were not quite as simple.

I disliked the whole arranged-marriage business. I minded

the twenty questions about my education and cooking abilities. I was not interviewing for a corporate job; I was looking for a loving partner in an intimate relationship. An arranged marriage seemed an unlikely avenue to get me there.

My mother listened to my expressed disdain for the process, nodded as I told her I did not know if I wanted any part of it, and then promptly told all her closest friends to keep an eye out for a suitable husband for me. One June afternoon, months after graduating college, I walked downstairs to hear my mother in deep discussion on the telephone.

"She's twenty-one years old. A teacher." A proposal, I realized. *Not again!* I thought with dismay, as I remembered a handful of awkward encounters at weddings and dinner parties with completely inappropriate suitors over the years. None had ever made it very far, but I did not want to relive any of that again.

"Do I have to?" I grumbled that evening, as my mother coerced me into lipstick and *shalwar kamiz* and handed my brother a camera.

"They asked for a picture," my mother said. "He'll send one, too, I'm sure."

I fumed as I slouched against the wall, wearing a beige and maroon shalwar kamiz, and glared at my brother, who was giggling. My enthusiasm ranked a notch below that of an inmate posing for a mug shot.

"*Beta*," my mother said, trying to elicit a smile, "Auntie Zaida met a nice boy on her visit to South Carolina. I talked to his mother. They seem very nice. There is no harm in sending a picture."

I had agreed to meet possible suitors, but now that the moment was at hand, I felt uneasy about having my picture sent to total strangers for inspection and approval. I envisioned a family circled around the photograph, pointing out blemishes or flaws, deciding if I was good enough to join their fold.

My apprehension showed in the photo. Instead of the traditional *ristha* picture of a shyly smiling girl, I stood with my arms crossed and my eyes fixed on the camera with a very clear expression of annoyance. As I watched the mailman drive away with my picture the next morning, I felt apprehensive. A rejection based on a photograph would hurt, but perhaps it would prove to my mother that this sort of arrangement was not for me.

Two weeks later, he called.

I took the phone to the study and shut the door tightly to grant myself privacy from curious cousins, aunts, and parents just outside the door. I felt my stomach turn over as I sat down and pressed the phone to my ear. I already knew what this conversation would be like before it began: awkward pauses, cleared throats, and a hasty hang-up. I wanted it done as soon as possible.

How wrong I was.

Talking to him felt anything but awkward; instead, I felt as if I were speaking to a long-lost friend who had suddenly ventured back into my life. We spoke for what felt like hours, our conversation moving seamlessly from one topic to the next. At the end of the conversation, he said, "Wow. I really liked talking to you." I could hear the surprise in his voice, and smiled; I had not expected this either. "Me too," I told him.

But then a month went by, and Kashif did not call. I tried suppressing my disappointment. It was only one phone call, but I thought we had had a connection.

I tried to forget about our conversation, until one day when my mother greeted me at the door with a smile as I came home from work. "Kashif's mother called," she said. "They were moving, so he hasn't had a chance to call again. But they want to come over this weekend to meet you."

The preparations for the visit began. That Saturday, I chopped the salad and helped set the table. A lunch of *biryani*, chicken *korma*, and *shami kebobs* sat on warmers. The curtains dusted, the crystal polished, we stared at the front entrance, waiting for the doorbell to ring.

Finally, the chime echoed through the house. I watched my parents walk to the foyer and open the door, greeting our guests. A friend who was an expert at this process had advised me to make a grand entrance, but my curiosity got the better of me. Though I had sent my picture, I had never received one in return, and now I was seized by fear: Why *hadn't* he sent a picture? What did he look like? As I heard them settle in the living room, I smoothed my beige shalwar kamiz and ran a hand over my braided hair before walking out to join everyone.

It felt surreal to walk into a group of strangers who might one day become my family. I greeted his mother and sister, and then for the first time I met Kashif: tall and lean, crisp white shirt, black pants, brown eyes, black hair, and a nervous smile that he flashed my way.

After a few minutes of polite conversation about the weather and the drive from South Carolina to our home in Florida, my father cleared his throat and stood up.

"We have orange, grapefruit, and guava trees outside. Why don't we take you on a tour?" he asked with a smile and an unusually loud voice.

We all stood up to follow him.

"No," my father said, shaking his head. He smiled at Kashif and me. "You two sit and talk."

Blushing furiously at my father, I watched as he led the others outside. We sat quietly in the living room and looked at each other. Kashif looked as uncomfortable as I felt. *Was our earlier conversation a fluke?* I wondered.

Finally we began speaking, making small talk at first but falling quickly back into the easy rapport that had captured my interest four weeks earlier. Later, over lunch, I listened to the sound of laughter and saw the smiles on my parents' faces. Our two families seemed to blend together seamlessly; I could see myself considering Kashif's parents family someday.

Over the next few weeks, Kashif and I continued to talk on the telephone. Like any newly dating couple, our conversations ranged from light topics to serious ones. One minute we were talking about our favorite movies, and the next about how many children we wanted. I was amazed by my own comfort level and how naturally I found myself sharing personal information with him. All my life I had thought I would detest this process, yet I found myself waiting eagerly for his phone calls and the hours we spent discussing life.

A few weeks into our weekly conversations, I had just taken my earrings off and placed them on the dresser, when the phone rang. It was Kashif, calling at our usual time. I smiled as I answered the phone. I had had an interesting day at work and hoped to get his take on it. But as soon as I heard his voice, I knew something was up. He sounded different.

He began our conversation by mentioning the first photo he had received of me and laughing. "I saw your expression, and I knew you were being forced to stand there and pose," he said. "You seemed so uninterested that you interested me!" I laughed, too, as I shared the story behind the photo. Then he grew quiet. His silence unsettled me. What was going on?

Finally, he cleared his throat. "I wanted to talk to you about something," he said finally. "These past few weeks, I have really loved talking to you. I feel like we have a connection. I know we met just that one time at your parents' house, and I could say that we should meet again and talk for months or years before I say this. But the truth is, I don't need to meet you again to know I want to marry you. I wanted to ask you—will you marry me?"

I sat down on the bed, letting his words settle over me. I had met him once. Spoken to him a handful of times. And now here he was, proposing we take the ultimate leap of faith, defy the logic and the norms of the world we lived in, and commit to spending our lives together. I should have been feeling trepidation, anxiety, or doubt. Before meeting him, I had thought with certainty that I would be unable to answer this question from someone I barely knew. But the truth was, *I did know him*.

I knew all I needed to. I knew he was kind, that he promised to support me and my dreams, and that we shared common goals and interests in life. Yet what I knew above all these things, a knowledge I could not then articulate, was that somewhere deep inside me, I knew I wanted very much to know him—and grow with him—for the rest of my life.

"Yes," I said into the phone, tears welling up in my eyes.

I had never been more certain of anything in my life.

We have been married nine years now, and I feel even more certain today than I did then that I made the right choice. What I did not expect, however, what I completely underestimated, was that I would continue to fall more deeply in love with him as time went on. *Alhamdullilah*.

Love in the Time of Biohazards

Melody Moezzi

There are few things less sexy than having the word "biohazard" plastered across your arm.

It's a predicament I've found myself in on more than one occasion, thanks to an annoyingly recalcitrant pancreas. Last time I was in the hospital, I spent three less-than-fun-filled weeks there, and "sexy" was the least of my concerns. There's nothing romantic about needing help stumbling to the bathroom, nor is there anything attractive about catheters, bedpans, or central lines. It's a pretty foul state of affairs for me, and it's a terrible time for witnesses.

Matthew and I were married in 2002, and in the decade since, he has always been my primary witness and assistant in such scenarios. He's learned from prior experience that it isn't always best to heed my directives. *Leave me alone; I don't want to shower; I don't want to go for a walk; I don't want to get up to pee; I don't want to move.*

I'm extraordinarily sedentary by nature, so it's hard enough getting me to move on an average day. Leave me in a hospital alone, and my indolence can reach lethal levels.

The first stint Matthew spent with me in the hospital was in the summer of 2004, and it lasted a little over a week. In his compassion, he respected my refusal to shower. Showering was torture for me, and required more energy than I could muster. After several days of Matthew's empathy, however, a strange smell began to permeate the room, and it didn't take long to notice that the stench was emanating from *me*. I have never before nor since stunk that badly. I knew I was wrong to ignore it, but, since I was frequently unconscious, it didn't affect me much. For those around me, however, it was all but intolerable.

Thank God one of the nurses was finally kind enough to give Matthew some advice without insulting me to my face. "You can't listen to her," she told him. "If you don't do something, we'll have to. And you don't want that." Water had to be involved, as fumigation was apparently not an option. So Matthew at last familiarized himself with one of the many uses for a biohazard bag.

After procuring one such bag from the nurses' station, Matthew cuts the bottom out and slides it over my arm, taping it around whatever mess of tubing happens to be there. He tapes it so tightly that I temporarily lose circulation, as even the slightest moisture can lead to infection. Matthew then helps me undress, undresses himself, and prepares for my torture chamber. Not exactly the stuff of romance novels. There's nothing like the smell of bleach and a surplus of handrails to kill the mood. He proceeds to do whatever my hands would do themselves in normal circumstances, and I follow his instructions (arms up . . . back to me . . . lean back, etc.). By the end of the hour-long ordeal, he generally has the added honor of having to support my body weight as well, since by that time I may have lost my balance and ability to stand. He helps my limp, exhausted body out of the shower and dries me off.

Back in the room, he pulls my hair back into a bun or a ponytail,

holds up a fresh hospital gown for me to walk into, and finally
reattaches all of my tubes to the IV. Then I generally ask for my
next dose of Dilaudid and pass out in the bed.

I met Matthew in the fall of 1997, less than a year after I first
got sick. I was seventeen and he was eighteen. It was my first
semester at Wesleyan University in Connecticut. Going there
was the smartest decision I've ever made—not just because of
the stellar education that I received, but because it brought me
to him.

I was walking home from the library one early autumn afternoon and had nearly made it back to my dorm, when Matthew
popped up out of nowhere. Trying to look nonchalant, though he
had clearly been running to catch up with me, he immediately
pled his case. He said he had noticed me and "noticed me noticing
him," which was a total crock of shit, as I'd never seen him before
in my life. Then he asked me out. His stealth tactics and physical
resemblance to Harry Connick Jr.'s serial-killing character in the
film *Copycat*, which I had just seen the night before, freaked me
out somewhat. Still, his audacity was impressive. I gave him my
number, and though I must have had fifteen pens in my bag, I told
him I didn't have any, so he would just have to memorize it. This
was the first of many tests I put the poor boy through.

He said he wanted to cook for me on our first date, and I told
him that would be fine, but that he would have to cook something fat-free because I had a bum pancreas that was unable to
digest too much fat. I told him how overindulging could easily
destroy my pancreas, which could result in organ failure, which
could then kill me. Talk about high maintenance! All of this was
a true possibility, though admittedly unlikely and melodramatic.
But if it scared him, he didn't show it, and either way, I didn't
care. It was just another test.

He cooked some sort of chicken, and later that night when he tried to play with my hair, I told him that there was no way I would ever date him. I told him that if I *did* date him, it would last maybe two weeks, and then I would lose interest. I also told him that as a good Iranian American Muslim girl, I planned on staying a virgin until I got married—always a shock to white American boys. It didn't seem to bother him, though. I said we could be friends, fully expecting this to end as every other such encounter had ended for me, and believing that I would never hear from him again.

As it turned out, however, he actually *did* want to be my friend, and we kept it that way for more than two years. Matthew spent the year after we first met studying abroad at the London School of Economics, so I didn't see him again until my junior year. Email wasn't too big in 1998, so we wrote letters and talked by phone. Our exchanges remained platonic, but the more I learned about him, the more I thought that if I ever had to be a man, I'd want to be him. I'd never felt that way about anyone before. It was sincere admiration.

I had to take a leave of absence during the second semester of my sophomore year in order to finally have surgery on my pancreas. It was becoming increasingly painful since the mass had been discovered days after my graduation from high school. Matthew was happy for me, especially because I told him that if I had to live on that damn diet any longer, I'd have to kill myself by eating a jar of peanut butter.

It was a risky surgery, however, and the doctors weren't prepared for what they would find. While they had originally thought I had a cyst, it turned out to be a tumor. The first few days, they told us it was malignant. My family was devastated. Pancreatic cancer has a less than 5 percent survival rate, so this diagnosis was nothing short of a death sentence. And at twenty years old, I wasn't ready to die.

My mother, a pathologist, fought the diagnosis, emphasizing that I had lived for two years with this mass. Had it been cancerous, I should have been dead already. So the doctors took a closer look and found that my mother was right: I had a very rare tumor that looked malignant but was in fact benign. I didn't understand all of the medical details then, and I don't understand them all now. I do, however, understand that this experience was the greatest gift God has ever given me. Few people have the privilege of facing and defying death at such an early age. It changes you.

I remember walking into a religious shop several years later and meeting the owner, a jovial, middle-aged Indian man who was missing several front teeth. As I browsed through the prayer beads, rugs, Qur'ans and other Islamic books, and paraphernalia, the owner approached me and asked, "What happened to you?"

I was confused. "What do you mean?" I asked him. He explained that I was young, and young people aren't interested in religion without some sort of serious impetus. He told me that he had had a near-fatal car accident, and that was what had brought him to God. I understood him immediately and told him that my pancreas was like his accident.

Shortly after my surgery in April 1999, I spent a summer in Montana. I had wanted to go there for years, and with my new lease on life, I was determined to make it happen. I headed out to Glacier National Park, where I worked in a gift shop and a café when I wasn't climbing mountains. I set out to do all the things I had always wanted to do, and I was in a rush to do them—the kind of rush I'd be in if I were running late for an important interview, but the interview was with myself. I had to figure out what I wanted to do with my life and how I was going to do it.

When I first called Matthew from Montana, I must have sounded crazy, and in many ways, I was. I had seen God in everything there—the people I met, the lakes I swam in, the glaciers I slid down, the wildflowers I couldn't pick, even the bears and moose that terrified me—and I had fallen in love with Him. It helped that I was reading the Qur'an and beginning to pray regularly, but what really brought me closer to God was this love and gratitude for creating a place like this for us humans to play in, however briefly. And just as northwestern Montana was in many ways the *place* that brought me to God, Matthew was the *person*.

I left Montana and headed back to Wesleyan with an entirely new mentality. Up until then, most of my education had been through books. Over that spring and summer in Montana, however, I had learned more from experience than I had ever learned from books. Drunk with a new love for life and for the God who had given it to me, I was ready to meet Matthew again. We were soon inseparable.

One night, we went to Staples looking for office chairs and ran into this crackhead, high as a kite, trying out the chairs as well. He was spinning as fast as he could on as many different chairs as he could find. Having failed to secure the perfect chair, and losing interest in the crackhead's new take on the Sit 'n Spin, Matthew and I proceeded to chase each other around the store and were nearly kicked out. Somewhere between the aisles of Post-its and highlighters, I realized that I was in love with him. I had never been in love before, but I knew this was it, and I prayed that God would never take him away from me.

I had seen so many of my friends fall prey to love. But this felt different. I knew that God would never give me more than I could bear, and I knew that after all that I had already been through, I couldn't bear to lose Matthew. Still, the probability of marrying my first love seemed painfully low, especially at the turn of the twenty-first century. Somehow, though, this reality didn't faze me. I fell.

Matthew and I were married in the fall of 2002. He converted to Islam in the spring of that same year. Though he was brought up Catholic, he had never been religious. He grew up to become a curious agnostic, and when he saw what Islam had done for me, he became interested. He's always been a voracious reader and delighted in embarking upon a close read of any book. So, when he did this with the Qur'an, I didn't think anything of it. I didn't expect or want him to convert; I wanted him to be who he was and to use whatever religion or philosophy he thought he needed to get him to where he wanted to go. It turned out for him, however, that Islam was a part of that religion and philosophy. I have to admit that I now consider his conversion a sort of bonus, but at the time I just thought it was unnecessary. Some of the best "Muslims" I've known have not identified as such, and some of the worst have pigheadedly insisted on doing so.

What I love most about Islam is its focus on actions. We are or are not Muslims on the basis of our intentions and actions, *not* on the basis of our words. And no one is fit to judge those actions and intentions save God Himself. So *calling* yourself a Muslim doesn't make you a Muslim any more than calling yourself a goat makes you a goat. Likewise, simply *saying* you're in love, with God or any of his creations, doesn't *mean* that you're in love. You have to *act* on it, even when you're not feeling particularly loving, lovely, or lovable. More than anything else, Matthew has taught me this, not by telling me, but by showing me.

Toward the end of my last hospital stay, after that final shower, as I was walking into the gown that Matthew was holding up for me, I had enough energy to pull off an imitation of Dr. Frankenstein's monster. Arms held up in front of me, walking toward the gown, rolling my eyes into the back of my head, I announced, "I'm alive!

I'm alive!" And I felt it. While these showers are always draining, they never fail to bring me a sense of rebirth in the end. My hospital memories tend to be vague, thanks to the fog that accompanies a stream of steady IV narcotics, but I have a clear memory of my last shower in the hospital.

Matthew laughed at my pathetic parody, then tied up the strings on the back of my gown and helped me back into bed. As he was reattaching the dreaded tubes, ignoring my persistent pleas for just a few hours of "freedom" from the rolling IV contraption, I looked up at Matthew and realized that *this* was love.

All the romance in the world couldn't match that moment. Overcome with devotion, I pulled his head toward mine. I told him that he was my favorite human and that I loved him more than anything or anyone else on Earth. He kissed me, laughed, and told me that maybe it was time to lower my dose of narcotics.

A Prayer Answered

Tolu Adiba

I suppose I've always known that I am gay. That did not deter me from converting to Islam when I was eighteen years old. Nor did it prevent me from becoming engaged twice to men I barely knew. Thankfully, both of those engagements fell apart. One wanted to move overseas, and the other was a married man who asked me to be his second wife. I was open to both options—I thought I might be able to improve my Arabic by living abroad, and being a second wife would ease some of the responsibilities of marriage. But when neither situation worked out, I was reflective, not heartbroken. I immersed myself in learning and practicing my faith. Given Islam's seemingly stern textual prohibition on homosexuality and strong emphasis on marriage, I uncritically accepted that I would eventually get married to a good man.

But my earliest and most innocent crushes, going back to fourth grade, were on girls. Although it didn't seem strange to me then, I did not yet have the vocabulary to describe my feelings. My attraction to women became clearer to me in adolescence, just as Ellen DeGeneres was coming out on television, but the pressure of disapproval from my family and peers kept me firmly in the closet. Also, because I was not completely averse to guys and because I wanted children, marriage to a man seemed much more realistic than ending up with a girl and having kids.

When I began the process of learning about Islam, I put my thoughts about my sexuality on the back burner. At the time, I was still reeling from an unrequited romance with a female friend. We had grown close our final year of high school, before we both went away to college and into the unknown. I spent months working up the courage to tell her that I loved her and wanted to be with her, even if the distance between our universities separated us. But when I told her, she recoiled and said, "I like guys." Ah—my gaydar had missed the mark. My proclamation hurt our friendship, so I quickly learned to become much more cautious and renewed my vow to remain closeted.

I was drawn to Islam's simplicity. I set out on a path, like so many lesbians and gays, trying to reconcile my faith and my sexuality, both of which I believed stemmed from God. But I lived in a state of fear, careful not to react externally to the harsh rhetoric I heard from imams and Muslim friends about gays, while cringing internally. I told myself that being gay was a test. This was the message I kept hearing, sometimes from leaders whom I looked to for guidance, even as they expressed a special revulsion reserved for homosexuality—or, more specifically, the thought of men having sex with other men. I thought—if my faith was strong enough—I could pray, fast, or marry my way out of my sexuality.

I vowed to remain closeted and celibate and eventually submit to marriage as a means of fulfilling my desire for companionship and to have children. I tried to push the thought of sex with a man out of my mind. I wouldn't be the first woman to grin and bear it, and polygamy was becoming an attractive option. At least I wouldn't have to fake it on the days reserved for the other wife.

Then, slowly, I began to discover the hidden world of gay Muslims. I was both excited and reticent. I was amazed at the courage of the writer Irshad Manji, who spoke openly about being both Muslim and a lesbian. Yet I could not embrace her as a role model, because we approached theology in very different ways.

Remaining mum on issues of homosexuality was my shield. But that shield began to crumble as I met other gay Muslim women who shared my level of religious devotion. There was Zain, a Somali Canadian in Toronto, whom I met while taking Islamic studies courses. Our friendship was slow to develop, but we kept in touch. We were both shy and introverted, which always makes it harder to confirm initial suspicions, and even when we finally did admit our attraction to each other, it became clear that our relationship could never work: Zain had more progressive views and wanted to be out, so she grew impatient with me as I so desperately tried to remain in the closet.

I didn't realize it then, but my conversion to Islam led me to embrace a very conservative form of Islamic belief, even though I'm rather liberal politically. I had created an identity that revolved around conservative religious piety, a sort of "ideal Muslimah," yet that very same identity was what would cause enormous spiritual and emotional turmoil for me as I tried to understand my conflicting impulses. Remaining in the closet did violence to a part of my identity, but it also allowed me to move comfortably in conservative Muslim circles. I feared the social rejection that would inevitably accompany coming out. I didn't want to lose the love and social support of my Muslim friends and the community that I had grown to depend on over the years. And I feared that I would have to withdraw from that community—which is such a vital part of my life and identity as a Muslim—in order to protect myself from the hateful looks and words toward gays and lesbians I've heard so often from those I considered friends and teachers.

Ramadan began soon after my second engagement ended, and I found myself absorbed in the rituals of the month, from fasting and praying to reading the Qur'an and giving in charity. Many nights I broke my fast at my local D.C.-area mosque, chatting with other Muslim women over spicy *iftar* dinners, and inevitably one would ask if I was married or looking to get married. Marriage, it seemed, was being pushed as a panacea for every problem, including loneliness, financial instability, immigration, unemployment, and the issue of educating and keeping new Muslim converts in the faith. In my community, a single woman not looking to get married is viewed with some suspicion and as a threat to an idealized conservative social order.

I prayed many nights during that Ramadan for Allah to provide me with a pious spouse. I didn't have a specific set of qualities or must-haves in mind; I just wanted someone I was compatible with in terms of religion and personality. Everything was negotiable.

Then I met Hafsa. We met online through our blogs and eventually realized we lived in the same area. We kept in touch through email. She was a convert like I was, and we agreed to meet, to exchange gifts for Eid. She was even more conservative then I was—she wore full niqab and abaya.

I don't remember saying much at our first meeting as we stood shyly on the sidewalk while crowds of Muslims in their brightly colored finery streamed out of the mosque all around us after Eid prayers. We exchanged simple gifts, books by Ibn Qayyim, and then parted to celebrate the day in our different ways.

Shortly after Eid, Hafsa invited me to her place to hang out, so we could get to know each other better. She called me twice to follow up: "So, when are you going to come over?" she asked. I'm not the most outgoing person—email and text message are my preferred means of communication. I felt shy but nervously agreed to meet her at her apartment the following Wednesday.

That Wednesday morning, I was anxious but I made sure to arrive a few minutes early—Hafsa had mentioned that she liked to be on time. I pulled up and waited in my car, trying to figure out how I could back out or turn around and go home, which is my usual way of dealing with social anxiety, always heightened around new people and situations. When I glanced up at the apartment building, I saw Hafsa staring at me through the window. *No turning back now*, I sighed. Somewhat reluctantly, I got out of the car and walked up to her door.

During our only other meeting, at the mosque, Hafsa had been wearing niqab, so I didn't know what she looked like. This time, she was wearing a flowery, soft yellow–colored, one-piece prayer garment. She opened the door for me, and I said "salaam" to her as I stepped inside to take off my shoes. She smiled at me, her eyes alight behind her glasses.

As I entered, Hafsa took off her prayer garment. Underneath she wore a long red tunic and black pants, and her dark brown, shoulder-length hair was tied back. That first sight of her took my breath away. I quickly lowered my gaze and pretended to be distracted by where to put my shoes on the shoe rack. *Tolu, behave*, I reproached myself internally. She was married and completely unavailable.

To my great relief, our conversation that morning flowed effortlessly. We found that we had much in common, despite our very different backgrounds and experiences. She was of mixed European descent, grew up in the Midwest, converted to Islam while in college, and married soon afterward, hoping to start a family. I grew up on the East Coast in a small college town, the daughter of African immigrants, and, after my conversion, took an extended break from college. But we connected over our shared American cultural nuances and values, our love of reading and tuna fish with apples, and our fondness for all things Mac. We quizzed each other with all the litmus-test questions for conservative Muslims:

Do you listen to music?

We had both thrown out our massive CD collections at some point after our conversion.

How do you celebrate the holidays with your non-Muslim family?

While neither of us consciously "celebrated" the holidays, we did nonetheless join in family gatherings on these occasions.

What do you think of hijrah *to a Muslim country?*

Hafsa mentioned that she'd like to make *hijrah* to learn Arabic, live surrounded by other Muslims, and wake up hearing the *adhan*. I told her that I was quite happy right here in the United States. It was hard for me to imagine anywhere else feeling like home.

Then, suddenly, Hafsa began to tell me about a friend she had met soon after her conversion. This super-Salafi niqabi sister had gone from being married with kids to being an out lesbian living with her partner, and had left much of her Islam behind. The community had ostracized her.

I reacted to Hafsa's story with compassion and said that we all have our tests and that I hoped for the best for her friend. Hearing stories like this one always hurts and scares me, because I fear being forced to choose between two integral components of my identity: my faith and my sexuality. I didn't know it then, but Hafsa was testing me to see if I was a homophobe. It never occurred to me that she might also be gay.

Over the next few months, our friendship deepened and we began to spend more time together. We met regularly at Hafsa's place every Wednesday; sometimes we went out, and other times we stayed in and chatted about everything from the news to our favorite books to how we dealt with our non-Muslim families. No matter how many hours we spent together on those Wednesdays, the time always seemed to pass much too quickly. Our days would end when her husband returned home from his long day at work. We parted reluctantly, but with the comfort of knowing we would meet again the following Wednesday, *inshAllah*.

Two months after we met, Hafsa went to visit her family for several weeks. It was only then that I realized how close we had become. I missed her terribly; she was always on my mind. So I wrote an email to tell her in a gentle and open way that I loved and missed her. She responded warmly, and we agreed to meet up when she returned. I had no intention of professing my true feelings for her—I was still fully inside the closet and intended to stay there. Hafsa and I had even discussed finding a husband for me, and she had sent me one brother's typed one-page marriage profile.

In the meantime, the pressure from my community to get married didn't ease up. While I was volunteering at a fundraising dinner for a local Muslim school, a sister tried to hook me up with a Ghanaian man from New York. I thanked her but said no thanks. Even though I was flexible in terms of the specific qualities I was looking for in a partner, I knew I wanted to marry an American—someone born and raised in the United States, who understood and shared a similar cultural outlook.

The Wednesday after Hafsa returned, we resumed our weekly routine. I was delighted but also troubled. I mentioned that there were things I found difficult to talk about and recounted an earlier incident I had witnessed, involving gay Muslims who were told they couldn't be gay and Muslim at the same time, perhaps as my own way of testing whether Hafsa was safe for me. She did not press or try to pry more information out of me, and I was grateful for that.

That night, reflecting on my past experience and on my growing closeness to Hafsa, I was in turmoil. I had fallen in love. But she was married. I didn't think I could ever tell her that I loved her, because I didn't want to lose our friendship. And I didn't want to be a home wrecker.

Perceptive as ever, Hafsa wrote me an email that same night and asked me if I was going through my own trial:

You've been thinking a lot, it seems, about other people's trials. I wanted
to make sure that you're okay, that you're not going through some
major trial of your own without me even knowing. I'm good at handling
people that are extroverted with their emotions, but you're not so much
like that. Even if you were falling apart inside, I wouldn't expect you to
burst into sobs and fall into my lap and ask for a hug and a cup of tea
(that's what I generally do at the peak of crisis, so watch out).

How could I tell her that my trial, my inner turmoil and
struggle, was my love for her? My trial was one that gay Muslims
rarely feel comfortable enough to talk about with anyone fearing
rejection—or worse.

Her email continued:

I sometimes get the feeling that I know exactly what you're not saying.
I recognize the look in your eyes when you talk about it. Sometimes, I
just want to say, "Yes, I was there. Can't you tell? That's my story, too.
Have any advice?" And then I realize I'm probably just projecting. But it
is sort of a comforting thought, isn't it? To think that we're not all alone
in these trials—the ones we can't talk about.

That Saturday, I went to her house to talk. The conversation
was painful and stilted. I wasn't ready to open up; I was afraid.
But Hafsa was determined and insisted, and soon we were talking
about my previous unrequited love. As always, I told my story
without the use of any pronouns, and Hafsa asked me if I was gay.
It was a relief to say yes, though terrifying at the same time.

To my great surprise, Hafsa didn't reject me; she told me that
my story was also her own. Years earlier, unable to reconcile her
faith with her sexuality, she had broken up with her girlfriend
and married one of the first men "with a beard and short pants"
who came along.

I loved her and she loved me. Had we both been single, maybe things would have been different. But she was married and wanted children. She wanted normalcy, something a relationship or a marriage between us (could we even get married?) would never provide within a conservative Muslim community like ours. "I don't want to have to hide, not from my friends and not from my family," Hafsa said.

Knowing that I was not alone in my struggle, and being able to talk to her openly, was a relief and brought us closer together. But my inability to reconcile my faith and my love made me want to run far away from her. I thought about moving back to my hometown. It was too painful to stay. I shared with Hafsa part of Graham Greene's heartbreaking novel *The End of the Affair*, in which the character Sarah breaks things off with her lover:

SARAH: Love doesn't end just because we don't see each other. People go on loving God all their lives without seeing Him.

BENDRIX: That's not my kind of love.

SARAH: Maybe it's the only kind.

Hafsa was also in turmoil. Not knowing what to do, she called her mother for advice. She told her mother that she had fallen in love with a friend, someone she could never marry. Hafsa's mother asked, "Is it Tolu?"

Two months later, Hafsa asked for and was granted a divorce. She didn't tell her husband that she was gay. We moved in together, though publicly we remained closeted. *We are just good friends*, we'd tell everyone. *We are living together to help with the rent and live closer to the mosque.* Those early days were some of the happiest of my life; our relationship was fulfilling, and I was content. We encouraged each other in our acts of worship, and we learned from each other's experience.

The pressure to hide as we lived together, reconciling our sexuality with our faith, exacted a high emotional price. After a few months, I tried to come out to my mother to share with her the happiness I had found with Hafsa. I told her that we were very good friends and that we had become very close. When she asked, "Are you a lesbian?" I froze and I lied, retreating back into the closet. She asked me again several years later, after increased media coverage of a spate of gay-teen suicides. Although I thought it was a sweet gesture that she was reaching out, perhaps afraid of losing me, I still couldn't tell her the truth. Today, when I see out gay women or couples, I'm awestruck and a little envious of their courage to live openly and hope someday I will be able to do the same.

The prayer for a pious spouse that I made repeatedly during those long nights in Ramadan was answered in a most unexpected way. Hafsa and I were in love, two orthodox girls with an unorthodox love, not willing to give up on our faith or each other. We moved forward, happy but conflicted. Though our relationship didn't last, I am ever so thankful for our years together.

Is being a gay Muslim and finding love a contradiction or disgusting? I don't think so. Does it really get better? Sometimes, but not always.

Love at Third Sight

Patricia M. G. Dunn

"You converted because of your husband," people would tell me.

"No" was always my answer, whether they had meant it as a question or not.

I lied, of course. I lied to the world. I lied to myself. The truth is, if it weren't for Ahmed, I might have never found Islam. But I couldn't admit it, even to myself. I was a feminist, and I wasn't changing religions for any man. I wasn't changing anything for any man.

He never asked me to convert. It was fine with him that I was a feminist Marxist. "I respect all religions," he said. And Marxism was the most evangelical of all the faiths either of us had ever been exposed to. But it was through my questioning—badgering—of his beliefs that I found my place in Islam, a place big enough for this Catholic-Italian-White-Marxist-Feminist-Forever-a-Bronx-Girl. It was comfortable. It was home.

But really, my conversion to Islam is a love story. A love story between God and me. Well, eventually—but before God, there was a man named Ahmed.

I was a hardcore-feminist, do-the-right-thing-and-fight-for-it, type-A personality when I met Ahmed. He was also a hardcore-feminist, do-the-right-thing-and-fight-for-it, type-A personality, but he was a type A from L.A., which meant he was a bit more laid back than my type A from New York. He never stressed about showing up to a party late or not showing up at all without calling. "It's L.A.," he'd say. "People don't expect you to call." He was right, though in the ten years I lived in L.A., I never became comfortable with that.

According to him, it was love at first sight. Well, maybe second sight.

It was early 1988. My friend Leila and I were giving a talk at UCLA about the women of the Intifada. We had just returned from a two-week student delegation to the West Bank and Gaza. There were a good number of people in the audience, but during the question-and-answer period, there were very few questions. I couldn't tell if it was because we had already given all the answers or because people had long since stopped listening. On our way out, I was feeling a little unsure of myself, when a tall redhead stopped me and introduced himself, extending his hand to say, "My name is Ahmed."

I had never met a twenty-three-year-old guy who was so formal and polite, without being the least bit strange or creepy. He told me humbly how impressed he was with all that I had said, and how it was great to hear people at UCLA talking about the Palestinian struggle. I was flattered, and thought he seemed very nice. He also had the best-shaped nose I'd ever seen on a guy—a nose that could be on the face of a lion. It gave him a majestic yet humble look. He was hot, but dating, relationships, and love were the last things on my mind when I met him.

Who had time for men when there were flyers to hang and phone banks to organize? Well, I guess I did, but only if it was the right kind of man. I was getting tired of dating, falling in love, and having my heart broken, but was still in a falling-for-charismatic-jerks phase. I had a weak spot for the kind of guy who sweeps you off your feet and then, after he's convinced you that he's the one for you, takes out the dustpan and, well, let's just say you wake up with eyes swollen from crying and wonder how long it will take this time for the sharp pain in your gut to dull.

I thanked Ahmed for his kind words and walked away. On our way back to our Venice Beach apartment, Leila said, "He was totally into you. Couldn't you tell?"

I couldn't. Besides he wasn't my type. "Not interested," I said.

"Because he's a nice guy," she said.

"Exactly," I said.

She huffed and then said, "Nice could actually be good for you."

Maybe she was right. Why not?

Then she told me that the guy who had spoken to me was Ahmed Nassef, the head of the Muslim Student Association (MSA) on campus. *That* was why not. At that time in my life, the word "Muslim" meant religious and possibly fanatic, and I had spent too many years distancing myself from my wacky Catholic upbringing to even consider dating a religious guy.

Of course, when I was in the West Bank and Gaza, many of my host families were Muslim, and I remembered how in awe I had been the first morning when the call to prayer had woken me up. I had watched through a crack in my bedroom door as the mother and daughter who were hosting me prayed, and I had felt calm, something I had never felt before in relation to prayer. When I was growing up, prayer meant obligation, confession, and begging for forgiveness—in other words, it was, for me, an anxiety-ridden experience.

Still, in my mind, watching this mother and daughter share what looked to me like a true spiritual experience had nothing to do with Islam, or my idea of it then. Besides, what people did in the privacy of their homes was one thing, but God had no business getting involved with politics.

Leila tried to explain to me that the MSA at UCLA was one of the most progressive groups on campus, and that Ahmed was totally cool.

"Haven't you ever read his column in the *Bruin?*" she asked.

I had thought he looked familiar. I, too, was writing a column for the university paper, and we were both considered to be on the left. I think the paper even ran our columns on the left side of the page. And when I read Ahmed's commentaries, I always thought they were smart, cool, and very progressive, but the Muslim thing threw me for a loop. There were no Muslims when I was growing up in the Bronx—just FUCK IRAN T-shirts during the Iran hostage crisis.

I didn't give Ahmed another thought until the next time we met, eight months later. It was the day of the 1988 Dukakis vs. Bush debate, which UCLA hosted. I was in a room with my supposed comrades, who were all shouting at me because I refused to support either Dukakis or Bush. "Dukakis is the lesser of two evils! We must support him!" my good friends yelled in my face.

"No. We don't!" I heard a voice shout from behind me. It was the president of the Muslim Student Association, coming to my defense. "We need to support who we believe in."

That marked the beginning of a great friendship.

And we stayed friends for years. Ahmed wanted more, he asked for more, but I wasn't into him in "that way." I wanted to feel "that way" about him, though—he was smart and sweet, and for every joke I made, he had an even funnier response. I'd be upset after a call from my mother during which she'd spent an hour telling me all the ways I needed to change my life—the same call I got every Sunday at three—and Ahmed would just spring into Steve Martin's "cruel shoes routine." No guy ever made me laugh or think as much as he did.

So of course I loved him. But I was not *in* love. Being in love meant feeling sick to your stomach most the time. So we stayed good friends and then, after one of those guys who did make me sick to my stomach broke my heart, my friend Leila said, "Hey, maybe it's time to give the nice guy a chance." And I did. And after a year of giving "the nice guy" and "love" a chance, we decided to get married. But it wasn't until we'd been married almost four years that Ahmed and I would share an experience that would finally get me to shout, "I am *in love* with this man!"

It started on the morning of Ahmed's thirty-third birthday. He wanted only one thing. It was the same thing he wanted every weekend, but—between family obligations, work, and a wife who treated lounging during daylight hours like it was a sin—something he rarely got: a Sunday morning in bed reading the newspaper from front to back, drinking a triple-espresso nonfat latte, and snacking on a French baguette and cheese.

Grateful I didn't have to make a trip to the mall to buy him a present, I woke up early, and before Ahmed opened his eyes, he had the *Times*, coffee, bread, cheese, and a bouquet of his favorite purple and yellow tulips at his bedside. "Happy birthday," I said, kissing his dry morning lips.

"Thanks," he smiled.

I did good, I thought, and was turning to leave him to his fantasy Sunday, when he said, "Don't go. Stay with me."

I thought, *I should have just gotten him a CD player instead*.

I was one of those women who are up and on the move as soon as they awaken. There was always something to do, and in my mind, it was always dire. This was one of the fundamental differences between Ahmed and me: He loved to nap, and I could barely sleep.

But it was his birthday.

I took off my shoes but left my street clothing on, and got back into bed.

He put his arm around me, which felt nice. *Maybe this would be fine*, I thought. Then he lifted the front section of the paper to his face and handed me the book review section, one of those "should-reads" for writers that had never become a "want-to-read" for me. I flipped the pages, until all the reviews of books that weren't mine started to make me feel that I had to get out of bed. I had just started my MFA in fiction; I needed to be writing. But Ahmed's hold around my shoulders was tight.

I looked at the Paulo Coelho novel on my nightstand and wished I hadn't finished it the night before. I had to do something, because I was close to sighing mode. When I sighed, Ahmed always stopped what he was doing and said, "Okay, let's do something you want to do." But it was his birthday, and I knew that even if I said that I didn't want to do anything but lie there with him, that sigh would make it impossible for him to relax. *And just look at him*, I thought, smiling as he read and chewed and sipped. There was something else on the nightstand. I reached over to get it.

"Where are you going?" He sounded sad.

"Nowhere. I'm just reaching for this," I said, pointing to the blue-and-white booklet on the nightstand.

"This is nice. Thank you." He kissed me on the top of my head and went back to his paper.

The blue-and-white booklet was the coverage information for our new health plan. For most people, reading this sort of material was as stimulating as drinking half a bottle of NyQuil. But I wasn't most people. I was a need-to-know-it-all personality who liked reading about medical procedures and was always up for any test a doctor wanted to prescribe. I was actually disappointed when a doctor told me there was no need for me to have a colonoscopy.

So this was a good way to pass the time. This plan covered a whole slew of procedures and treatments that our old plan hadn't, like acupuncture, which I knew could be costly. I had tried it before, but it was hard to tell whether it was working or not, because I wasn't treating any particular symptoms. I just thought it would be interesting to try.

Then I got to the section on infertility testing. We were covered. For everything.

"Ahmed," I whispered.

"Yeah," he answered, with his eyes on his paper.

"Don't you think it's strange that we have been together for years—barely using protection—and I've never gotten pregnant?"

"No."

Come to think of it, I had made a few stupid choices before Ahmed and had never gotten pregnant then, either.

"What if I can't?"

Ahmed put his paper and his plate with the last bite of cheese and bread on his nightstand, and released my shoulders.

"Sit up a second."

I sat up and looked at him.

"Are you telling me you want to have a baby now?"

I didn't hesitate. "No."

I wasn't ready to have children. Until Ahmed, I hadn't even wanted them at all. But I knew the first time we took a twelve-hour flight to Cairo together that I wanted to have a child with him. Every kid on the plane was drawn to him. Toddlers took turns sitting on his lap, and none of the mothers flinched. They trusted this stranger. He was too good with children not to be a father, and I figured he probably had enough maternal instincts for the both of us.

"Okay, so, what are you saying?"

"I just want to know I can have one. And since we've got this great coverage right now . . . "

"Pat," he said, in a tone that told me I had broken his mood, "the reason we have never gotten pregnant is because it's just not been the right time . . . When we are ready to try, we will just have to have a lot more sex, and Allah will take care of the rest, *inshAllah*."

Even after having been Muslim for almost seven years, I still got thrown when Ahmed played the *inshAllah* card. "God willing" was the translation, and sometimes it was comforting to know that God was going to take care of it all. But sometimes, especially recently, it said to me, *How dare you question God's intention*?

When it came to our faith, this was the major difference between us. Ahmed had been born into his faith, so there was a lot he could take for granted. As a convert, I had to work for everything I believed. I had to think about the whys of my choices, which, in the early days, meant looking a lot to Ahmed, not necessarily to God, for answers.

This wasn't to say that Ahmed didn't study and question what it meant to be a Muslim. He did. All the time. He might have left his Islamic studies graduate program with everything but his dissertation done, but there was never a time when he wasn't reading or writing about Islam. For this reason, I turned to him with almost all of my questions. They started with the rudimentary ones—"If you swallow accidentally while you brush your teeth, does that mean your fast doesn't count?"—and eventually, after more studying and searching on my part, became more sophisticated: "Can a woman really divorce her husband if he doesn't please her sexually?"

Though Ahmed encouraged me to lead the prayer when we prayed together, I refused, even when he insisted. He was the authority. Besides, he sounded so beautiful when he recited the

Qur'an in Arabic. I sounded completely ordinary when I recited the translated version. In those early years, I was translating constantly, and not just language, but also rituals and belief systems. I was still very much a Catholic who believed that an individual could not have a one-on-one relationship with God. You needed an intermediary, some authority, someone more worthy to intervene on your behalf. I realize now that for a while I didn't just make Ahmed my teacher; I made him my priest. When it came to matters of faith, I wanted him to call the shots.

But on Ahmed's birthday, as we discussed the possibility of having a baby, I didn't repeat *inshAllah* and let the matter go, as I usually did. This time I repeated it . . . and kept talking. "I think Allah has given us these tools, and I want to use them. Besides, who knows how long we will have this kind of coverage?"

"It's your choice," Ahmed said as he got out of bed, bringing the conversation and his dream Sunday to an end.

Life continued on fast-forward, and while balancing graduate school, writing (or agonizing about how I wasn't writing), my family, Ahmed's family, and all of my other obligations, I took tests. All sorts of tests.

In the beginning, I felt like a fraud when I went to my fertility-clinic appointments. I knew the women waiting with me in the reception area weren't there because they just happened to be curious about their fertility and had good health insurance. These women were like the ones I had watched so often in movies—women who wanted to have children. At first they left it to fate and spontaneous, passionate lovemaking. When that didn't work, they took the more calculated, scientific route—temperatures taken every morning, ovulation pinpointed to the day, bedrooms turned into laboratories. It wasn't until they felt like failed science experiments that they came to the clinic. These women were now desperate for children, which made every test either the possible answer to their prayers or the proof positive that their worst fears were true: They couldn't conceive, and no amount of medical intervention could change that.

After two years of blood, urine, and cervical-fluid tests, ultrasound scans, an endometrial biopsy, and a hysterosalpingogram (which inspired "The Blue Dye Up My Uterus Blues," my first and only blues poem), my own fertility started to matter.

The hardest thing about the medical field is that—as many answers as it has—it doesn't have them all. In my case, it didn't have any. The tests all came back negative. Everything looked okay. Ahmed's sperm tested well, too—plenty of good swimmers, the doctor said. So why, after five years of unprotected sex, were we not pregnant? The fertility specialist hadn't a clue. And neither did I.

After almost another year of now trying to get pregnant and failing, Ahmed and I flew to Northern California to attend a Sufi retreat led by Kabir and Camille Helminski, of the Threshold Society. We met many lovely people that weekend, and Leila, one of our closest friends who lived in the area at the time, was there with us. It gave Ahmed and me something we both desperately needed: calm time together, without having to answer phones or emails. I especially needed a break from the fertility question.

I took away a lot of ideas from that weekend about faith and my relationship with God. What grabbed my heart, as opposed to my head, and hasn't let go of it since, is the idea that spirituality is not something found only in the monasteries of Tibet or the retreat centers in the mountains of Santa Cruz. True spirituality can also be found while working at an office, shopping at a supermarket, riding a subway, or looking for one's fertility.

I can't say for sure if it was the experience of that weekend or just the timing in our lives, but it was soon after that retreat that I knew I was ready to have a child. I also knew that the answer to my fertility, or infertility, was not going to be found in a medical laboratory. That's when I went back to saying *inshAllah*. The idea of God's will didn't shut me up as it once had. Instead, I accepted who was in control.

Six months after I stopped testing, Ahmed and I were driving home after an early movie.

"Where do you want to go for dinner?" he asked, checking his side mirror.

"I'm tired," I said.

He pulled the car over. I understood his reaction. I was never too tired to eat.

"You've been tired a lot lately," he said, turning his head to me.

"I think I'm just coming down with something," I said. "No big deal."

"Let's get a pregnancy test," he said.

"It's just a cold," I said.

"Let's get one anyway," he said, and this time he reached over and covered my hand with his. He knew I couldn't go through another disappointment, another failed test.

"It's going to be okay," he said.

"Whatever happens?" I asked.

"Whatever happens."

I didn't know then that when we got home that night, I would pass the test. We were going to have a baby. But as we drove to the nearest pharmacy, Ahmed steering with one hand, never once letting go of me, I knew, without a doubt, that I was in love with this man. The man who told me *it's going to be okay*, and believed it enough for the both of us.

Wild Wind

Nijla Baseema Mu'min

I met him while interning at a film festival in San Francisco. His eyes surveyed the crowd as if he was searching for something. His long, fuzzy locks hung past his shoulders. I liked the sharp angle of his cheekbones. I thought to myself, *He's cute*, then continued to work, greeting guests and making sure the screenings started on time.

As festival patrons gathered in clusters, sipping red wine and eating hors d'oeuvres, he and I engaged in a visual game of tug-of-war. The look on his face carried some sort of longing. And it was this look that led him over to me. He pushed past overdressed attendees as the next screening was announced. He revealed his name. *Theo*. We chatted a bit. I told him about my upcoming trip to South Africa and discovered he had traveled the world through a Semester at Sea voyage the year before. *Cute and well traveled*. We exchanged phone numbers. Our eyes met many more times throughout the evening.

A week later, I went to South Africa to help film a documentary—an independent project a colleague of mine had developed—about community development and self-sufficiency in a township called Mamelodi. I served as the director of photography and still photographer, capturing the everyday nuances of the Mamelodi society on video and film. I was gone for a month and a half, and immediately upon my return, Theo's number appeared on my cell phone. I didn't recognize the number, but I recognized his soft, lazy voice.

"So, how was Mamelodi?" he asked. "Anything like Cape Town?"

His South African awareness was an instant turn-on. I was surprised to find out that he'd remembered our conversation at the film festival and waited exactly six weeks to call me, knowing I had no cell phone reception in Mamelodi. By the end of the conversation, we had set up a date.

Dating was always an interesting but difficult concept for me to understand. All my life, I have possessed a dual, conflicted religious existence that has complicated socially accepted practices, like dating, courtship, and boyfriends. My mother and father divorced before I could say my first words, and with their divorce came a variance in the way I saw the world. My mother believed in Allah and regarded Islam highly, but she didn't pray five times a day, drank Corona beers, and eventually married a non-Muslim man. My father was a disciplined Muslim who converted to Islam and changed his name after moving to Oakland in the late 1960s from a small Christian town in Louisiana.

After my parents' divorce, my siblings and I lived with our mother but went to our father's Oakland home every other weekend. We'd go to the *masjid*, where I found immense joy in praying side by side with sisters, our feet touching. I loved going to the halal pizza joint, eating beef pepperoni, then running my fingers across the rayon scarves that my father sold after Jumma.

I also adored the popular R&B guy groups of the time: Immature and what was left of New Edition. I taped their posters to my wall, dreaming of going on a date with one of them, or even marrying them. I didn't care about what their religion was or that, according to my father, I wasn't allowed to date—I just loved their songs.

My father always said that when I was old enough, I'd have a *strong* Muslim husband. Dating was never mentioned. When I asked my father how I'd get to know the man who would be my husband, he said that a parent had to chaperone us. My mother echoed these sentiments most times, but with less conviction. She didn't always include religion in her marriage prediction, just said she hoped I would end up with a nice, respectful guy.

As her relationship with her boyfriend (and my soon-to-be stepfather) progressed, I realized that my parents and others within my immediate community were not adhering strictly to the ideals they advocated to me. With Lil' Kim blasting through my boom box speakers and the Qur'an sitting atop our mantel, I came to recognize the layers of our existence, even if I didn't fully understand them.

During my teenage years and into my undergraduate career, I navigated a loose, confused understanding of religious and personal obligations, especially when it came to my body and sexuality. My mother maintained that because we were Muslim, I shouldn't wear the cut-off halter tops that my friends wore, though tank tops were permissible. Dates weren't encouraged, so secret "meet-ups" resulted. When I was ten, I watched from our apartment porch as my older sister French-kissed her "friend" on the round patch of dried-up grass downstairs. The kiss was sloppy and rushed, an attempt at romance before our mother came home from work. A strange mixture of excitement and disgust ran through me as I watched them.

That same weekend, we went to our father's apartment. In the evening, when we were all settled in, Daddy went out to dance at Geoffrey's nightclub. Alone in his apartment, my siblings and I created games to overcome boredom. "Step on back" was our favorite one; it consisted of someone's running across the floor with a sheet draped over him or her, and others chasing that person to see if they could step on the sheet and make the other person fall. This caper resulted in laughter and painful carpet burns, but it was worth it.

I never thought my father was breaking any Islamic code by going out on these nights, just that he loved to dance. Whether he courted women during these excursions remains unknown, but I do know that he danced with women, and in my mind, there was nothing wrong with that. In the morning we'd go hear the imam's *khutbah*, make *salat*, and buy mini–bean pies.

The next time I saw Theo, it was a wild, windy day in San Francisco. He didn't tell me what he had planned for this date, only that I'd enjoy it. He swooped up to the curb outside the BART station in a burgundy Buick. Bob Marley wailed from the speakers as I got in the car. Two small wineglasses sat in the middle compartment between our seats. I squinted my eyes, confused as to why they were there.

Theo spoke of many things as he drove to our surprise destination, starting with a question that brought an immediate awkwardness into the car.

"So, do you consider yourself spiritual or religious?"

I didn't know how to respond. I stated drily that I fostered a relationship with God.

He stated proudly, "I've been *saved* . . . What about you?"

I started to giggle because I didn't know if he was joking or not.

"I'm not sure if there's an equivalent to that in Islam."

"Oh . . . you're a Muslim."

There was a long, uncomfortable silence.

"Do you attend a mosque?"

"Yes, but not regularly."

He nodded his head slowly, massaged his beard, and sang along with Bob Marley. Slight perspiration gathered on my forehead, and I started to feel like I was on a job interview. Theo spoke mostly of his love for God. Most of his sentences began or ended with "God," "the Bible," and matters related to Christianity. He briefed me on his previous stint as a New York City gang member, and how God had pulled him from that life just as a rival gang member had laid a near-fatal blow to his face. I was interested in his convictions and life experiences, but somehow that wasn't enough for Theo. The fact that his fervor failed to convert me made things tense.

I thought back to the initial look in Theo's eyes at the film festival—the longing that had radiated from them. He was looking for someone to believe in him, and to believe in God the way he did. Memories clouded my mind. I remembered high school, when my best friend insisted I was going to hell because I didn't proclaim Jesus Christ as my lord and savior. Then a slumber party when I was ten and my friend's father insulted me because I didn't eat the pepperoni pizza. No matter the year—it seemed religious tolerance wasn't a factor in some people's minds.

As the car rolled through familiar San Francisco terrain, I could offer no more than halfway nods and smiles that masked my discomfort. How could I convey to Theo that while I respected his religious beliefs, I still had my own? How could I let him know, without seeming apathetic, that I wasn't overly religious? Upon hearing his proclamation that he needed to find *a wife to support him in his aspirations to become a preacher*, I couldn't help but let out a confused, but genuine, laugh. The absurdity of the car ride had become funny.

No matter how much Theo probed, I wasn't going to give him the answers he desired—that I was interested in becoming a

Christian, that I attended a church or *masjid* every week, or even that I wanted to. It wasn't because I eschewed his ideals; it was because I wasn't going to compromise my identity in order to make him feel better about his.

There I was, in the car, on a date with a man I hardly knew. Bob Marley was singing when we arrived at a beach. Theo picked up the two wineglasses in the middle compartment and opened my door, and we walked. The sand made our balance uneven, almost as uneven as the conversation we'd had in the car.

He laid out a lint-covered sheet and pulled two Subway sandwiches and a bottle of champagne from his backpack. The scene was like one from a movie, only I couldn't drink a sip.

"I don't drink alcohol."

"Oh, yeah—I forget about that."

An uncomfortable silence mixed with the wind, which plastered my dress to my legs. We ate warm sandwiches and watched the waves fight with each other. We talked more, this time about our world travels and how we both appreciated South Africa.

"I met some amazing people there, like this one woman who was a filmmaker. I should connect you guys," he said.

I was relieved that the conversation was starting to veer away from religion and joined in without hesitation: "That'd be great, Theo. It's amazing how complex the cultures there are. Most people speak about ten different languages."

Theo and I practiced clicking our tongues, as is custom when speaking the Xhosa language. "The next time you go, you have to visit Cape Town," he said. "You'll love the ocean."

I nodded and felt myself relax for first time that day. Later, when I exited his car at the end of the date, he looked into my eyes and stated, "God loves you." He was like one of the televangelist preachers on late-night TV. All I could do in response was give him the same uncomfortable smile I'd had for most of the date.

I was left with an unfinished impression of Theo. I knew he

loved God, but not much else. I wasn't sure what response of mine could match his conviction. I saw that same look in Theo's eyes: He wanted something from me, for me to be a "believer" the same way he was, but I wasn't. I just walked away.

I haven't seen Theo since that day.

I've been walking away from him, and from the idea that I must lose myself in order to be with someone, ever since. I no longer perceive my nebulous spirituality and romantic life as faults. The waves of my identity are more complex than my simply being a "pious Muslim woman" or a "God-fearing Christian." Now, at age twenty-six, I am thankful for my upbringing, which, though difficult to understand when I was a child and a teenager, helped me build a "both/and" perspective about people and the world. I had a Muslim father who read the Qur'an in the morning and loved dancing at night, a mother who kept a Qur'an on her mantel but had a boyfriend, and a sister studying Sufism and sneaking kisses outside our apartment. And we were all Muslims.

I like and love things and people based on passion, interest, and conviction, not according to categories and social boundaries. I sometimes think about what kind of wedding I will have if I do marry a non-Muslim man. Will we read from both holy books? Will we walk down the aisle or have the imam speak to us while we sit, as my parents did? And, like my mother, will I wear a sari or don a white gown instead? Will I jump the broom, as part of African American tradition, or have *mehndi* applied to my hands? I am aware of the potential clash—or the merging of beliefs—that will arise from my choice. I am willing to take the chance.

The Opening

Ayesha Mattu

In the name of God, the Merciful, the Compassionate
All praise is for God alone, the Cherisher and Sustainer of the
Worlds,
The Merciful, the Compassionate,
Master of the Day of Requital.
You alone do we worship, and to You alone we turn for help.
Guide us to the straight path,
The path of those whom You have blessed,
Not of those who are lost.

Al-Fatiha (The Opening, 1:1–7), Qur'an

It's two weeks after 9/11 and I need to dance. My heart and mind are burned out by double sorrow: for that terrible day, and for the bitter end of a long relationship. I've got to get away from the relentless TV coverage and remember happiness again.

I call up Brian, my old college buddy. "A local funk band called Superhoney got a great review in the *Metro*. They're playing at some place called Harpers Ferry down in Allston tonight. Let's go."

He says he'll meet me there. I smile as I hang up the phone. He's the kind of guy a girl can rely on to show up looking good enough to stir up the envy of other women, while being smart enough to hold sacred the delicate friendship between a woman and a man.

Riding the orange and then the green line to the club, I think about how I was supposed to be in Pakistan by now, visiting relatives during a sabbatical. But Logan Airport was still closed on the date of my departure, shortly after the attacks. When it came time to reschedule the flight, I found I couldn't leave my country, not after all that had happened.

I also think about the man who, after spending years mired in indecision about me and everything else in his life, finally walked away. I start making resolutions about the future. *From now on, I'm only going to date Muslim men*, I tell myself firmly. At twenty-nine, I've never limited my love life in this way, but I'm heartsick after failed relationships with non-Muslims. And, after years of estrangement, I'm drawn to and curious about Islam again.

My spiritual search started a year ago and has only been accelerated by the events of 9/11. I was raised with the Islam of "no," which had no place for joy or creativity, questions, or doubts. But since I discovered the ecstatic mystical poets of Islam—Rabia al-Adawiyya, Bulleh Shah, Hafiz, Rumi—I've realized that a deeply personal connection to a loving God and joyful Islam not only is possible, but is my birthright.

Up until now, I've avoided Muslim men who share my South Asian heritage as much as I have the Islamic faith. But I'm cautiously optimistic that somewhere within the diversity of American Muslim men—white, black, or of Arab, Asian, and other heritages—my soul mate awaits. Most of all, though, I just want a good man who will make it through my traditional Pakistani parents' front door. How to find him is a question I don't yet have an answer to, but as I walk into the club, I already know that this isn't the best place to begin.

The venue is a bit too divey for my taste, vast and dark, with a large, elevated stage and filled with a casual crowd of what appear to be, disconcertingly, mostly Boston University under-grads. Brian and I, acutely aware of how even a few years stretch wide between the young and the younger, separate ourselves by sitting at the bar and talking about the events of the last two weeks while the band plays.

"I saw men in trucks circling the Common, waving American flags and yelling. I could understand where they were coming from. It's not anti-Muslim, it's pro-American," Brian insists in his deep voice and matter-of-fact way.

The image makes me shudder. "I get it, but it makes me uncomfortable, like if you don't wave a flag or yell, you don't really love your country," I respond. "It's the first time I've ever felt how white Boston really is. Erin called me and said I should come stay with them all the way up in Milford. I think she was afraid I'd be lynched here just for being brown. And Muslim," I add, almost as an afterthought; it's a word for which I now have to figure out a place in my life again.

We sit with this thought for a minute, and though I wait for a reassurance, it doesn't come. There's so much about my country and circle of friends that I don't recognize or understand right now. On the one hand, colleagues in the social-justice movement are organizing to protect local mosques and congregations, and on the other, a friend asked if I would hang an American flag outside my home to prove my patriotism. I have few Muslim friends to compare these experiences with, and most of the ones that I do have are secular, without the strong spiritual roots or religious depth to help me navigate the stormy waters in which I, like most American Muslims, am being asked to defend Islam and our Americanness.

I sigh and decide to lighten the mood because, after all, didn't we come here to forget?

It's at this moment that I notice him. He's standing in a knot of friends, close enough for me to see clearly without the glasses I refuse to wear, but far away enough that I can steal covert glances at him. He's gorgeous, but it's something else that holds my attention. He is dancing alone, confident and graceful. Most guys in their twenties just don't do that, not even after they've had their obligatory two drinks to loosen up. Heck, most *people* don't do that, ever. Case in point: His friends stand around stiffly, drinks in hand.

It's a pleasure just to watch him move. He reminds me how good it feels to have a body that's young, and still alive after the recent tragedy. I can't stop glancing at him, and soon enough, he looks my way. Too shy to hold his gaze, I will him to come over, assuming that my six-foot-three male companion will not be a lasting deterrent.

Surely at some point Brian will go to the restroom, I think, and then the tall, dark stranger will approach. But I've underestimated Brian's Irish-Italian genes, which have fused together to form a superbladder, impervious to the vast quantities he is drinking. It's getting close to closing time, and, though we're still exchanging glances, the man has made no move toward me. Brian is still planted obliviously at my side.

My new resolution about Muslim men flies temporarily out the window as I try to formulate a plan to talk to the stranger. In a conversation with a more orthodox friend, I summarized our approaches to life as "I'm happy, and you're good." Tonight, the promise of an immediate thrill pulls me in again, even though I am becoming more aware that my actions rarely bring me long-term happiness.

I feel shy about approaching him myself, but it doesn't cross my mind to enlist Brian's help. As an "exotic" beauty in Boston, I've always been the one who is approached, never the one who approaches, so this is a novel situation. Before I've thought of my opening move, the man appears at the bar, standing behind Brian. Without thinking, I lean across my friend and tap the stranger on the shoulder.

"Hello," I purr smoothly. "I couldn't help but notice we're wearing the same shirt."

The man looks down at his shirt in confusion. We are not wearing the same shirt. They are both baseball-style shirts, but his is gray and green, with some sort of sports motif, and mine is blue, with sparkly letters that spell out SWEETHEART. I am mortified. I feel a rush of sympathy for the men I made fun of over the years for approaching me with inane pickup lines. Why couldn't I have just stopped at "hello"?

"Yeah," he says with a kind smile, "they're sort of similar."

"I'm Ayesha," I push on, heart racing and cheeks flushed, barely noticing when Brian finally realizes what's happening and smoothly gets out of the way.

"I'm Brandy," he replies—or at least I think he replies, in my confusion and over a spike of noise in the hall. *Oh boy*, I think to myself, *now, that is not going to go over well with my teetotaling parents*.

I realize my mistake a few minutes later, as the lights go up and I look down at his actual name—Randy—on the business card he hands me in exchange for mine. Thankfully, he still looks good in the sudden glare, and his hazel eyes and wide smile tell me that he feels the same way I do. I feel the tingle of potential, the excitement of something new, the attraction of a stranger and all the things that he could come to mean to me. The possibilities send blood rushing through my veins as I stand radiant and powerful under his gaze.

We part, playing it cool but sure that we will meet again, and soon. I think about my new resolution and file it away to consider again later. Brian appears, smiling, and we stand for a minute before parting.

"You're going to marry that guy," he says in that creepy, prescient Irish way he gets sometimes at last call.

I laugh off the idea, still riding high from the thrill of the chase. But when I look down at the card, the black letters of his name dance with possibility.

"I have a surprise for you," Randy says one day, two months after we met. "I can't tell you anything else besides: Wear shoes you can walk in. I'll pick you up in an hour."

I once went camping in Armani jeans and clogs, attempted to cook a frozen pizza on the campfire, and was eaten alive by mosquitoes. I have no shoes appropriate for the sort of walking he means, but I gamely search for a pair.

Wearing the most stable heels I own, I stride from the coed vegetarian cooperative where I live to his waiting BMW M3. The sight of the car makes me laugh each time I see it, remembering how my flatmate Marcy asked what kind of car he drove and I answered, "I think it's a Honda." I may not be interested in the type of car a man drives, but I'm beginning to like the soft black leather against my bare arms, the way the BMW hugs curves, and how Randy's large, elegant hands handle the wheel expertly.

While I have lived in Boston on and off for a decade, I have explored little beyond the reach of the red line between Davis Square and downtown. We have already driven past the areas I know, the city skyline dropping behind us as we arc north on Interstate 93.

I've rarely met a native of the area. Most of my friends and colleagues are transplants like I am, drawn here by the creativity, diversity, and possibilities that colleges seed in the communities around them. I'm fascinated by Randy's stories about growing up in a small, insular town only six miles away in geographical distance, but decades apart in practice from the politically correct campuses in the city.

Randy lost his Medford accent in college, but he retains the town's lack of pretension. He may work in the booming, money-drenched tech industry, ski in Austria, and dine on tapas at Dalí, but he can just as easily watch a Pats game while eating ribs with other locals. Used to peers who refuse to socialize outside certain scenes or neighborhoods, I find this quality of his attractive.

Born in Chicago and brought up all over the United States, I spent my high school years abroad and am used to being in between countries, homes, and friends. I've never been able to point out "home" on a map, but Randy feels like home to me—he accepts all that I am, who he is, and who we are slowly becoming together. I love the way his roots gnarl deep and wide in one place, back to his immigrant Albanian grandparents. With him, differences feel complementary and strengthening, instead of being points of contention or weakness. He is grounded but open to new experiences, and, after years of moving between continents, I am adaptable but looking to build a deeper community.

Maybe that's why I'm not afraid of the critical difference between us: religion. After eight weeks together, I already have a certainty as solid as my bones that I will marry this man. What is uncertain is how we are going to get there, though that doesn't faze me. Some of this unusual calm on my part is due to Randy's easygoing and optimistic personality, but mostly I believe there will be a divine smoothing of our lives into one, somehow. If I just keep walking this unmapped path one day at a time, have faith, and stay as wide open as he is, we will figure it out, together.

Today he takes me to the Fells. Stumbling in my ridiculous shoes over the forest floor gives me a chance to hold his hand, palm to palm, in the clean autumn air. Aside from our footsteps,

there is little sound. Or, rather, the sounds are ones I have forgotten after living in the city: the susurration of the wind through
the branches above, fiery leaves crunching underneath our feet,
and rocks tumbling against each other as we climb. I would not
have found this place without him—this breathing, green-and-
gold forest—and I love him for sharing it with me.

We stop in a clearing at the crest of a hill near the old stone
watchtower and look at the city gleaming in the distance. Randy
spreads a blanket and pulls all the essentials from the basket:
bread and cheese, fruit and poetry. With any other man, Sonnet
116 would be only a carefully rehearsed step to seduction, but
because he was a fellow English major, his gesture is also romantic
and sincere. I relax into his voice, the cadence of the poem, and
the sensations of the forest around us.

In the world of low expectations that is dating in one's late
twenties, where one steps lightly, never letting on that feelings
might be running deeper than simple enjoyment, for fear of
scaring the other person off or moving too fast, I realize I've been
dating boys up until now. Dating a grown-up man who is not only
unperturbed by, but the initiator of words and phrases like "I love
you," "girlfriend," and "commitment," is delightful. I'm playing
catch-up to Randy's maturity, trying not to sound stunned when
the words roll out of his mouth.

I don't seek out large, green spaces often enough, which is
another reason why today feels like a gift from him. It reminds
me of one particular summer day when I sat watching the breeze
blowing through an oak tree nearby. When I closed my eyes, all
of my senses came alive and suddenly, after years of distance and
doubt, I just knew that He existed, and realized that there must
be *more* to everything around me.

I share this story with Randy, and end by saying, "When I was
a kid, I believed because I was afraid of punishment, or the judgment of other people. Then I didn't believe much at all for a long

time. But now I believe because creation resounds with Him. I'm so curious—I want to know the Being who created this beauty all around us," I gesture, encompassing both forest and city.

I feel a little nervous, as I always do when I've shared something intimate and a response is slow in coming. But Randy isn't afraid of silence the way I am. Instead of filling the space between us, I focus on emulating his stillness, breathing slowly, and internally reciting my favorite *dhikr*, the opening verses of the Qur'an.

"I like that," he says, finally. "Not a God who punishes and demands, but One who creates, and wishes to have a relationship with us, too."

He smiles and continues, "You know, if we'd met a few years ago, I would have written you off as crazy. I couldn't stand religion or religious people back then. I'm not sure what I believe in, but I'm curious, too."

"I still feel the same way about most religious people. They scare the heck out of me!" I laugh. "But the more I read, the sorrier I am that I ever took their word for it. I wasted years because I didn't think I fit into their conception of Islam or God. And I don't. But God is greater than all that. There are as many ways to Him as there are people on the planet."

With my hand nestled safe in Randy's, we sit in the clearing until it's time to go home.

On the first day of the new year, Randy and I are shy with each other. The night before, he asked me to marry him and I said yes. There was no ring or bended knee, no parental knowledge or consent. And today it's just the two of us, unable to stop smiling, feeling a little awkward, and wondering what this means for us now.

I decide to call my dad, always the easier of my parents to approach. He met Randy briefly in November when the latter dropped off his digital camera to capture the arrival of our family's first grandchild. Although I have not mentioned Randy to my father since then, I detect no shock when I screw up the courage to tell him that I have met someone I want to marry.

"Is it that boy who came to the hospital?" my father asks gently. I blink in surprise. Once again, my parents know far more than they let on.

"Yes, Abuji. I've known him since September, and . . . " I hesitate, unsure how to talk to my father about a boy, something I have never done before. "He is a good man—gentle, loving, and kind. I want to be with him, but I also want your consent and blessing."

My father is silent for a few minutes. My face is slick with anxiety as I wait for his answer.

"*Beta*, I have only two requests," he says finally. "First, that he loves and cherishes you your whole life. And, second, that he studies Islam and considers converting."

The second request is not a surprise, but the openness with which my father has greeted this news is. No one in my family has ever married a non-Pakistani, or considered someone who was not born Muslim. What a long way my father and I have come from the night we sat on the porch a decade ago and he told me I had to marry someone who was not only Pakistani, but of the same clan and caste as ours. I know that both of my younger sisters' being spoken for makes it easier for him to bend, as does the looming threat of my spinsterhood. But I am humbled by my father's love, by his willingness to consider and make room for his daughter's happiness, in spite of the censure he and my mother will face from some of their friends and family members.

Upon hearing my father's request, Randy immediately stands up, takes down Charles le Gai Eaton's *Islam and the Destiny of Man* from my bookshelf, and starts reading it. I don't interfere, wanting him to find truth in it for himself instead of performing a conversion of convenience. I know that for a man journeying from agnosticism to faith, nothing less than belief will do.

Six months later, Randy goes to the Cambridge mosque to convert and has a conversation with the imam that will impact him for years to come.

"Your family is Christian and may have fears about your conversion, especially now," the imam says. "Instead of debating or arguing with them about the merits of one religion versus the other, let your behavior speak for you. Let them see the change in you. Let them see that being a Muslim has made you a better son, brother, and man."

I sit beside him in the car, listening to him tell the story. There are tears in his eyes as he grips my hand tightly. I know he did this for himself, that it was a truth that spoke to him. But I also know that he did it for me, that he considered a faith he might not otherwise have in the aftermath of 9/11, because he met a Muslim woman and fell in love with her.

I have broken down so many times on the roadside of belief over the years that his clarity feels holy to me. I know I didn't do this alone. The factors of religion, parents, and culture were too complex for me to have sorted them out by myself. I know for a fact that an opening was created for us.

Eleven months after Randy and I first met, I finally reschedule that flight to Pakistan to celebrate our wedding in Islamabad with my huge extended family. Randy and his mother will join me soon for the festivities.

As I watch the continent slip by underneath me through the oval airplane window, I am stunned to find myself in this unimaginable place. I thought I knew myself so well the night we met, and had a list of all the values and qualities I wanted in a lifelong partner—headed by "Muslim," though I wasn't sure where or how to find one. Randy embodies all of these criteria, as well as many others I never knew to ask for but needed so very much. Such complementarity seems cosmic and beyond my control. And thinking about how I found my future husband while sitting on a bar stool immediately after making my resolution to stop dating non-Muslim men makes me certain that God is imbued with a sense of humor as well as infinite, loving mercy.

On paper, we might never have chosen each other, but in life, we were made for each other. The woman climbing her way back to Islam found her soul mate in a self-described agnostic. In my choosing Randy, and in his choosing me, we chose to create a new home in and with each other. There is no map or chart by which to plot our course of brown and white, of American and Muslim, of Pakistani and Albanian; we are simply creating a blended road as we walk forward, hand in hand, together.

A decade after we met, all I can say for sure is that my beloved's search for the truth led him to embrace Islam, and through his beautiful embodiment of those values, he made my own path back to the Beloved easy.

Alhamdulillah.

Punk-Drunk Love

Tanzila Ahmed

A punk-rock circle pit is like tawaf *around the Kaaba. It looks like circular chaos of pushing and shoving, but there is an internal order, love and spirituality in the perceived chaos. And—every now and then—some guy copping a feel.*

I've always been a sucker for a man with a Mohawk.

The first time I saw him, on the West Coast, he was standing on the sidewalk outside his band's hitched trailer. I had just driven eight hours from Los Angeles to Oakland to make it in time for that night's show. The members of the three punk bands were unloading into the venue. I jumped out of my car and raced over to hug them. I'd built online friendships with each of them, so, though it was my first time meeting most of the band members, I felt like I knew them all.

Yusuf was tall, with broad shoulders and Arabic tattoos lacing his muscular biceps. His hair was shaved on the sides, a shock of purple down the center, swept limp to one side. His jawline was firm, but his high cheekbones and intense, thickly lashed, dark eyes softened the effect. A pretty man all the girls wanted to get with and all the guys wanted to be. I saved his hug for last.

Our eyes locked. I walked over, feigning nonchalance. We mumbled greetings. An awkward hug. He let go quickly, as if he didn't want his bandmates to know. Were we just friends, then?

We had rendezvoused in New York City only four weeks earlier, at midnight on my thirtieth birthday. It had been a one-night make-out thing, with nothing defined the next morning. Though we'd never met in person before, we had felt as if we had known each other for years. I had interviewed Yusuf for an article on his band three years earlier, and we had struck up a deep online friendship that consisted of sharing lyrics and MP3s and having GChat conversations about life. For years, he had told me stories of his latest conquests over late-night IM sessions. I knew he wasn't relationship material. He went through girls like candy, and I had no plans to be the flavor of the month.

I sat at the bar alone, drinking my Red Bull on ice while the opening act continued in the other room. I was overwhelmed. I had been following Yusuf's band since I had first written about them, six years earlier. They might have been a bunch of broke, punk misfits, but in my mind, they were celebrities.

Yusuf found me. He grabbed a stool. My heart thumped. "You look great," he said.

"Do you like my hair?" I asked, playing with the pink tendrils. I had just been laid off from my day job, and dyeing my hair was my personal rebellion. I was untethered, collecting unemployment, and ready to play. I looked at Yusuf slyly.

"The hair." He looked down at my DIY T-shirt, with a profile of a Mohawked man sitting in prayer. "The shirt. All of it. You look awesome." He paused, stumbling over his words, before they started spilling out. He talked about feeling lonely while driving cross-country. The overwhelming testosterone on the tour. The homoerotic cuddling. He talked about how it all made him long for female energy.

His words tumbled out in continuous run-on sentences that blended into each other. I listened, awestruck, feeling as if one of our IM conversations was manifesting itself in real life. It was electric. But after a moment, we were interrupted by someone joining us. That was how it would be—stealing intimate moments when we could.

"This is going to be the first time I've seen Yusuf's band perform," I whispered to my friend as we stood in the audience, waiting for them to take the stage.

They were a Muslim punk band—though the moniker "Muslim punk" didn't really fit. Instead of praising the Almighty, their lyrics were controversial, toeing the line between Islamophobia and orthodoxy, and having fun doing it. They were the marginalized, playing raucous music with political, in-your-face intentions and not giving a fuck. Punk, through and through.

"Oh yeah?" my friend responded. "How are you feeling?"

"It's surreal," I responded. As a Southern Californian teenager in the '90s, I was the one brown Muslim girl crowd-surfing at the local punk shows on Saturday nights. On Sunday mornings, I'd don a headscarf and head out to the local mosque's Sunday school. I was defiantly proud of being *desi* and Muslim in an Islamophobic and racist America, and to me, that translated into punk. If I told fellow punks that I was straight edge—meaning, I didn't drink or do drugs—they didn't bat an eye. And when I went on to work in political organizing because I wanted to make the world a better place for my people, that wasn't just an Islamic value—it was a punk value, too.

As the band set up, I stood near the back, feeling too old for the front-pit action. But when Yusuf jumped on the mic, it reminded

me of those countless Saturday nights I had spent at punk venues
as a kid. Only this time, for the first time, it was a band that was
Muslim, *desi*, and punk like me. I sang along to all the lyrics and
jumped right on in.

"I wish I was sitting next to you," his text said.

I looked over in his direction. We were at a chicken-and-waffles
place in Oakland. The entire entourage had stumbled here after
the show. He was surrounded by people: his own band members,
fans, and the members of the opening bands. There was no space
for me, so I stayed put.

Eventually, though, he came over to sit next to me. We talked
closely and intimately. He leaned in for a kiss, but I paused before
we made contact, and pulled back. "What will your band members say?" I asked, in a flirty, hushed tone.

"It's only a kiss on the cheek. That's okay." He leaned in, lips
pressed up on my right cheek. Quick and tender, soft and longing.
And that was it.

The next day, we were at the Muslim punk wedding of the year—
the bands' national tour intentionally planned around it. My
sari was gorgeous black chiffon with pink sequined flowers that
matched my newly streaked hair. With my big black shades on, I
looked the part of the quintessential California *desi* punk girl.

My friend Fatima and I met some of the boys in the parking
lot in front of the Indian restaurant. Piercings and saris, dyed hair
and kurtas, sunglasses and *cholis* . . . this punk wedding entourage
was a real-life, slow-motion musical montage.

Yusuf met us at the entrance, looking at me silently. He was
dressed in a gray kurta top, cut to fit him perfectly. He sat next
to me during dinner. He kept looking at me and grabbing my leg
under the table so no one could see, rubbing it up and down. "You
should really stop looking at me and eat your food," I said, blushing.

A few minutes later, I was fidgeting. My sari was coming undone under the weight of the sequins and my lack of grace. When I mentioned it to him, he said he wanted to help me unravel my sari later that night at the hotel.

While the rest of the wedding party was having late-night drinks by the pool, Yusuf and I snuck out to go skateboarding in front of the hotel. He jumped on my skateboard and skidded away on the black, moonlit pavement.

"Be careful!" I shouted. He wasn't a skater, was too broad to be nimble, and hadn't been on a board in ten years. I chased after him on foot, caught up, and stood in front of him, slightly out of breath.

"Give me a kiss," he said. I looked up and he gave me a quick, closed-mouth peck on the lips.

"I wait for two days and that's all I get?" I teased.

I leaned up and in for more. This time, he kissed me deeply. Open mouth, tongue on teeth, breath on breath. His wide hand reached around my waist and scooped me in, pulling me close and tight. It was the kiss I had been waiting for. I didn't want it to stop, but he pulled away.

"Not here," he said, looking toward the hotel entrance.

I bent down, grabbed my board, and skated to a far-off, empty corner of the parking lot that was illuminated only by dim street-lights and moonlight. I looked over my shoulder. He was chasing me. I squealed and jumped off the board as he reached for my waist. My board rolled away but I remained behind, held in his arms.

We kissed, the endless kind of kiss where the world stops to revolve around you. My hands roamed, trailing his neckline and tracing his tattooed arms. I craved him, even though he was right there in front of me. It had been four weeks since our last kiss, and my anticipation was finally being fulfilled.

"I could probably kiss you like this forever," he said into my lips.

"I don't mind. I could forever, too," I responded.

We reexplored each other under the streetlight. He was the perfect height for me to lean my forehead into his neck, rest my cheek on his chest, and wrap my arms around his waist. His kisses were even better than I remembered. We would have stood there longer if we hadn't been interrupted by his band members' voices. They were looking for us. I grabbed the board and, with Yusuf chasing on foot behind, skated farther away.

Everyone else had gone to bed, so we snuck into the backseat of my car. It was dark outside, but we still felt like we could get caught at any moment. The energy in the car was explosive, the windows steamed immediately.

The lyrics "Why won't you milk me all through Hijrah? Am I burning up your oil fields? *Subhanallah, lehnga utaar* . . . " kept running through my mind. And I knew listening to Yusuf's album would never be the same again.

I left the hotel the next morning without a proper good-bye. I had to hit the road to go back home to Los Angeles. But I knew the punk entourage would be close behind: They had a show in L.A. three nights later.

As I drove down I-5, I felt changed. Complete. After only forty-eight hours, I had fallen in love with each of the people I had met in this so-called scene, individually and as a collective. It was a space where connections were instant. We had prayed together behind the punk venue and prayed together to honor a marriage. At the intersection of prayer, punk, and love, I had finally found my people.

My parents had never understood why the intersection of being Muslim, an activist, and a punk was so important to me. Growing up, I led a life of duality—the secret life of a punk-rocking activist combined with the home life of a pious Muslim daughter. As the oldest of three daughters to Bangladeshi immigrants, I was the guinea pig who wasn't allowed to do anything. Sleepovers were out of the question, and when I became a teenager, the only way I was allowed to go to a punk show was if my mother waited in the parking lot while I was in the pit. And Allah forbid that my dad ever found out about it—I would have been kicked out of the house had he known I was crowd-surfing, with the hands of boys holding my body up.

So I learned early on how to keep secrets. As long as I was home in time for Maghrib prayer and in my room doing homework, my parents left me alone. Little did they know, I was listening to punk music and reading Rachel Carson's *Silent Spring*. They wanted me to become an engineer, but I went against their wishes and became a political activist. They wanted me to buy a status-symbol car, but I drove a hooptie ride while starting a nonprofit organization. And forget boys. They learned early on that with my piercings, colored hair, and "independence," I wasn't the biodata type. I dated throughout my twenties; I just didn't tell my parents that. As far as they knew, I was a thirty-year-old Muslim virgin who had never kissed a boy.

That weekend in Oakland was the first time I felt completely free to be myself. I could talk about Rancid lyrics and fighting against racial profiling in the same breath, and top it off with a "fuck that shit, *inshAllah*," and no one would blink. Secrets? These were the people at the heart of living secret dual lives—with them, there were no secrets. They just knew.

And Yusuf. He knew all my secrets and adored me for all my parts—whether punk, Muslim, or activist. Unlike any other guy I had dated, he understood me through and through. The last thing I wanted was to be his groupie. Maybe it was because of our three-year online friendship, but I felt connected to him. He wasn't a one-woman man, but my heart pulled me toward him anyway.

• • •

I was sitting on a sofa, wearing a summer dress, my bare legs on Yusuf's lap. He caressed my skin, periodically kissing my knees and playing with my toes. It was 1:00 AM, and the band members were spread out across every spare inch of carpet in a friend's two-bedroom Los Angeles apartment, sleeping.

It was hard for Yusuf and me to downplay our chemistry. We were being silly, laughing at everything, as he kissed my knees. I'd never seen him act goofy before, and it was adorable. It was the first time that I thought there could be something more between us.

"We have roof access!" a punker proclaimed, after returning from a quick exploration of the building. Sleeping under the stars sounded perfect.

Yusuf and I went down to my car to get my futon and air mattress and take them to the roof. But when we got into my car, he pulled me in for a kiss. The attraction had been building. We sat there, getting our fill after having not kissed in two days.

"We should go; they're waiting for us," I mumbled into his lips. "I'm going to miss you when you leave Los Angeles."

"I haven't left yet. I'm still here." He kissed my lips tenderly. "Come with us to Austin. You'll love it there. It'll be fun."

The truth was, I had been thinking of joining the tour and had even mapped out the drive to Texas on my laptop. But I hadn't wanted to plan anything until I knew what the vibe was between us, and of course, I had been waiting for an invitation.

He took my silence as hesitation and leaned back in his seat. "You have to work on your book. I know, I know . . . "

My original plan had been to work on a book as soon as I became unemployed. It was a reason, yes. But it wasn't *the* reason. "No, no. It's not that. It's driving back solo from Texas. Let me think about it . . . But we should go inside now. Your friends are waiting for us."

We went upstairs and cuddled on the apartment-building roof, babbling incoherently while gazing at the moon. We talked about stars, palm trees, and planets. But the topic didn't matter. All that mattered was that we finally got to lie in each other's arms until we drifted off to sleep under the Los Angeles sky.

We held hands under the table like giddy teenagers. It was another 3:00 AM meal after another sweaty show; this time, the Muslim punks were at a Jewish deli. There were probably fifteen other people around us, but we were in our own little bubble.

"Can we talk outside?" he asked. As soon as we were out of the band's view, he grabbed me. "I like you. I really, really like you," he said in a singsong voice.

"Oh yeah? How much?" I teased.

"Like . . . a whole lot."

"I'm not just another one of your groupies?"

He hesitated. "Do you *want* to be one of my groupies? Why do you keep bringing that up?"

I shrugged, unsure of what to say. I had mentioned it a few times already. I felt we had something deeper, but I needed to know if the feeling was mutual.

"I like you, *jaanu*. I really, really like you. I've had this huge crush on you. I'd make up excuses to get you to talk to me online," he revealed.

My heart fluttered. I didn't know what to say.

He continued, "And I think you're super cute. I didn't think you'd be this cute. I knew you'd be hot, but you are so cute."

What could I do but lean up and kiss him?

The last California show had just wrapped up. People were milling around the band's trailer. I sat on the back of my car, devastated. The five days of L.A. bliss had come to an end. The guys were leaving the next day to drive twenty-six hours to their

Austin show, and eventually back to the East Coast. I had a horrible ache in my heart. I had just found them. I wasn't ready to be alone again.

Yusuf came over to upload stuff into my trunk and saw me sitting there. I took a deep breath and asked, "What if . . . I came with you guys to Texas?"

"I would love it. And we will totally help on the drive out there." He kissed me quickly, and just like that, I was driving to Texas.

"Can I ask you something, T?" he said, in a voice saved for serious late-night pillow talk. "Did you hook up with my brother?"

It was chilly in LA. The post-Fajr sun was rising as we sat on the roof. My head rested on Yusuf's little brother's shoulder. He was nineteen, the youngest person on the tour; he was following the band for his college thesis and had gone from mild-mannered researcher to two-tone-Mohawked hype man over the course of the journey. He knew Yusuf's brilliance and downfalls better than anyone.

I wasn't sure how to respond to his question. Though we were now friends, he was still the younger brother.

"Yes," I responded cautiously. "Back in New York, when we first met."

"That's what I thought," he responded in a monotone.

He talked about girls on the scene and how Yusuf went through them rapidly, whereas he was piously saving himself for love. I wondered if he thought less of me now. He questioned me more pointedly, asking for details. But I demurred.

"He's dating someone that he really likes now. It's the happiest I've seen him with someone since he's been divorced," he revealed.

My heart sank. It seemed implausible, since I had met Yusuf in New York City the weekend after he had broken up with his latest girlfriend, but what did I know?

"Where does she live?" I asked.

"In Washington, D.C. He's really happy with her. I think things could work out with this one."

My gut wrenched. Yusuf and his brother lived outside Philadelphia; this girl was closer to him than I could ever be way out in California. D.C. was on the way home from the tour. He'd see her in a couple of days, after he left Austin, and I would be forgotten.

"What do you want with him?" he asked protectively.

"I don't know. He chased me. He talked to me online for years. He pursued me." I didn't want him to think of me as just another groupie, but I also wanted to believe it went deeper that that: "I'm not looking for anything; I'm just open to what the universe sends my way and giving everything a chance," I said, trying to convince myself.

I thought back to my last serious relationship, two years earlier, with a black Muslim convert I had met at a Muslim spoken-word event in Los Angeles. We had dated for eight months, but I had never felt I was Muslim enough for him.

Regardless, by our third date, he had been ready to commit, but I hadn't been sure he was the one. And at the moment when I had finally trusted him and started falling for him, he had dumped me. I had waited too long.

Ever since then, I had made a point of giving every guy who crossed my path a fair chance. I wouldn't close off my heart anymore. I wasn't going to pass up the chance to show that I could love—and be loved—again.

We sat quietly as the sun rose in the sky. Maybe I *was* just some West Coast groupie, but who was I to ask for more? Our situations were complicated. We lived across the country from each other. Yusuf was on tour, and I had just lost my job. I knew about his six-month itch, his unwillingness to commit. He had told me he never wanted to get married again. I had known what I was getting into before I had gotten into it. But did that mean denying love when it was presented to me?

I snuck out and left without saying good-bye while everyone was still deep in slumber. I drove home to the 'burbs, wavering between going to Texas or not. I wanted to continue the adventure of the tour, but I no longer knew if I wanted to risk getting hurt. How real could Yusuf's feelings for me be if he was seeing someone else? I felt like a fool for not knowing. And I would be a fool to follow him to Texas, knowing what I knew now. But in spite of that, I found myself thinking, *What if?*

My house was on the band's route to Texas. I texted Yusuf my address and told him to swing by before they left Los Angeles. I decided to go with my gut and make my choice when I saw him later that night.

My little car wound its way east over starlit desert roads, with Yusuf at the wheel. I sat in the passenger seat while the band's drummer slept in the back. We were like nomads caravanning through the late-night desert; the rest of the band was in the tour vehicle far behind us. When the entourage had stopped at my house earlier that evening, my heart had filled me with a longing to complete the adventure. I needed to know how it would end.

"Tell me a story," I asked, after I realized just the two of us were awake. I was having the kind of nerves you feel on a first date. We were facing twenty-six hours of nonstop driving before we arrived in Austin, Texas, and we were only on hour one. What if we ran out of things to talk about?

It was the first time we had been together at length without interruption. Confined by the car, with the radio off, we talked. Yusuf wove together stories of his life from his days of being a writer in South Asia—tales of violence and music—and described his passions and goals.

He was different—intelligent, thoughtful, sweet—when he knew it was just the two of us awake. I felt a fluttering in my gut. I tried to quell it, reminding myself about what Yusuf's brother had said that morning, thinking about how risky the situation was. We drove through the night, until his words lulled me to sleep. As my eyes closed, I knew that I was done. I had fallen for him completely, in spite of the risk.

We arrived in Austin two days later, at 3:00 AM. All nine of us crashed on a college kid's living-room floor. All I wanted to do was to cuddle with Yusuf and sleep, but the local hosts were excited to have the band in their town and wanted to party. And, of course, Yusuf was the center of that party.

I left them, found a corner, and fell asleep. An hour later, Yusuf pulled me onto the air mattress with him, wrapping himself around me.

"T, I love you," he whispered. Even though I had been half-asleep, I turned to look at him in the dark. My heart leapt to my throat, rendering me speechless.

I waited a moment before I whispered back, "I think I love you, too . . . " But by the time the words left my mouth, he was already asleep.

The Austin show was my fifth and final one on the tour. I bounced, skanked, and sang along to every song, wilding out like a teen-ager. It was the most fun I'd had at a punk show, ever.

Yusuf found me at the bar after the show. He looked dazed.

"Are you tired?" I asked.

"Yeah, but don't worry," he said, leaning forward to kiss me. "I have enough energy for you."

My breath caught, and nervous energy flooded me. I had gotten a hotel room for our last night together. I grabbed his sweatshirt, pulled him into a back corner behind a wall, and kissed him fiercely, trying to get a taste of what was to come.

The drops beaded on Yusuf's brown skin and soaked his purple hair as he turned his face toward the water. His wet body pressed me up slowly against the hotel shower's tiles. Cheap yellow light shone off his slick skin. My heart raced as my soul was set on fire.

My fingers ran over him. The light emphasized the muscles on his shoulders, biceps, and forearms. My hand trailed down his chest, his ribs, his waist, his hips, grabbing hold of him and pulling him closer. His calloused rocker fingers tenderly followed the natural trail of water from hair to neck to waist and below. He licked me. Sucked me. Bit me. I took it all in, took him all in, until my nerves, my knees, melted like the water around us and I could stand no more.

We finally satiated years of attraction and weeks of tension. Skin to skin, lips to skin, teeth to skin, we melded together with a fierceness and urgency found only in the most intense of punk-rock circle pits.

"I love your hips. And I love your thighs," he whispered huskily, his voice cutting through the darkness.

"What else do you love?"

"I love your eyes. I love your waist. I love your fingers. I love your touch," he continued as his fingers trailed lightly over me.

"What else?"

"I love your hands. I love your skin. I love your *ras*. I love your taste. I love your lips. I love your neck. I love your legs." His voice trailed as he pulled me in for a deep kiss, and more.

• • •

It was impossible not to cry. The next morning, I drove Yusuf to meet up with the rest of the tour. They'd hit the road immediately for Louisiana. Then Georgia. Then D.C.

I wanted to ask him about the D.C. girl. I wanted to ask him about us. But I didn't want to ruin the moment. I needed to appreciate this for what it was, didn't I?

Whatever the future held didn't lessen the truth of what I was feeling right now. I believed that our hearts are intended for use; now, I was putting my beliefs into practice. I was letting myself fall in love, and in the end, wasn't that what was important?

Yusuf paused, drumming his leg with his fingers, and looked over at me soberly.

"What is it?" I asked.

"I'm going to miss you," he said.

"I'm going to miss you, too," I said. I grabbed his hand and kept my eyes on the road, blinking away tears.

In the end, I never told him that I knew about the girl in D.C. I just didn't have the heart to.

Allahu alim.

"You are so super cute in real life. I didn't expect this," Yusuf said, amazed. We were standing outside, taking last-minute pictures while the rest of the posse packed the trailer.

"Well," I said, looking up at him, hands around his waist, "I didn't think you'd be such a goofy dork."

We got our last kisses and cuddles in. The photos from our last moments alone together are my favorite pictures ever.

And then he was gone. They were all gone. I was alone in Austin, Texas, 1,500 miles from home. I pulled my car over to the side of the road and cried.

My pilgrimage—a week spent with a rambunctious posse of Muslim punks, all misfits on a personal journey trying to define themselves and not let others define them—was complete. It had been a pilgrimage both unlike and very similar to the one I had performed in Mecca years and years earlier—a journey into my internal spiritual self, finding a collective people I connected with, and finally feeling like I belonged.

I had fallen in love in the best way—with a boy, with like-minded people, and, maybe most important, with being honestly and truly myself. I had found a family that was cut from the same contradictory cloth and going through the same blasphemous struggles as I was. I had found myself, and I had let myself go. I had punk-rocked, prayed, loved, moshed, laughed, skated, cuddled, rocked, touched, kissed, and cried.

It wasn't just a story about my falling in love with a guy, or following a band, or going on an adventure. It was about love, punk, and punk-drunk love. People who got me, really got me, and all that I came with.

Ramadan was around the corner. It was time for the slow roll back home to Los Angeles and Khalifornia. I charted a two-week course, one that would take me through the site of John F. Kennedy's assassination, a Muslim graveyard on the border of Texas, a Native American reservation in Santa Fe, and the rim of the Grand Canyon. My life would never be the same—but my adventure wasn't over yet.

With reckless courage in my heart, I wiped away my tears. "*Bismillah*," I whispered, starting up my engine, and turned west, toward home.

Alif:

Where It All Begins

The Birds, the Bees, and My Hole

Zahra Noorbakhsh

Finally. My first year of high school was over, and summer was here. My mother was dropping me off to go to the movies with Jen, Kim, Laura, and Ryan. Wait. Oh, crap, I had forgotten about Ryan! There he was, walking with my girlfriends to the ticket booth. I knew that if my mom saw him, she would never trust me again and would confine me to the house for the rest of the summer.

My parents were so strict that I couldn't go anywhere without their practically doing a background check on everyone who would be there. Regardless of how chaste the event was, they had to be sure there wouldn't be any boys present to tempt me down the path of loose women. The thing is, I was a late bloomer and had absolutely no interest in dating—what I knew of it, anyway, based on Molly Ringwald's characters in John Hughes films like *Sixteen Candles* and *Pretty in Pink*. Though I could barely admit that I "liked" guys, my days of blissful ignorance about the world of dating were about to be over.

I had told my mom that it would be just my girlfriends and me at the movies. How could I forget that Ryan was coming?

There was no adjective in the world that would make my mom see past my geeky, lanky, pasty, computer nerd, Mormon classmate Ryan's Y chromosome. She was totally going to freak. She was going to remind me that we were Iranian Muslims, not Americans. These lectures always reminded me of when she'd explained to me in kindergarten that Christians believed in Santa and got presents, and we didn't . . . so we simply didn't. It just wasn't fair.

There was no way she was going to let me go to the movies with a man. Ryan was only fourteen, but to my mom, he was a man. He could've been eight or forty; it was all the same. When I was in middle school, she didn't approve of all the "men" exercising with me in gym class. She didn't like that I was friends with so many of the "men" in my sixth-grade history class, or that girls and eleven-year-old "men" were playing coed T-ball at recess.

As we made our way through parking-lot traffic in our Danville, California, suburb, I strategized about ways to navigate our argument. I could already hear her in my head: *Zahra, what do you mean this man is just your friend? A young girl is not friends with a man! It is not right.* Mageh Kafir hasti? *You want to be like these filthy American ladies who go home with dis guy and dat guy, and blah blah blah . . . ?*

This is such bullshit! I thought to myself.

I had a pretty good feminist rant stashed away that just might hit home: "Mom," I'd begin, "you didn't raise your eldest daughter to stay quiet and avoid making friends or talking to people because of creed or stature or even sex . . . " *Wait, I can't say "sex." She'll flip out. "Gender." Remember "gender" . . . Forget it. Take the easy way out: Lie. Just lie and say you don't know him. He's not with you. You don't even know whose friend he is.*

I snapped back to reality when I realized how close we were to where my friends were now standing . . . without Ryan. I looked around, scanning the crowds feverishly, but couldn't see him anywhere. *Perfect!*

"Zahra! Hey, Zahra!" It was Ryan, tapping on my window. "I got your ticket."

Godammit, Ryan, you polite-ass Mormon, I thought. *You don't need to come say hi!*

My mom rolled down the window.

"Is this your mom? Hi, my name's Ryan! I'm a friend of Zahra's. We've got Algebra together. Hey, Zahra, I got your ticket already and saved us seats. You saved me on my math test, so I figured I owe ya. Anyway, great to meet you, Mrs. Noorka-baba-kaka-kesh."

He shook my mom's hand, gave me my ticket, and ran into the theater, waving.

Thanks, Ryan. You just ended my summer and any hope I had of a normal adolescence. I couldn't even look at my mother, so I kept staring straight ahead. I could feel her glaring at me.

"Zahra," she began.

Here we go, I thought.

"Zahra, are you going to go?" she asked.

"What?" I asked, confused. Was this some kind of reverse psychology?

"*Maman jaan*, there's traffic behind me—get your bag," she complained.

I grabbed my bag, undid my seat belt, and reached for the door handle of salvation.

"Wait," she said.

Fuck! I waited too long.

A spot opened up in front of us, so she rolled in and parked the car. We sat in silence for what felt like forever. What the hell was going on? She didn't seem mad. I didn't know what to think or what to prepare for.

Maybe Ryan's politeness impressed her, I thought. *Maybe she's going to take back everything she's said about men. Maybe she's going to apologize for all the times she yelled at me, because she now realizes how great my friends actually are. Wow. I really underestimated my mom. I guess the toughest thing about being the firstborn daughter of immigrant parents is that they have to catch up to you as they assimilate into a foreign culture.*

Maybe I needed to initiate this dialogue, to tell her it was okay if she felt bad about all the mean things she'd said before about my guy friends or the "American ladies."

"Mom—"

"Zahra," she cut me off, "I just wanted to tell you . . . " She had a distant look in her eyes, but then suddenly zeroed in on me with intense concentration.

"Zahra, you have a hole. And for the rest of your life, men will want to put their penis in your hole. It doesn't matter who you are, what you look like, who is your 'friend.' Even at the movies, *maman jaan*, wherever—it does not change. Ri-anne seems like a very nice man, but he is a man. And all he wants is your hole. So, I will pick you up here at five o'clock. Have fun, *maman jaan*," she said.

I got out of the car and staggered toward the theater. I was horrified and astounded. *I have a what?! A hole? Where?* Was that what I had missed in sex ed the one day I had the flu? Was I the last girl on Earth to find out about my hole?

I'd never felt so completely clueless about or protective of my body in my entire life. I'd thought I had a pretty clear idea of sex. It didn't look all that complicated: a lot of kissing and touching and groping and people mashing their bodies together under bedsheets. There were no "holes" in *Sixteen Candles*!

Suddenly, crossing the parking lot to the theater was like being a scared, limping animal in a wide-open meadow with sleazy hole-hunters lurking about. I couldn't look a single guy in the face.

I busted my way through the double doors of the theater and accidentally made eye contact with the concessions guy, who was lasciviously filling up a large swirly snow cone and staring at me. I imagined him halting mid-ICEE, flinging it in the air, and then leaping across the counter, making a beeline for my hole.

I had to find my friends.

I saw Ryan sitting third-row center, with an empty seat saved for me next to him. Nothing about my relationship with him felt platonic anymore. I felt awkward and clumsy. I felt like . . . like . . . like I was on a date. Omigod, was this a date? My vision was blurring. I couldn't think fast enough.

He bought me my ticket.

He met my mother.

We're sitting next to each other.

Did he ever really *need help with algebra?*

I sat through all of *Johnny Mnemonic* with my jeans pulled up to my waist and my legs crossed tightly together. Every time my legs started to relax and slide open, I felt like I was exposing my hole to the world, and clamped them back together again. The longer I held my legs together, the angrier I became at Ryan. *Look at him, all stupid-faced and smiling, sitting there dipping his disgusting hands into the greasy popcorn. This movie sucks. Why is he smiling? He's probably thinking about holes. Gross!* All I knew at that point was that, date or not, he'd better not be thinking about my hole, or I was going to kick his ass.

I was twenty-two years old when I lost my virginity. That's right, twenty-two. And no, I wasn't married, or engaged to be married, or even in an exclusive relationship.

By Iranian standards, I imagine the response to be: *Why are you talking about your virginity publicly? You are totally embarrassing your parents; your two million first to fifth cousins, aunts, and uncles around the world; their Iranian friends and the Iranian friends of their friends; Iranians who know them or of them; Iranians who know you; and Iranians who live near you. Just pray to God that word of this never gets to your grandparents.*

By Muslim standards . . . well, I suppose it depends on how observant you are. By the standards of the Abrahamic religions, I imagine the response is something like: *Whore!*

By mainstream American standards: *That's a little late. Did you have some kind of personal issue?*

Yes, I did! It's called being the firstborn, first-generation daughter in an Iranian Muslim household. I thought I could skate through life as a happy, assimilated American woman if I could just make my "hole" invisible to men.

My mom's crash course in sex ed was a scare tactic that kept me at arm's length from guys throughout my teens. American culture only reinforced that fear with the confusion surrounding sex in high school. If a girl had sex, she was a slut or, at the very least, the victim of endless gossip. If she didn't have sex, she was either naive and sheltered or a frigid prude.

The only place where I felt I could be safe from judgment was asexuality: a place of fist pumps, video games, oversize black hoodies, and comfortable physical distances.

But by the time I made it out of high school and began college, I didn't want to be invisible anymore. I wanted to be seen, desired, even. I was no longer hiding from "men"—I wanted to be found. I did not want to save my virginity for marriage. I hadn't yet been in love, but didn't want to be in a relationship defined by the status of my "hole."

When I started UC Berkeley, I found myself in a land of hipsters where androgynous, Cartoon Network–watching tomboys were a catch. I went on my first-ever date with Dean, a nerdy, Nietzsche-loving philosophy major and "minimal house music" DJ from the Midwest.

I first fell for him in the car on our way to a mutual friend's house. We had the same propensity for dark and often inappropriate humor, peppered with unidentifiable foreign accents. Our jokes degenerated into silliness, until I was dying with laughter and had to pull the car over to catch my breath. Dean turned to me, eyes twinkling, and said, "This is the most fun I've had since I hung out with my best friend in high school."

Two weeks later, Dean did not want to have sex with me. It was a beautiful Berkeley summer afternoon, and I was sitting on the bottom bunk of the bed across the room from him, listening to him explain that taking my virginity just put too much pressure on him. He said he couldn't handle the weight, the responsibility, and the attachment I might feel after the deed was done.

There I was, offering myself up, and I was being rejected . . . by a guy? A man! A hole-hunter! I wondered what my mother would say if she knew.

What was I supposed to do now? Rub his back and tell him it was okay? Assure him that it'd be painless and that I wouldn't think less of him afterward? Maybe I could offer him a drink, something to relax . . . like a roofie, a few hits of Viagra, or just a slap in the face.

What the fuck, Dean? I wanted to yell. *I shaved my legs. I got Brazilianed. I lotioned my entire body. I got my nails done. I'm wearing a hundred dollars' worth of fancy underwear. I attended Pilates this morning so my abs would look hot. I risked UV rays and got a tan! I made an appointment with my doctor to discuss birth control options! I illegally downloaded porn to figure out some moves and blamed the computer viruses on my brother!*

I had come to Dean's dorm room that day on a mission. I was my mother's daughter, after all, and frankness among the women of our line was a virtue. So, from where I sat on the bunk bed, I said to the distraught man across the room, "Dean, I think it's really wise to consider the repercussions of taking my virginity. This is certainly new turf for me, and I appreciate your honesty in telling me that you are not seeking a relationship. I'm not looking for a relationship, either. You see, Dean, at fifteen, sixteen, even seventeen, a girl hopes to find someone she trusts, before she . . . you know. At eighteen, nineteen, even twenty, she still kinda wants to be seduced. But by twenty-two, Dean, she pretty much just wants to get fucked. Does that clear up the confusion for you?"

Dean stopped smiling, jumped up from where he was sitting, and kissed me hard on the lips. We fell against the bed, and he started taking off my clothes. He reached under my shirt, grabbed my bra by the sides, and pulled my top off with it. He grabbed hold of my belt buckle, stretched its leather, and tore off my jeans. I was in awe. His desire for me was incredible. His eyes, intense and possessed, were locked on my body. *Oh my God,* I thought, *this ravaging, pillaging beast wants my hole!*

His crazed, panicked rush mesmerized me. I had no idea why he was in such a hurry, but I was totally into it. I grabbed hold of his undershirt to help. He flung it off and we started on his pants. My hands ran up his bare chest as we lay back down. My heart was pounding.

As I watched my pink panties fly up in the air, the sunlight from Dean's dorm room window shining through the $50 lace, I felt giddy. Inside, I was screaming, *This is it! This is it! This is it!* I was jumping out of my skin with anticipation and excitement. I had to breathe. I had to clear my head. I had to relax, but I kept thinking, *From here on out, Zahra, nobody can put the burden of virginity back on you. No man can claim it, because you've given it up to a man who doesn't want to own you.*

Afterward, Dean asked me if I was okay and wanted to know how it had been for me. I said I wasn't sure. It seemed dispiriting to ask if I was supposed to feel . . . more? Or if he had actually been inside me? Or if it was supposed to last longer? Instead, I asked him if we could try it again. He said something about "refractory periods," then slid to my side and fell asleep. And that was it.

I mean, I hadn't expected Kristin Scott Thomas's spasms in *The English Patient*, the acrobatics of *9½ Weeks,* or a round from Jenna Jameson's "best of" clips. But this was supposed to be a rite of passage for me.

This was the point at which I was supposed to look over at Dean in an irrational postcoital fog and think he was the one to whom I must forever bind myself because he'd shown me a whole new world, taken my virginity, owned a piece of me. Based on what? The fact that he had penetrated my hole for less than a minute?

I started to feel overwhelmed by just how underwhelmed I was. It seemed like the most uneventful act of my life, and yet, based on everything I had heard up until this point, it was supposed to define me. Where was the transformation? The heavens were supposed to open up and reveal the secrets of the world! I didn't feel any different.

The only thing that was different was Dean. He started to change. Our evenings together became awkward, as if we were moving backward in time to the clumsiness of a first date. When I'd sit down next to him and snuggle up close, he'd scoot back. When I would hold his hand, it was like he was keeping track of how long I was holding it for. If I laughed too loudly, he looked at me like I was hiding something. And then I got the speech:

"Um, this is really hard to say, but I thought I was pretty clear that I'm not looking for a relationship, you know . . . I think you kind of like me too much . . . It's awesome hanging out with you, and I still want to be friends, but I kind of need my space."

I felt like a fool.

Though I had come to see that not all men were after only one thing, I also realized that men could be duped by the emphasis on virginity, too. Dean had felt my virginity as a burden, and now he thought he had to decide whether I would become his whore or his wife.

I was heartbroken about losing my friendship with Dean after he panicked over his "responsibility" toward me. But I felt freer, too. My mother had been right about the significance of my hole, but for me it wasn't about protecting my virginity. My experiences and choices were being guided by something much more sacred than that: I had learned about my body, and about what it was like to get what I wanted. I felt much older and wiser than the girl I had been only weeks before. I finally felt like a woman.

Sex by Any Other Name

Insiya Ansari

t was two in the morning, and I was frolicking on an air mattress in the middle of my living room with a guarded man. We'd met a month earlier while I was on a work-related trip. After an extended period of phone flirtation, he had flown in from the other end of the state for the weekend so that we could get to know each other better in person.

At the beginning of his trip, we were just friends, but by the third night, we'd advanced to benefits. We were fondling and flattering each other to a soundtrack of hungry, labored respiration, when he bumped up against the sexual glass ceiling that had loomed over all my serious relationships to date.

We'd been chatting between kisses, and the interstitial conversation had just turned to sex. I delivered the bombshell: I'd been with my last boyfriend for five years and we had never done it. The groping froze. A moment later, he proclaimed firmly, "Well, that definitely ain't me." Meaning: *I'd never wait five years for sex with any woman—capisce?* The familiar acidic disappointment hit my gut, and then I felt indignant. A slow-unfolding relationship wouldn't satisfy this one, even if biding his time without sex meant he could end up with a queen like me.

I am a girl with an ample sense of self-worth. I possessed it even during my awkward teenage years, because I was cosseted and adored by my family. Unlike with many other first-generation American Muslim girls, my parents didn't impose rules to mirror the strictures of their own upbringings in India (which had, nonetheless, been forward-thinking for their time). I hadn't been reduced to sneaking around with boyfriends, and my parents even tolerated it when those boys were "Americans," as they referred to anyone who was either white or black.

With these affordances, I cycled through at least one boy-friend every year. But each relationship played out in my home, under the watchful eyes of my parents, who allowed us to hang there only if my bedroom door was wide open. One of these boyfriends, a chocolate brown South Indian whom my father dismissed as a raffish thug, managed to get me alone in his bedroom regularly during my sophomore year in high school. He'd ease me onto the bed hopefully, and we'd kiss and grind, never even toying with the button of his baggy purple denim shorts.

About a half hour of that would bring us to the outer limits of my sexual concession zone. I'd unfailingly extract myself with a semiapologetic smile and walk down the hill to my parents' house. This relative chastity was a direct outgrowth of parental enmeshment, as described by a crude maxim in our dialect that essentially means I was "all up in my parents' armpits." Collective values went unspoken. I understood that unlike for the loose Americans I'd grown up around, having sex was tantamount to growing dreadlocks, stretching my earlobe with a gauge, or declaring myself agnostic. And I'd never experienced any counterpressure that was convincing enough to make me disrespect my parents. Therefore, I never had to endure that most embarrassing of parent-adolescent rituals, "The [don't get pregnant, use a condom] Talk."

My parents have always called themselves liberal Muslims. While I was growing up, they prayed *namaz* about as often as they drank beer and wine—neither was regular practice, nor occasioned only by a holiday—and they paid interest on our home. These behaviors countered conventional orthodoxy; some are considered haram. My parents weren't the sort to pull the "because I said so" card, and for the most part, my brother and I didn't push the limits. But bohemian and secular my parents were not. They were devout believers in the Qur'an's historical narrative, and their cultural values were dictated by an Islamic worldview that was shared throughout our community, a close-knit Shiite minority sect. Within the extended community, news of a hellion child spread fast. I was not very newsworthy until, at eighteen, I met my first love.

Much as I cherished the notion that my relationship with Michel was a love for the ages, it looked a lot like a pop-culture trope: Virginal, Coddled Ingenue Gets Stars Crossed with Dangerous/Broken Casanova. (See: *Grease*, *Dirty Dancing*, various Molly Ringwald flicks.) I met him in a program that attracted young writers from divergent backgrounds. He'd throw smoldering looks across the room, before he turned his attention to our peers in the program and let rip with impossibly confident, cogent rants about everything from criminal justice to teen moms to the conspicuous consumerism of his broke friends dizzied by their obsession with the latest Jordans. Michel had nearly been denied his high school diploma because of a pitiful attendance record, but I wasn't alone in believing that he was brilliant.

Initially, I was much more taciturn than he was in those meetings, slightly intimidated by the big personalities and strong opinions. When Michel first began flirting with me, I assumed it was because I was fresh meat. When we weren't at work on projects, the testosterone-amped office atmosphere regressed to locker-room antics, the boys assiduously ranking each girl's dateability.

But when Michel and I were together, he'd lose the machismo. He'd make himself vulnerable, dropping his lids over huge, almond-shaped eyes to fully appreciate an affecting song on the radio, while urging me to do the same. He was genuinely present, and I responded with rapt attention. We were both as inquisitive as we were voluble, and a conversation that started with the typical exchange of childhood anecdotes would spiral out into a full-throated debate that folded in topics from gangsterism to interracial dating to international water rights to maternal attachment.

He told me that I was the first girl with whom he wanted to talk as often as he wanted to kiss her. And I was a "faith over fuck-ups" type, constantly expressing my confidence that he could climb out of hood life to attain the professional victories that he dreamed of.

My parents, in our first truly painful schism, decided Michel was a scoundrel the first time they met him. As I became more wayward, serially ditching my college classes, they blamed him for sucking me into his vortex of troublemaking. They didn't appreciate his intelligence. Rather, my father seemed to feel Michel was too slick—even when, or maybe because—he stooped his long neck, softened his voice, and answered questions with "Yes, sir . . . no, sir."

I, on the other hand, was outright disrespectful, challenging my parents to "give me just one reason!" why they didn't like him, and becoming sullen when they came up with five or more. I began to stay out until dawn, sometimes leaving the house just a few hours later with no more than ten words to my parents in between.

Even as Michel's appearance in my life felt transformative, my parents' concerns about our differences weren't entirely off the mark. We were each bewildered by the others' sexual values. Michel was a monument to virility, a playa's playa. I made it clear at the beginning of our relationship that I was "waiting until I was married" to have sex. Never mind that the notion of marriage was an abstraction to me. All I knew with certainty was that it was a handy demarcation for the Before and After of sexual intimacy. My sexual values had never caused problems in my relationships before, and since I didn't know what we were missing, I never knew how much I was asking Michel to give up.

This presented a moral quandary for Michel, since he was falling in love with me, despite my abstinence. To attest to how smitten he was, he'd describe his peers' reactions when they heard that Michel was in a celibate relationship: "You, patna? C'mon." "So, y'all still ain't f&*#ed?" They were counting down to the day when I'd inevitably give in to Michel's charms. He was magnetic and sexually experienced in equal measure. He'd begun having sex when he was fifteen. Before he knew of my jealous streak, which was voracious for anecdotes of past girlfriends to obsess over, he'd share tantalizing details, curious to see my reaction. He told me a story about being jailed briefly, and then released in the middle of the night. Hungry for sex, he sought relief with a repulsive-looking girl from the neighborhood known for her loose lips. Although the anecdote shocked me, it also comforted me as I placed it squarely in the rearview: I figured that was the kind of behavior that he had gotten out of his system after all his teenage exploits. Unfortunately, it wasn't.

It took only six months for Michel to begin cheating—at least, as far as I was able to trace. But it took a year before I was faced with evidence that, even through my fog of infatuation, was undeniable. I caught a friend of his in a lie about a night they'd supposedly been together, when I called to inquire about the friend's injury. Short of his saying, "What broken leg?" everything about his response made it clear the story was a cover-up.

The truth tumbled out over the phone while Michel was out of town. He was in the rural South, helping a friend relocate from California. I was still in college and living at home with my parents. Unwilling to wait for him to return, I made my first big purchase on a credit card to fly out to meet him and seek an answer for my bewilderment. I held on to a faint hope that the irregular phone connection had produced some grotesque misunderstanding on my part, even though at some point he'd quietly said of the first indiscretion, "Baby, this is just a rock from the mountain of lies that our relationship is built on."

After I arrived, we spent the first night crying, with his head buried in my lap as he apologized again and again. The next day, his friend's batty auntie who lived next door to the guesthouse where he was staying told the rest of her family that we'd spent the night moaning bawdily. In a twisted attempt at defending my honor, Michel poured sugar in her van's gas tank. The engine easily revved to life the next morning and she drove away, leaving us on the lot alone. I spent the morning feeling angry and ashamed. Couldn't she tell the difference between sex and elegiac despair?

Stockholm syndrome is the only plausible psychoanalysis I can come up with for what happened that night, and for my overall reaction to the greatest betrayal I'd experienced. Michel and I were bored and frustrated, stuck in the backcountry without transportation. We'd been staring each other down from opposite ends of the thin mattress, and his explanations for the transgressions hadn't gotten any more coherent—how could they, when the acts were so muddled within his own psyche? I'd pressed him all I could.

Seized with a panicked thought that I would have to return to the generally unchallenging life I'd had without him, I folded myself into his arms. The role reversal commenced in earnest, and suddenly I was the one stroking his brow and kissing him.

The warmth turned to heat, and the mutual comforting transitioned into desire. Later that night, we had sex.

Sex. It's been more than ten years since that night, and this unequivocal label still makes me recoil. In my mind, what Michel and I did that night was something different—what a friend later called "The Dip." I finally let him enter me, but I didn't give in to the throes of unbridled intercourse. It was an approximation: controlled and tentative, and haunted by post-cheating sadness. When I reflected on the "why" soon after, I told myself that some act resembling the sexual activity he was used to would satisfy the desire that had brought us to this point in the first place.

Of course, it was a fool's bargain, a circumscribed compromise that I also assumed would keep me, within the most narrow of definitions, a virgin. By then I'd read several novels in which a night like this ended with a white sheet on a backyard clothesline, fluttering in the breeze and dotted with blood: the victory flag of a man newly married to a God-fearing Muslim girl. I threw out the superficial physiology lessons we'd all snickered at in junior-high sex ed and instead called upon this definition, which I took to mean that if there was no penetration, we were still engaging in heavy foreplay and nothing more. So on this night, and a few others, I crossed a line without crossing The Line. We'd be fooling around, and when I thought we were in a danger zone, I'd press my palms to his stomach and guide his body away from me slightly, like intuitive adjustments made to a ship's course according to shifting winds. Most of the people whom I've shared this tale with can't quite believe that I could have been so reckless, and confused, and naive.

Oh, trust me, I tell them. Before that fateful phone call from the South, I had ignored plenty of evidence about Michel's flirtation with other women, because I believed (and still do) that he loved me deeply.

For more than a year, I had watched Michel struggle with his duality: the tender, impassioned humanist, contrasted with the *napuck*, or brat, that my parents had recognized in him from the start. It was contagious; I turned into the poster child for Trying to Please Everyone While Pleasing No One. I was even worse at the balancing act than Michel.

When I was home, I was acutely aware of how disappointed my parents were that I was still dating him, and how they seemed to glower even more when I became antsy to leave, hogging the cordless phone as I checked for messages from you-know-who. When he did call, I'd up and leave at a moment's notice to meet him. I couldn't remember the last time my parents, my brother, and I had eaten dinner together as a family.

And what's more, The Dip itself was a bust. There was no freedom in it, and guilt flared up in both Michel and me and repelled us from the temporary bonded state we'd reached. He knew I was unhappy defying my parents, and with him, my suspicion fueled increasingly controlling behavior. Within six months, Michel was cheating again, and more flagrantly than before.

Partly, I stayed so long because I believed my youthful indiscretion would be justified if we managed to stay together and vanquish our obvious incompatibility. After Michel and I had to let go, through my next relationship, I tried to vanquish the sex itself.

My next long-term boyfriend was utterly devoted, loving, and willing to be patient with me, even in the shell-shocked state I was in after Michel. Our sex life unfolded completely on my terms. I remember reading an article at the time about "born-again virgins"—Christian girls who had sex and then decided to return to abstinence, presumably to reclaim a moral and spiritual high ground. I hated the term but decided to try out the approach.

Like Michel, my new man wasn't Muslim, nor was he other-wise religious, but he was willing to entertain this "born-again" status. He was significantly older and had already been in several long-term relationships. He seemed settled, and he was focused on the horizon, hoping we'd get married. We were together five years, and he was just as devoted to my newfound piety as I was, never once implying that I'd lose him if I didn't loosen up. But the sexual repression I was imposing on myself didn't feel right. I wish I could say that from being with Michel, I'd gained clarity that sex before marriage is ruinous. But it taught me more about what I *didn't* believe: that because I had pushed up against a pro-hibition, I'd also traded in my status as an observant Muslim.

That's not because I took issue with Islamic precepts around premarital sex, like some of my friends, who wrote them off as irrelevant to their modern lives. I just wasn't convinced that this one transgression negated all my other religious virtues.

In that sense, getting right with God was the easy part. But the post-Michel celibacy wasn't driven by conviction—it was a shelter under which I could heal, without having to reconcile my past experimentation with a religious and sexual practice that would feel right moving forward.

Ten years after Michel, I came to the brink again, faced with the toll of the hard work I'd shirked. This time, it was with the guy on the air mattress. A year after we met, the struggle over sex was again driving a wedge in our relationship. He was asking for an open relationship, and rather than feel the pain of that betrayal, I decided to go whole hog. I gave him everything that I'd physically withheld in my prior relationships.

At first, my heart wasn't in the decision, and the fact that I wasn't holding anything back scared me a bit. This anxiety begat paranoia. How could the man really love me and at the same time have pressured me to have sex when I felt so ambivalent about it? Was this my pattern: becoming infatuated with selfish men who would do me wrong? I dizzied myself with these thoughts, and gave of myself tentatively. Moreover, the sex was often disappointing.

So it might sound delusional when I say that I considered our intimacy over the next few years to be redemptive. But finally confronting the ambiguity in my sex life allowed me to be more accepting of all my purported contradictions. And when the obsession with my sexual status fell away, my religious identity came into relief. I focused on maintaining the practices that are core to my spirituality and my connection to God.

Ultimately, when Air Mattress Man and I fell apart, I didn't regret what I'd chosen. So much for that compartmentalized existence that parents, and many men, would like to impose: that a good Muslim girl doesn't engage in sex before she's committed for life. It's a specter I'm glad to be rid of. Here, finally, was that unambiguous status I'd been refusing to claim. I'm an unmarried, Muslim nonvirgin. I've said it aloud; still, I don't disappear.

Otherwise Engaged

Huda Al-Marashi

My first year in college, I went home every weekend. My parents viewed my staying in the dorms as the unavoidable consequence of living in a small California town without a four-year university. Since I didn't have my own car, Baba would drive an hour and a half to pick me up in his late-1980s Mercedes. If motor vehicles had rights, that poor car would have had Baba reported to Automobile Protective Services. The backseat and trunk were so covered with papers and books, their original surfaces had become invisible. The cup holders were filled with half-drunk coffee thermoses and Ziploc bags of gummy candies he called sours. Sours, Baba claimed, kept him awake on long drives. Since Baba had been known to fall asleep behind the wheel (and had been in two accidents because of it), sours were as important to his safety as seat belts.

Given Baba's driving record, I never let him drive me home. I'd throw my duffel bag on the paper mountain behind the driver's seat and slide in behind the wheel. I spoke little during our rides together. Baba was a storyteller, and he filled our time together with anecdotes—tales from the lives of the prophets and memories from his childhood. But that changed after my engagement to the son of our closest family friends. Then Baba started using our time in the car to ask me a question that was weighing heavily on his mind.

"You know, Huddie," he'd say, "I never got a chance to ask you if you really like this boy."

Baba always worded his question the exact same way, his voice never exceeding the volume of a loud whisper. It was as if he felt shy to ask, and he may have been. Baba wasn't in the habit of questioning our choices. He usually waited until my siblings and I had made our own decisions, and then he invariably voiced his support. Out of respect for him, we only allowed ourselves things we knew he'd approve of. It was a surprisingly effective parenting strategy.

"He's a nice boy," I answered. "I like him."

"Because if you don't like him, you don't have to marry him," Baba offered in an even quieter voice now.

"I know."

"What about your cousin, Fa—"

"No, Daddy."

"Why not? He is a *sayyid*."

My family belonged to a clan that claimed descent from the Prophet Muhammad, earning us the honorific title of *sayyid*. A man could marry a non-*sayyid* woman and still pass the title on to her children, but a woman could not. Mama loved my fiancé, Hadi, too much to bring up his not being *sayyid*. Baba loved being a *sayyid* too much not to mention it.

"That's not so important to me, Baba," I said. "It's more important for me to marry someone I know."

Within our Iraqi community, the only marriages I knew of had been arranged. Most couples spent little to no unsupervised time together before their wedding. When Hadi's father had asked my father for my hand in November, I had hoped that my engagement would be different. Our families had gone on road trips to national parks together. We'd been to each other's birthday parties and graduations, and both Hadi and I had been born in America. In my mind, the latter was the best guarantee I'd have some kind of romance before my wedding. Hadi had grown up watching the same television shows and movies. He had to know that in spite of the understanding between both our families, I still expected a private proposal that only the two of us shared.

"Well, it will be a great honor to their family if you marry their son," Baba said with a pleased smile. "Now their grandchildren will be *mirza*. This is the name they give people whose mother is an *alwiya*. You know this is the word they use for the lady that is a *sayyid*?"

I nodded.

"You know my sister's husband is not a *sayyid*, but he always calls his wife *alwiya*. It is so nice." Baba dragged the "o" in "so," and I felt there was a hint there, a tiny suggestion, that it would be equally nice were Hadi to call me *alwiya*. It was as if Hadi could make up for his lack of *sayyid*-ness by being overtly appreciative of mine.

I nodded again, because that's what we did around Baba: We listened and nodded regardless of what we were thinking.

My engagement party had been planned around the Christmas holidays so that my uncles and their families could fly in from their adopted homes in England. My Aunt Zena joined us from New Jersey with her three kids—a boy and two girls who shared her sea-blue eyes.

We would be renting a van and driving to my cousin Marwa's Southern California home for the party, but before we left, Mama wanted to do her share of the cooking. There were grape leaves to be stuffed with rice and layered into a deep pot, and cigar-shaped *boorek* to be wrapped and frozen in aluminum trays.

After dinner one evening, my mom, Zena, and I sat around the breakfast nook table with a stack of phyllo dough in front of each of us. We dug our spoons into a pan of sautéed spinach and feta cheese and then dropped their contents onto the center of a strip of pastry.

Bringing up the sides of the dough around a dollop of spinach, Zena said, "She's only eighteen. You should've waited. She is beautiful, *mashAllah*. It's nice for a girl to see how many suitors she can get."

"I'm not trying to sell a sheep," Mama answered. "What does it matter how many people come?"

"You know what I mean. It's nice for a girl to feel wanted, and then her future in-laws will value her more when they know how many people came for her."

"They already know what they're getting. They've seen all kinds of girls. They know there is nobody like my Huddie."

"Of course there's nobody like her. That's why I'm saying maybe you could've gotten everything: somebody with a good future, a good family, maybe *sayyid*."

I didn't make eye contact with Mama or Zena. I busily wrapped my dough, knowing that soon Mama would come to Hadi's defense. But as much as I tried to dismiss what I'd heard, something nagged at me. It was as if Zena thought I was marrying down. My thoughts drifted away on a wave of disappointment. In a world where people didn't necessarily marry for love, whom you married and what he or she was mattered. You married names, reputations. It never occurred to me that by Iraqi standards, Hadi's "who and what" might not have been that impressive.

"He's a good boy," Mama said. "And good boys aren't easy to come by. Maybe we wait for somebody *sayyid* and he turns out to be a jerk. You think it's so easy to find someone *sayyid* with a good job, and close in age, and whose family you know and trust. Wait until you're looking for someone for your daughters. Then all you'll want is someone who really knows the value of your girl, and this boy loves her. You know that."

"She's not that hard to love," Zena said.

My Uncle Mazen walked into the room and caught Zena's last remark. "Who's not?" he asked.

"Huddie."

"Of course not. She's lovely," he said, his voice lilting with the British accent that he'd picked up along with the language.

"I was just saying maybe they should've waited."

He shrugged. Uncle Mazen was Mama's youngest brother, and he wasn't about to get involved in an issue between his older sisters. In our family, he was the comic relief.

"He looks a bit Indian, no? Makes me feel like speaking Urdu." Uncle Mazen accompanied his jab with a stereotypically Indian head bob and the hum of what was supposed to be a Hindi song.

I placed another *boorek* in the tray so I wouldn't have to react. *Uncle Mazen didn't mean it*, I told myself. *He said that for a laugh.* But weren't jokes a disguise for what people really felt? Blue-eyed Zena and Mazen were unimpressed by Hadi's bronze skin and brown eyes. My family had more than its share of fair skin and light-colored eyes. This, among typically dark-haired, dark-eyed Iraqis, was a source of pride.

Or maybe Zena and Mazen were doing nothing more than what families did. Make fun. Joke. Act like their side was too good for the other. But then again, what if they truly weren't impressed? Maybe if I had been marrying someone different, someone better, they'd be saying nice things about him now. Maybe they'd be telling my mom we were lucky to have found such a good guy.

I plopped another spoonful of spinach onto a strip of dough, feeling a lot like the *boorek* I was wrapping. Zena and Mazen had dropped a helping of doubt at the very center of me and were now wrapping me around those thoughts so tightly, I wondered if they'd ever escape.

We had reserved four rooms at a Holiday Inn Express in Anaheim. This was done for the sake of my young cousins, who'd been promised a trip to Disneyland the day before my engagement party. Otherwise, we'd have thought nothing of adding sixteen guests to the five household members living in Cousin Marwa's four-bedroom home. In Iraqi culture, there is no such thing as not enough room. The only BYOB in our world is "bring your own blanket."

We arrived at our hotel in a sixteen-passenger van, overloaded with adults, children, luggage, and trays of food stacked in a cooler. Being within walking distance of Disneyland had filled the children with an anticipatory glee I shared. Hadi would be joining us the next morning, and it would be his last chance to give me the special proposal I'd been hinting at for weeks.

Since we'd been promised, Hadi and I had spoken on the phone every night. So far, all my hints had been the cause of more trouble than good. I didn't want to tell Hadi exactly what I expected, because that would've ruined the surprise. So instead I'd suggested, "You haven't really asked me." This had prompted the completely undesired response, "Will you marry me?"

I'd answered, "You can't ask me over the phone," and he'd followed with proposals over email, fax, and greeting card. Not wanting Hadi to think these amateur attempts had satisfied me, I'd picked up the phone after each effort to inform him that, although cute and flattering, these proposals still did not count. In fact, they were only making the real, official moment less special.

I called Hadi from the hotel room that night to confirm our plans for the following day. He told me he wouldn't be coming, that his parents thought it was too much for him to make the two-hour drive to Anaheim only to make the same drive the next day for the engagement party.

I responded with the one thing I knew worked—tears. If I cried, Hadi would ask me what was wrong, and I could reluctantly say what I wanted without feeling like I had asked for anything.

After a round of unconvincing "nothings," I sniffed about wanting to spend the day together before our engagement party. About how we'd gotten engaged and hadn't had an outing together since. I did such a good job presenting my case that I began to feel sorry for myself. My one chance to experience something like a date with the boy I was going to marry had been ruined.

I hung up the phone, grateful that only Mama had been in the room to overhear my conversation. She put down the dress she had been hemming and entered the narrow space between the room's two full-size beds. Her hands on my shoulders, she comforted me with "It's okay, *hababa*. Maybe they want some time together as a family."

"I just wanted us to have one fun day together before our party."

Mama picked up the phone, frowning as if I'd pleaded with her to call Hadi's mother. My tears stopped instantly. Mama would fix things. She always did. I stayed seated at the edge of the bed and listened as she worked her conversational magic. First, an exchange of the many ways people say, "How are you?" in the Iraqi dialect: "What is your color?" "What is your news?" "How is your health?" And again, "What is your news?" A little catch-up talk. Another round of "how are yous," this time in reference to other members of the family. And then to the point: "So, what's the story with tomorrow? I got this one in tears over here."

Mama listened to Hadi's mother's response, nodding and laughing. "What is this talk? He's our son. Of course we want him with us."

Their conversation moved into a discussion of the party, but I knew all I needed to know. Hadi was coming tomorrow. I stretched out on the polyester bedspread, my thoughts bouncing. Maybe he would ask for my ring early. Maybe he'd ask me to go with him alone on a ride. We'd be waiting in line, and he'd get down on one knee and say, "I've loved you for as long as I've known you. Will you marry me?" I'd cover my face with my hands in surprise. Then I'd cry and say, "Yes." We'd hug for the first time. Maybe even kiss.

The next day, I put on my planned outfit. I wanted to be wearing something comfortable but cute, so I'd packed khaki pants, loafers, a cap-sleeve denim shirt, and a cropped navy blue peacoat with small buttons. I styled my hair, put on my makeup, and hoped Hadi was as ready to propose to me as I was ready to be proposed to.

Hadi was waiting for us in the parking lot of our hotel by the time all sixteen of us trickled down the concrete stairs. I was happy to see him but unhappy that he'd chosen to wear his puffy Lakers jacket. He loved that jacket, and I wondered when in our relationship it would be appropriate to tell him I hated it. All Hadi needed was a pair of oversize tennis shoes and a couple of gold chains, and he'd look like a hip-hop star. If he did propose to me today, we were going to look like such a mismatched couple.

Later that afternoon, Mama gave Hadi and me permission to slip away from the group to go on a few rides together. We went on four rides alone, each one offering us an hour of wait time in line. And yet, despite ample opportunities, Hadi still did not propose. The only thing that surprised me about our time together was that this did not upset me. I was too happy to be bothered. I finally felt like the girls I'd watched in line, summer after summer, with their denim shorts and Minnie Mouse ears, their hands and lips locked with their boyfriends'.

I had a boyfriend now. When we were alone, we held hands

and said nothing of it. We carried on talking as if our hands had accidentally bumped into one another and latched of their own accord. All this to avoid acknowledging we'd touched before we were Islamically married, something we'd been taught since childhood was haram.

"Sorry about the crying yesterday," I said.

"Don't be sorry. I wanted to come."

"I know it's a drive, but I thought it would be nice to be together."

"I'd drive anywhere if it meant I got to spend more time with you."

I thought to affectionately squeeze Hadi's hand, but that would've drawn attention to the fact that our hands were still linked. Instead I smiled and said, "I hope your parents aren't upset. I feel like I made you come."

"Naw. I think my mom didn't want me imposing on your family time."

At the end of the day, we rejoined my family on the Disneyland asphalt to watch the evening's last presentation of *Fantasmic*, a light show projected over the park's man-made lake. The ground was still warm from the afternoon sun, and with my hands on my waist, I arched my sore back. From behind me, Hadi offered, "You can lean on my legs."

This warranted a quick scan of the adults. My aunt and uncles were each busy with their own children. My mom and dad had run off to buy everyone popcorn, so I allowed my back to rest against Hadi's propped-up knees. By the time my parents returned, the show had started. They squeezed in next to my sister, Lina, glanced at me, but said nothing. And so I stayed right where I was, watching lit-up boats filled with dancing characters move through the water, feeling a rush of conflicting emotions. The day was over, and Hadi hadn't proposed. I hated the jacket he had draped on my shoulders, and I hated that he was the kind of guy who not only liked sports but liked them enough to buy a team jacket. And yet still, my heart and everything next to it was pounding. Hadi's shins felt warm against my back. I'd never been so close to a boy.

The next day at my engagement party, I studied my hair and makeup in the magnifying mirror attached to the hotel room's bathroom wall and asked my mother, "Since I'm pretty much engaged now, do you think I could pluck my eyebrows?"

In my family, hair removal required permission. Plucking, waxing, shaving—these were the pursuits of married women with an audience for their smooth skin. I'd won the battle to wax my legs in junior high by crying that my girlfriends were calling me a gorilla, but shaped eyebrows were another symbol entirely.

I stepped out of the bathroom to hear Mama's response. She walked over to me and took my chin in her hand.

"If you really want," she said, her voice heavy with reluctance. "Just don't pluck too much. Your eyebrows are beautiful already."

"You do it. I don't know how."

I wiggled myself onto the bed in my sheath dress as if I were a mermaid with a lace-and-sequins tail. Mama sat down on the bed and leaned over me. As she tugged away at the stray hairs along my brow bone with angled tweezers, I squealed in pain and surprise. I'd assumed that tweezing couldn't hurt any more than hot waxing, but it had an entirely different kind of pinch.

"How come it doesn't hurt you when you pluck?" I asked Mama.

"I've been doing it forever. My eyebrows are dead."

Mama was already dressed in a beaded blue dress suit. I thought of all the times I had watched her getting ready for a wedding, and I couldn't believe that I was the bride-to-be now.

As soon as Mama was done helping me get ready, she gathered up the family and left in the van. Hadi came to pick me up from the hotel shortly afterward. Lina and Baba had stayed behind as chaperones. They slid into the small bucket seats in the back of Hadi's two-door sports car, and then Hadi held out his hand for me as I stepped into the front seat. Unlike the day before, I was pleased by Hadi's appearance. He wore a pin-stripe suit, a cream-colored shirt, a tie I'd bought him, and a new pair of dress oxfords. I liked Hadi in a suit, and I wondered if there was a way to arrange for him to wear one daily. It was much easier to think positive thoughts about us as a couple when Hadi was dressed nicely.

Lina and Baba went inside as soon as we arrived at Aunt Marwa's house. Hadi and I stayed in the car, waiting to make our entrance. It was our first moment alone, but I hoped he wouldn't ask me to marry him then. I wouldn't be pleased if he'd let a perfectly good day in Disneyland pass, only to ask me in the car. There was only one opportunity left now. He had to ask me at the party, and he had to do it right.

When Mama gave us the signal, we walked through the front door together. Arabic music, heavy with the beat of drums and tambourines, was playing on the tape deck plugged in beside the door. The women in our families sent their tongues to the roof of their mouths to welcome us with their ululating cry. Hadi's grandmother threw a mix of candy and coins over our heads as we sat on the chairs parked at the front of the room. Our families and guests crowded in on the sofas and folding chairs along the living room's perimeter.

Hadi's father took the microphone plugged into the stereo and welcomed our guests, before announcing that we'd be exchanging our rings. I took a deep breath. My special proposal had to be now. Oh, my God. Yes. It was now. Hadi took the ring box his mother handed him and turned around in his seat. Wait a minute. Why wasn't he kneeling like an American boyfriend would? *Get down on the floor, man. Please.*

Oh. No.

It was worse than I'd thought. Hadi leaned in and was whispering something about spending the rest of his life with me. Why was he whispering?

"Say it loud," Baba called out from across the room.

I smiled awkwardly and prayed. *Please, God, make him say it out loud.*

"Say it loud," Baba called out again.

"*Yella*," everybody chimed in.

This was so embarrassing. Hadi was supposed to profess his undying devotion to me so that my family would finally understand why it didn't matter that he wasn't *sayyid* or fair-skinned. His love for me was so beautiful and pure that it trumped all other status-bolstering criteria.

"Will you marry me?" he whispered.

There it was. The question. It was over. The words were spoken, and they could not be taken back. My long-awaited moment had been cheek-reddening and dull. What now? Was I supposed to whisper, too?

"Yes," I said, because there was no other answer to give at that point. I smiled so no one would suspect that I was unhappy, but my heart wobbled with disappointment and I felt a burning in my nose that meant I was dangerously vulnerable to tears.

Don't go there, I spoke to myself firmly. *Your only chance for a beautiful proposal is gone, but your chance to have fun at your only engagement party is not. Smile and be happy now. Be sad about the proposal later.*

Hadi opened the velvet ring box sitting on the gold tray his mother brought to him. My ring. Yes. Everything would be fine as soon as I started wearing my ring.

The ring was awful. I grinned like a beauty queen, but my mind raced, *No, no.* The two trillion cut diamonds sandwiching the brilliant round center stone had all the shine of dirty glass. *Stop it. Stop it. Don't think like that. You love it. You have to. It's the only ring you have. Okay, you love it. Yes, I love it. Who am I trying to kid? I hate it! Try a different angle. Maybe it's okay from a side view. Phew. Yes. A side view is okay. Look at it from the side, always the side.*

Arabs wear their engagement rings on their right hands and then switch them to their left on the day of their wedding. When I pushed Hadi's ring past the joint on his right ring finger, the ladies in the room gave another ululating cry. Hadi's grandmother returned to shower us with an additional handful of coins and candy.

Mama ushered us into the family room, bringing along the tape deck. As the music grew louder, the guests migrated about the house. Those who thought it was okay to listen to music and dance in mixed groups of men and women stood up and formed a circle around Hadi and me, clapping as if to cheer us on. Those who had no objection to music but frowned upon dancing in mixed groups stayed in the living room or mingled around the appetizer table set up in the hallway. Those who thought music was haram stepped outside, far away from the grasp of its sinful notes.

Since we'd announced our engagement the month before, Mama, Lina, and I had practiced dancing on the weekends. There was an *aroosa*, a bride, in our house now, and so there was a reason to play music and celebrate. Mama would tie a scarf tightly around my hips and coach me.

Hadi had not received similar instruction. On the phone, he had told me that he did not like dancing, nor did he care to learn. I'd insisted it was because he didn't know how. I'd teach him, and he'd like it. Now, for my sake, he stood in front of me. I told him to extend his arms, but instead of picking up on the classic Arab male shoulder shimmy, he moved his arms up and down like a bird trying to take off in flight.

I'd always pictured marrying someone who loved to dance. During the parties in our honor, we'd dance and laugh, our heads thrown back, ours smiles wide, just like the happy couples in movies and magazines. My groom was supposed to be so excited to be with me that he wouldn't be able to contain his energy.

But three disappointments in one evening were far too much for a bride during the most important time in her life. The negative thinking had to stop. The party was fun; family had flown out; Mama and Marwa had gone to so much trouble; and Hadi looked so handsome in his new suit. I loved the contrast of his dark skin against his crisp, off-white dress shirt. Hadi Ridha was cute, and we were going to be happy together.

After the party, Hadi drove Baba, Lina, and me back to our hotel. He dropped them off in front of the lobby so that we could be alone while he escorted me back to my family's room.

Hadi opened the car door for me and then offered me his coat—a long, forest green leather overcoat that someone had led him to believe was acceptable for a five-foot-eight-inch twenty-one-year-old to wear. I took it even though it made me look like a Christmas tree. We walked in silence until we'd stepped into the glass elevator on the face of the building. Hadi reached out for my hand, leaned over, and whispered, "I love you so much." This time, his whispering didn't bother me. His voice was too sincere to judge and so heartfelt that I thought I detected the slightest hint of a crack.

I put my head on his shoulder because a moment like this called for reciprocation. "I love you, too," I said.

I meant it in the only way I was capable of meaning it then. I knew I didn't love him completely or unconditionally. I was too young to love anyone in that way. But I loved him for loving me, for being the one to play the part of the groom while I played the role of the bride.

"It's about time you said it," I said to lighten a moment that suddenly felt heavy with emotion.

"I've always felt it. For as long as I can remember, I've loved you. I was just waiting for us to be official before I said it out loud."

The elevator doors opened, and we stepped into the open hall overlooking the parking lot. I paused and took in a breath. I'd been so preoccupied with how Hadi had asked me and what my family thought of him that I'd paid little attention to what he had said when he'd offered me my ring. Only now did it occur to me that I'd underestimated the sentiment behind his words, the time he must have spent considering them.

"Why did you wait so long to tell me? It's not against the rules to love someone."

Our hands still linked, Hadi answered, "Because that's the kind of thing that you should only say to your wife, so I wanted us to be officially together before I said it."

I nudged Hadi forward with a slight swing of our hands. "So, if we didn't get engaged, you wouldn't love me."

"No. I'd love you. I just wouldn't have ever told you."

"I see," I said, stopping outside the hotel room door.

"What? You think it's silly?"

"No, I guess I'm surprised. I didn't know you had such strong feelings about this."

"You know what else I have strong feelings about?"

I knew, but I didn't know if I wanted to hear him say it. I had spent months thinking of how Hadi should profess his love to me, but I had given little thought as to how I'd respond. A lifetime of being taught that a girl was supposed to be shy and withhold emotion in the presence of a boy had left me at a loss.

"What?" I asked.

When Hadi answered with the anticipated "You," I smiled demurely and opened the door

The First Time

Najva Sol

I am old enough to know it is supposed to be a secret. The first time I ask a girl to let me touch her between the legs, I stand awkwardly in her room in the mountains near Karag in Iran. It is summer; we are both muddy-tan and salty from playful attempts to build a dam of branches in the nearby stream. She is wearing a thin cotton tank top, practically a soft sheet of paper. We are friends, but I want us to be closer. I have just discovered my clitoris. I think we can share it, like Barbies. I am six years old.

It isn't anything special, just the normal curiosity of hands going between and in, the sensation similar to finding a new fingertip, a new way to touch. In Iran, even the innocence our age affords us is not enough to shield us from the nagging bug-bite feeling that what we are doing is not for our parents to know. While we discover our bodies, our small frames hide inside the girl's closet, with space to spare.

I move from Iran to America at seven years old. I don't keep the girl's name, but I keep the memory.

The first time I kiss a boy, I am in seventh grade and I think I must be the last girl left in my little suburb in Maryland who still doesn't have that business taken care of. His name is Akbar—wayward curls, lanky body, and skin the color of a shish kebob. He is in my class at school, has a nipple piercing, listens to Nirvana, and says he likes me.

When I ask my strict Muslim dad about going to watch a movie with some girls and boys, his ears steam, his neck bulges, and his disapproval erupts. There is no sex until marriage; there is no dating; while I live under this roof, boys are not to be my friends.

My mom sneaks me to the movie. She can hear me on the phone after dinner every night, telling this and that friend that I can't make it to meet the group at the park or the mall. Maybe it's the feminist in her, or maybe she takes pity on me. Maybe being the wild child with two older brothers made her know enough to let me run free.

She drops me off in front of the neighborhood hot-dog joint, where I promptly join in on a six-person triple date. Akbar buys me a dog and a large Coke. We all shuffle our scuffed skater shoes and wide-leg jeans a few doors down to the local movie theater. We watch *Center Stage*, and right there, in between the blatant popcorn throwing and subtle armpit sweating, he presses his lips on mine. His tongue attempts to deep-sea dive into my throat. I don't like it very much, but I think to myself—*Finally*.

The first time I have sex with a boy, I am mostly just glad it doesn't hurt. I'm fifteen, and weave a teenage web of elaborate sleepover lies and ruses. This night my friend Vanessa drags me to get wasted with seniors from a nearby school who are friends with her boyfriend, Mike. I drink piss-flavored keg beer and write my number on a cute tattooed redhead's shirt in Sharpie. I giggle with him as we make fun of everyone who isn't us. Later I dance with a blond, blue-eyed boy who is Mike's friend, but I keep wishing I were kissing the redhead. We leave for the blond's house, where we are all staying. I don't know if the driver is sober, but I know that I am not.

The blond and I make out on the couch, and I suddenly find myself naked. He poses the question—may I? He has a condom. I can't think of a good reason to say no, so I say yes. In the morning, I take his sweater and tell my friend all about it. It's no big deal, I say. I mean it, too. I'm just glad it's over.

The first time a girl offers to go down on me, I am still fifteen. The invitation comes from my friend Samantha, who lives next door. We are smoking pot while her parents are out. The sunset is a melting sherbet and I'm telling her how I don't think I like sex with boys that much. I can't orgasm. It's not that I don't know how to reach my peak alone, but the other two times I tried sleeping with boys, I couldn't seem to get it right—like math equations where dyslexia ruins my answer no matter how well I grasp the theory.

"Do you want me to try? I'd love to," she says.

I consider it for a moment—I had forgotten girls were an option.

"No, thank you," I reply. I don't mean to be rude, but she isn't my type. I begin to wonder what my type of girl *would* be.

The first time I like sex with a boy, I have almost given up on its ever happening. I am eighteen and it's Valentine's Day. This day is also the first time I have ever said "I love you." My boyfriend, Alex, is visiting New York for the weekend from Maryland. In preparation, I have kicked out my roommate for the night, waxed, purchased strawberries and whipped cream, and bought a pair of fancy black heels. After traipsing around downtown Manhattan to hookah bars and cafés in said heels, I am ready to be taken. He undresses me slowly, as if I am an old book that may turn to dust.

He takes his time with me, and when we are both beginning to see stars in our eyes, I whisper in his ear, "I love you." His eyes lock on to mine and he says, "Me, too."

We sit together for a while, naked. *This is it*, I think. *This is love. This is my future. This is the boy I'm going to marry.* He has dropped out of high school. I tell my parents about him, but they are not as impressed as I had hoped. Every time my father calls, he asks me what I'm doing with my life. Living, I respond. Our conversations are short, and I stop mentioning details other than class and weather. My mother asks about Alex all the time, and warns me that he's no good.

Alex tells me that he isn't intimidated by my attraction to girls. He is far away and I am young, so I sleep with one and think it's my first time. I forget to count all the childhood explorations. The girl has pink, mermaidlike hair, I have a curly purple mane, and we bond over Facebook. We are best friends the entire school year, living in the same dorm, sharing coffee at 5:00 am when projects are due, reading too much Chuck Palahniuk. Finally, sweetly tipsy, the last night of freshman year, we fall into bed together. It is easy and satisfying, like a chocolate bar from a vending machine. *Ohhhh*, I think to myself, *this is what sex is like for most people*. It's cut short due to roommates and train schedules, but I want more. I want to sleep with a girl who isn't just a friend.

I tell Alex about the incident while we're in a car. He isn't heartbroken, but he isn't cheering, either. He grips the steering wheel tighter. It is not long until he asks me if I would prefer him with a more feminine figure. I am compelled to be honest. He closes the relationship. No more, he says, just me. I begin to wonder how long we can last. I can't stop craving girls.

The first time I tell my parents I'm queer, I'm twenty-one, and I'm not the one admitting anything. It turns out they have been checking my web history and reading my blogs for years—more specifically, the posts after I broke up with Alex and dated a string of girls. I come back to my hometown for Thanksgiving, as always. We gather under the premise that we are discussing my career. We meet in public, at a higher-end chain café. It's odd to walk in and see them, tea in mugs, a pastry casually lounging on a plate, as though they aren't recently divorced, don't live in separate houses, don't curse each other under their breath. When my parents, my sober Iranian Muslim parents, tell me they know Everything, I panic. I have never met a gay Iranian.

What do you mean, Everything? It's pointless to ask. If they read my blog, they know about the drugs and the booze and the girls and the boys, normal by America's MTV standards, but not for an Iranian family that refuses to have a cable TV sully the living room. My childhood drug talk can be summed up in one line: If you take drugs, you are a failure. My childhood sex talk was: Don't do it. This is where we left off, and here is where we pick it up again.

Do they hate me now? I feel my heart do jumping jacks. My dad speaks first.

"You're going to have to choose," he says. "When you have a husband you can't just be AC/DC."

What is he saying? Is that a drug term? It takes only a few seconds to realize he means bisexual. I stay silent while they speak, throat full of gravel.

Then there's a pause, and my words sputter out: I don't think you should plan on me getting married, certainly not to a man. I am not ashamed of the people and ways that I love. I am not planning on hiding it anymore. I can be gay, and a good daughter, and a good person. Right?

I cringe, throwing a boomerang speech, anticipating it back in my face. My mother's eyebrows are furrowed and her mouth is slack. My father's eyelids crumble like ancient ruins. Lips move and sounds come out. Yes, they say, you can be. It's the tone parents use when their kid single-handedly causes the soccer team to lose the state championships. I am not a star player, but they will sit in the bleachers for my team. What? Really? They aren't disowning me. I am shaky with disbelief. Perhaps their years of spying have given them time to grow accustomed to the idea. Wearily, my father tells me he just wants me to be happy. My mother nods, but then chimes in, "But I don't think we should tell anyone just yet. I mean, it's nobody's business, really."

The first time I realize I don't have to keep my secret, I am drinking a peppermint mocha and trying not to cry. For fifteen years, I have been afraid there is not enough room in my parents' hearts, in my family, my Iran, or my religion, for my truth. I am no longer the little girl hiding in the closet. Who knew how elastic parents could be? How they could wrap around the largest letdown? Perhaps the rest, too, has more stretch. Perhaps someday, I think, I will, with my own full shape, fit into all the spaces that seem, at first glance, too small for me.

It is all too much. I finish my mocha, place the cup with the dirty dishes, mumble a good-bye to my parents, and try to make it to my car before the relief makes my mascara run.

The Hybrid Dance

Chinyere Obimba

'm sitting in an Indian restaurant in Cambridge, Massachusetts, at my friend Melody's birthday party. I'm chewing absently on a piece of naan after a huge meal and imagining preparing a feast of similar proportions for Sadiq. Back when the two of us were in college, I had it all figured out: I would appease his mother by being her apprentice. I would spend hours in her kitchen, learning how to make her son's favorite dishes. I'm not *desi*, but at least I could fake being a *desi* cook.

But that never happened. I look over at Melody and I don't get that normal twinge of loneliness as she and her fiancé make eyes at each other. She just turned thirty-two and has waited so long to marry the man she loves. Meanwhile, I'm almost twenty-three, single, and still in love with an apparition.

I'm taking a night off from studying epidemiology to hang with a bunch of my medical school classmates—and to exchange furtive glances with James, who, like everyone else at the table, is non-Muslim. I glance at him just in time to see him gazing at me. I avert my eyes, but I cannot hide my smirk. I wasn't sure before, but I now know that he likes me.

I met James while we were both applying to medical school. I didn't pay that much attention to him until we became class-mates. He lived down the hall from me, and I soon discovered that we shared a love of Latin American culture.

"What did you think?" I asked him one evening, after a bunch of my friends had gathered in the dorm lounge to watch my favorite movie, *Black Orpheus*.

"I liked it," he answered, a little more enthusiastically than usual. "Thanks for letting me watch it. It was really good." He smiled as we walked down the hall.

And that's how it all started. James was kind of cute, but that wasn't why I was attracted to him. Not really. He had beautiful, smooth chocolate skin, but he had a small head. I liked him because he was brilliant but modest. He wasn't a loner but was happy by himself. He was content to travel the world alone, and I found that admirable.

So I started to like James, and he likes me, too. Attraction seems so simple for him. It has never been so simple for me.

My parents' story is a transcontinental boy-meets-girl tale: Igbo Nigerian Christian boy meets African American Muslim convert girl. As their daughter, I am black, American, Igbo, and Muslim, and sometimes I don't know what to do with myself.

I remember a nature show I watched when I was eight. The narrator described the mating dance of two related, but different, species of birds. In one species, the male birds puffed their chests and hopped about; in the other, they flapped their wings and shimmied along the ground. At some point, the mating signals got crossed and one of the shimmying birds was attracted to a hopping bird, and the two crossed lovers birthed a chick. When this chick grew up and it came time to mate, the poor thing stood alone in the clearing, caught between puffing and shimmying, and none of the other birds came near it. This chick was not an attractive mate.

Watch me as I do my hybrid dance.

I was almost nineteen, a freshman, and barely Muslim when I met Sadiq. At least, I felt barely Muslim. After assimilating into the agnostic masses in high school in Ann Arbor, Michigan, I started practicing Islam again at the beginning of college. My foundation was the Islam I learned from my mother, a few of my aunts and uncles, and my grandparents, all of whom had converted to Islam years earlier, after being members of the Nation of Islam. As I learned more about my religion, I was attracted to its multicultural nature, as exemplified in the last sermon of the Prophet, peace be upon him. I fell in love with a faith that demanded that we transcend the limits of race and ethnicity.

I didn't want to hide my faith any longer. I wanted to tell anyone who inquired that I was Muslim, but I was self-conscious about the fact that I did not have two Muslim parents and did not come from a "Muslim" culture. Even after I began rereading the Qur'an and started to resume the five daily prayers, I still didn't feel Muslim enough in the company of the members of my college's Muslim Student Association (MSA).

As if trying to negotiate my newfound spiritual identity during my first year in college wasn't hard enough, I was also a competitive premed student trying to stand out in a school from which six hundred medical school hopefuls graduated every year.

I really started noticing Sadiq one day when I presented a project with my group members in front of our Organic Chemistry discussion section. A few people chuckled as we hand-waved our way through the organometallic mechanism that was central to our project. Against the backdrop of our mechanism, as I scribbled on the chalkboard, my hands covered in chalk dust,

I looked nervously at Sadiq. He was one of the smartest people in class. I cared only about what he thought.

"Do you get help when you work, or do you find most of your information yourself?" Sadiq asked me, as I sat behind him at the end of our presentation. I was kind of surprised, because he hadn't really spoken to me before. Why was he asking? Had our presentation been bad?

I shrugged. "I usually like to find information myself."

He nodded and I wondered, *Is he just now realizing that I'm smart, too? Does he realize that I'm competing against him in this class?*

Sadiq was a sophomore, a little less brown than I was, and about a foot taller. At the time, I thought he was Indian and didn't realize he was Muslim. He had a loud voice and a wide mouth, and all of my classmates seemed to think he was the funniest person ever. I didn't like him at first—I found him to be arrogant. He always shouted out the answers to problems before anyone else had the chance, and beamed proudly when he got the answer right. Which he always did. But over the course of the semester, he started to grow on me. He was different from most other guys I'd met before, in a way that I couldn't quite place. He'd started asking me questions about myself, kind of offhandedly, like he was interested in me. And then I found out he was Pakistani and Muslim, the latter being more important to me, as a burgeoning Muslimah, than any other guy's being interested in me.

A couple of days after our presentation, Sadiq sat next to me during lecture, something he had not done before. I glanced at him to say good morning, and he greeted me with dialogue from *Chappelle's Show*.

"Did you catch the episode last night?"

I told him that I hadn't; I'd actually never seen an entire episode of the show.

"Aw, girl, you have to see it!"

He'd probably called me "girl" because he couldn't pronounce "Chinyere," if he knew my name at all.

"And have you heard Kanye West's new album?"

I shook my head. Dave Chappelle, Kanye West—apparently, these were all people that I should have been familiar with. Had he never talked to a black girl before? You don't have to sound black and talk about "black" things to talk to a black person.

As the lecture began, Sadiq leaned in closer to me. He smelled like soap.

"Hey, I missed the last couple minutes of lecture last time. Can you catch me up?"

I grinned at him. That was more like it—a conversation I could actually participate in.

Over the course of the semester, I started to find it endearing that Sadiq felt he could identify with me on the level of Kanye's lyrics. I also started to become attracted to his outlandish personality. I knew few other guys who could pull off wearing a purple-and-pink T-shirt, like he did to class one day.

I started telling my best friend about him, and she thought he sounded crazy. She called him "crazy boy" and called him out for his characteristic gelled hairstyle. "Who are you talking about? You mean that boy with the spiky hair?"

By the end of the semester, I officially liked him.

After class ended, Sadiq and I made a point to hang out with each other. It took us about a month to get it together. His first suggestion—to talk about our families over bubble tea—turned into lunch, then dinner and a movie. I looked up the movie he mentioned. It was a romantic foreign film that seemed highly inappropriate for two Muslims going out on a not-date. I assumed it was a not-date because he seemed to be a serious enough Muslim that he wouldn't date. Good Muslims weren't supposed to date, I'd learned, even when sex wasn't involved. There was a lot more to Islam than I'd known about when I was growing up and it was just my mom teaching me. I knew premarital sex was bad, but the good and the bad had now become the halal and the haram, the lawful and the forbidden.

He wanted us to meet up for burritos at a place not too far from my old dorm. "Hey, Chi!" he called to me, standing up from a bench in front of the restaurant. That's what he had started calling me after he'd finally pronounced my name right. He was the only one I let call me that. I waved and walked up to him, but didn't hug him. Some Muslims didn't seem to mind touching between the sexes, but I knew others believed even handshakes were inappropriate. I didn't yet know where he stood.

"So, what do you do on weekends?" he asked me when my mouth was full. I wanted to seem interesting to him, but then I blurted out, "Oh, I mainly hang out with my family. I have a lot of cousins and stuff. My grandmother's sick now, so we go up to visit her most weekends." As I said this, I realized that it was probably the antithesis of intriguing.

He smiled at me. "I think it's cool that you're so close to your family. So am I."

Over the course of the not-date, I discovered that Sadiq loved family and loved kids. He also wasn't what I expected from a Muslim boy. He seemed to be okay going out with girls and going to parties. He was definitely a social butterfly. He didn't eat only halal meat, which I discovered after he ordered his steak burrito. Knowing this made me more comfortable around him. I didn't feel like I was going to be judged by him, that he wouldn't think I wasn't Muslim enough.

Being with him that day also made me feel like there was a whole world that I'd been insulated from. I hadn't even known this burrito place was down the street. I had stopped listening to music I liked because my high school friends thought hip-hop was stupid. Through Sadiq, I was discovering that it was okay to be me, because he seemed to like me for who I was.

I was comfortable around him and could have talked for hours more, but the movie was supposed to start at seven o'clock. I was relieved when the romantic film wasn't playing and we decided to see a comedy instead. When we entered the theater, the movie had already started. I accidentally touched Sadiq's leg, and we both adjusted ourselves. He was shivering the whole time, just as he had shivered on the last day of Organic Chemistry, when he'd sat next to me and told me he was going to miss me. I had laughed in his face then, because I hadn't known what to say. I still didn't know exactly how to act around this Muslim boy. It was a dance I hadn't learned the steps to yet.

During the summer, Sadiq was very attentive. He cheered me up with corny jokes and compliments. He told me that I amazed him, with my love for family, my dedication to my premedical coursework, and my love of language. He sometimes teased me with bad Spanish, knowing that I was going to be a Spanish major. But then he offhandedly told me that his sister wanted him to meet Pakistani girls. We went out only a couple of times after that. By the time school was back in session and I'd begun my sophomore year in college, he'd disappeared. He never wanted to hang out anymore. Maybe he didn't want to be friends with me anymore. Maybe he had never liked me. I felt like a fool.

I began the semester crying on the floor of my best friend's dorm room. My eyes were bloodshot when Sadiq poked his head into the room and told me that he'd heard my voice from down the hall. This caught me by surprise, because he didn't even live in my friend's dorm building. He asked if I was okay, and I felt like an even bigger fool. Had he just heard me crying over him? I told him that I had gotten upset from watching a sad movie, but wasn't sure if he bought it.

"I was wondering if I had done something wrong," he told me the following week, at the first MSA meeting of the semester. I assured him he hadn't. We stood there, smiling awkwardly at each other, before he returned to the brothers' side of the room. I hung close to my best friend, on the sisters' side, because I didn't know anyone else there. He didn't know I'd been crying over him, but I still felt embarrassed. Had I been foolish all along to think that someone like him, a born Muslim and Pakistani American, could like someone like me, a Muslimah Nigerian American? Or was I just the black girl he thought he could talk with about hip-hop?

As my sophomore year wore on, I saw Sadiq less and less. But the less I saw him, the more my memory of him became distorted. In my mind, I morphed him into a man who could look at my bronze skin, my kinky hair, and the way I wrapped my large lips around my words and see who I was on the inside. I imagined a man who embodied the multicultural spirit that drew me to Islam initially, transcending the limits of race and ethnicity. This man recognized that we were just two Muslim young adults trying to navigate faith, college, and future careers in medicine. Music was our second common language, and Sadiq the apparition, through his love of hip-hop, understood the challenges of being a black man in society and the synergistic marginalization of black women. By extension, he could understand the difficulty of being a black Muslim woman, triply marginalized.

For the rest of the year, I couldn't help but grin widely every time I saw the real Sadiq on campus and hope that he suddenly, miraculously, would become the man that I'd created in my head. But he never did.

We're leaving the restaurant after Melody's birthday dinner, where I've spent the entire meal alternately thinking about Sadiq and trying not to flirt with James. It's been three years, but Sadiq was the last guy I really liked. On the one hand, I feel like I'm getting too old to be as hesitant around men, like I am around James. On the other hand, I feel brazen. He's non-Muslim. What outcome am I hoping for?

We're walking to the M2 shuttle back to the medical campus. James is walking beside me. I glance at him and see him staring at his feet. I'm generally uncomfortable with silences, so I start talking.

"How did you like your food?" I asked. I'm smiling too much, just like I used to do with Sadiq. I try to relax. I don't want to flirt openly, but at the same time I want to let him know . . . something. That I'm open, that I'm interested, that I care about him?

"It was good. I had the chicken tikka," he answered. His smile is more engaging than his conversation. I'm not used to his kind—the silent, nonbrooding type.

Even so, I think I want him.

Astaghfirullah, God forgive me, but I do. I usually ignore such feelings, because I feel they are haram and counterproductive, especially when the object of attraction is non-Muslim. Maybe I should ignore what I feel right now.

I'm looking at James in his ironed collared shirt, his dark-wash jeans, and his cap. I want to say that he looks nice, but I know it's going to sound flirtatious, so I don't. I'm trying to keep my inter-actions halal with a man who doesn't know what "halal" means. What matters so much to me matters little to him. In terms of my dealings with men, I still don't really know where I stand.

This is the hybrid dance I first learned in my dealings with Sadiq. I want to hop over and talk to a man, but as soon as I open my mouth, I shimmy back, because isn't it haram to be too familiar with men? But then I hop forward because, no, I think this man is interesting, that's all. Interest in a man, if it begins on platonic terms, should be halal, permissible. Plus, how else will a relationship begin? But in the midst of hopping forward, I pause and shimmy backward again because I'm well aware of where romantic relationships can lead: to sex. Premarital sex, fornication, one of the biggest sins in Islam. Hellfire! But is an act that may end in sin a sin when it begins? Is forming a relationship with a man whom I admire a sin if I never sleep with him? I hop and I shimmy, and the man is gone before I decide whether I'm coming or going.

It was bad enough with Sadiq. We were both Muslim, and even then I didn't know how to let him know that I liked him and still be a good Muslim girl. It's worse with James because he's not Muslim. My non-Muslim friends would say, "So what?" I'm usually so liberal that it would seem odd for me to draw such a hard line on whom I would consider as a mate. But if they saw me scurry from the dorm bathroom to my room with damp feet and arms after performing *wudu*, throw my prayer rug onto the floor, and pray, then maybe my difference would make sense to them. Maybe then they would understand why I might prefer a Muslim man, someone who could join me in my five daily prayers, over a non-Muslim who may not understand why I pray.

I'm not sure if James knows what he's getting into.

Our conversation on the way to the shuttle has grown uncomfortably silent. Thankfully, James breaks the silence. "There's this international bookstore around here . . . " James points, but I have no idea what street we're on. That's okay. It's the perfect excuse to have him show me later. "I was thinking of checking it out. They have both books and movies there, plenty of things in Spanish."

I shrug. "Well, that's cool. There's this movie I've been looking for forever, *Las Cartas de Alou* . . . "

"Oh, yeah, I saw that," he answers. I chuckle, because I'm pretty sure he doesn't know what movie I'm talking about. His was a nervous answer. I recognize it from many years of run-ins with Sadiq, in the research building or on the street. A nervous answer is a lie that escapes your lips when you are talking to someone you like.

James's brown eyes sparkle under the streetlamp, and I think of all the things he doesn't know about me. To him, I'm simply Chinyere, a half-Nigerian Muslim woman who goes to classes with him, occasionally watches Latino and Brazilian films with him, and has a weakness for off-color humor. He has no idea that I'm in the midst of dancing between dating and not, between relating to men and avoiding them to prevent sex or not. But I still like him, just because he is who he is. And he seems to like me for who I am, right now, in front of him. Attraction is easy for him. Maybe it could be easier for me.

Walking with James, I realize that I'm doing not the hybrid dance, but a unique dance of my own that someone someday will understand. I'm not just an Igbo who is not Christian. I'm not just a black American Muslim. I'm a woman who loves God and who strives in my everyday life to be conscious of Him. I am a woman who has chosen medicine as my career, believing that I'm serving God by serving my fellow human beings. I am much more than the labels I use to identify myself.

And ultimately the man who loves me will love me for all of those things, *inshAllah*.

For now, going forward with James is better than holding out hope for a Muslim man who likes me in spite of my race. Tonight I'm letting the Sadiq apparition die for good. While part of me would like a Muslim partner to help me grow in my religion, I'm satisfied enough with the Muslim I am that if that doesn't happen, I'm okay. I know I can grow into the Muslimah I aspire to be, alone if I have to be.

But *inshAllah*, I won't.

International *Habibti:*

Love Overseas

Love in the Andes

Angela Collins Telles

Maiza and I escaped the rain by dashing into an Irish restaurant in Bariloche, Argentina. A restaurant, that is, if I could ignore the pints of Guinness, the central bar, and the droves of men standing around drinking. *I shouldn't be in a place like this*, I thought to myself, guilty conscience awakening.

Not as a Muslim convert who directs a private Islamic school in Orange County. Not as an American Muslim about to have her picture and story in *People* magazine for sixty million subscribers to read. Not as the girl who would soon be on CNN, Fox News Live, *Inside Edition*, the *Today* show, and Al Jazeera as an "American gone Muslim" after September 11, 2001. And especially not as the woman who would cave in to social expectations and wear a hijab back home in response to requests from the media and her devout community.

My thoughts slowed my stride, and my blond hair and blue eyes caught the unwanted attention of the locals. Maiza and I were in Bariloche to get away from our lives. She had a demanding job and a bad separation happening back home in Brazil. I had a community expecting me to be the perfect example of a Muslim in America. These unreal expectations, combined with several marriage proposals from men fantasizing about marrying a Western Muslim woman without considering our incompatible backgrounds, had driven me to seek an escape through travel.

We did not want our last night together to be interrupted by men with the worst of intentions. Yet this restaurant—and Argentina, for that matter—invited precisely those types of advances. That is, until he arrived.

"Did you find a phone?" a man asked me in English.

I realized it was the same man who had met my glance when I first arrived. I needed to contact our hotel concierge and had decided to ask this man if I could borrow his phone, but he did not have it with him.

Now facing him again, I found myself tongue-tied. In spite of my flustered silence, he tried again: "Is this seat taken?"

I regained my ability to speak as I sized him up. "Sure. Have a seat." He was clean cut, fit, and nicely groomed, with a confident, warm smile. He was more attractive than I had realized during our earlier encounter. He sat next to me and extended his hand.

"Hi, I'm Marcelo. And you are?"

"Angela. Nice to meet you."

"Wow, you're an American."

"Yes, and you?"

"Brazilian. I am here with my brother on vacation. We're leaving for home tomorrow."

"Oh." My tone lowered a bit at this information. "My friend Maiza is from Brazil, too."

While they greeted each other in Portuguese, I wondered why I felt excited that he had asked to sit next to me.

"So, Angela, what do you do?" Marcelo caught me off guard with his English again.

"I direct a private . . . "—I paused on the word "Islamic"—" . . . school. I'm a principal." Why had I omitted the most important part of what I do? I had never done that before.

"You work with children? Really? That's great."

"And what do you do?" I quickly diverted Marcelo's attention to give myself time to figure out what I was doing.

"I am a financial analyst in Latin equity research. I visit clients in the States frequently from Mexico City."

Why wasn't I driving the conversation into one about Islam? Why was I not explaining how Islam makes so much more sense than our Catholic and Christian beliefs, as I usually do with any new person I meet? Was I afraid I would scare him away with my strong belief in God, which wasn't widely accepted in the Western world?

As though we were close friends reunited, we skipped over the awkward conversation of people meeting for the first time and jumped straight into one full of personal views and stories. From our mutual opinions about the food and noisy ambience to my tales of my amusing tree-climbing adventure that day and how I had mastered the technique of fighting off assertive Argentinean men, Marcelo and I clicked magically as we laughed the hours away. The noisy restaurant, lingering men drinking beer, and even Maiza faded into the background, until a lady approached our table.

"*Disculpe, señor. Estamos cerrando ahora.*"

It was 2:00 am. Somehow, four hours had passed like minutes while we shared our life experiences about places we had visited around the world, our families, our jobs, our likes and dislikes. I was entranced by this man who spoke four languages fluently, enjoyed international travel as much as I did, and took care of his whole family back in Brazil. He was attractive, well educated, and amused by my stories.

"I have to go." I said. "I have a boat trip early tomorrow on one of the lakes here before I leave Bariloche tomorrow night."

"Wait—I would like to be in touch with you. How can I reach you?"

I hesitated. He was not Muslim. I could never see him again.

In spite of my qualms, I handed him a tiny piece of ripped paper. "This is my cell number in Argentina. But remember, I can only receive calls on this phone, not make them."

I told myself it was safe. The number would exist for only another twenty-four hours, and besides, he was returning to Brazil the next morning.

That night, I couldn't sleep. Inexplicably, I had an immediate sense of loss, knowing that I would never see Marcelo again.

The next day, after nine hours in icy rain and fog, the tourist boat finally headed for shore. As the shore appeared, my phone rang.

I answered it, surprised at getting reception on the lake. "Hello?"

"Angela, it's Marcelo."

"Marcelo! How was your trip back home?"

"Well, actually . . . I didn't board my plane this morning. And now I'm watching your boat come in to dock. I'm so happy I found you!"

"You're *here*?" I asked in disbelief.

"I'll explain everything in just a couple of minutes."

I looked over the bow and was excited to see the waiting people, now that I knew someone was waiting there for me, too.

I was the first to exit the boat. Pushing through the crowds, I searched for his eyes.

He was standing by a taxi in the parking lot, wearing a cap, looking younger, sweeter, and more innocent than he had the night before. He opened his arms and pulled me into the type of hug reserved for couples who have been separated for days. I could sense he was nervous as he stumbled for the right words to say.

"Can I take you back to town?" he asked.

In the cab, he kept staring at me, grabbing my hand, and trying to hug me sideways. I felt myself resisting his constant need to touch.

"How did you find me?" I asked.

Marcelo began to tell his story. The previous night, he admitted, he, too, had not been able to sleep, for fear that he would never see me again. When he had arrived at the airport earlier that morning, he had sought advice from his brother, Alexandre, about what to do.

"If I leave, I will never see her again. All I have is this number she gave me here in Argentina. I won't be able to reach her after she leaves Bariloche tonight." Marcelo paused, realizing the significance of what he was about to admit to his brother. "I think she is the one."

"If this is the one," Alexandre responded, "there's only one thing you can do."

Marcelo admitted that the same thought had crossed his mind after spending just five minutes with me at the table in the Irish restaurant the night before. He wasn't afraid to say what was on his mind. It was frightening, but exciting, too. I restrained myself from thinking further about what had to be an impossible union, but listened attentively as he continued his story.

Marcelo had left the airport, hired a driver, and spent the day trying to find which boat tour I was on. He had happened to arrive at the correct port just as I was returning. Of the twenty-four ports that exist in Bariloche, how had he found the right one?

I couldn't help but wonder if this was more than a mere coincidence.

The taxi ride back to the center of Bariloche was treacherous, not because of the muddy roads so much as because of what I knew could unfold between us if we let it. So, as Marcelo continued to be physically demonstrative, giving me happy, affectionate hugs, I found myself pulling away. I started to fear that if I accepted his show of affection, I would be leading him on, and I knew I could not do that as a Muslim.

"Marcelo, look. I can't stay with you. I'm flattered by what you have done, but I don't want to mislead you."

"No, that's fine. I wasn't suggesting we stay together," he responded.

"I have a girlfriend waiting to meet me in Santiago in two days," I explained. "I have a ticket to leave Bariloche tonight at ten o'clock."

"Can I go with you?"

I was not prepared for his request. I couldn't say yes, but I didn't want to lose his company, either. "Well, it's a two-day bus trip. When is your next flight leaving?"

"All of the flights are booked for the next four days. It's high season."

I realized what a risk Marcelo had taken to find me. He had missed his flight to try to find a stranger, postponing his work in Brazil. If he hadn't found me, he would have been stranded in Bariloche for four days, alone. Or, worse, I could have told him that I wanted nothing to do with him.

"Marcelo, I doubt they still have tickets for the sleeper bus. I bought mine when I first arrived, five days ago."

His eyes grew wide with despair. He seemed to fear that this could, in fact, be our last meeting. I watched as goofy motions overtook his confidence, as he tripped on the curb upon our exit out of the taxi. He struggled to find more words to say. There was something truly authentic about Marcelo. I realized he had never done this before and had not rehearsed what move to make next.

We had arrived at the bus station. Sure enough, there were no more seats on my overnight sleeper. But we found tickets leaving the next morning, though they were not sleeper seats. While I dreaded taking a two-day bus trip sitting up, I was excited at spending time with Marcelo on this long journey.

"*Dos billetos para mañana, por favor.*"

Early the next morning, we took our seats on a bus full of sleepy-eyed passengers awaiting their passage over the Andes Mountains. That August morning showed the winter season's first clear blue sky, which seemed to symbolize a new consciousness I was developing. I no longer felt fear of the unknown with Marcelo, and I accepted that what was unfolding between us was real and growing from good intentions.

As we were reminiscing about funny life experiences, the tires of our charter bus slid on the terrain and the engine groaned violently. The bus lost control, skidded, and finally came to a stop on an unplowed road. We were snowed in. Panic built all around us, yet we somehow felt protected and welcomed this unexpected delay in our travels.

Hours later, the plow cleared the road and our journey continued down the spiraling cliffs to Chile. Later that evening, we arrived in the small fisherman's port of Osorno. We found a nice restaurant in town. We were seated close to the window, and within seconds, a popular Chilean liquor was placed in front of us, along with the only meal being served that day: an assortment of meats, including sausages.

"Marcelo, I can't eat this, and, well, I can't drink this, either." Finally, I felt confident enough to share what I had been withholding from Marcelo.

"Yeah, sausage is pretty fattening," he responded, trying to make me feel comfortable.

"Well, not for that reason. There's something I haven't told you yet."

Marcelo looked carefully into my eyes and breathed in deeply.

"I am a . . . well, how do I say this?" I halted, as if I had completely misled him by withholding this huge part of myself but sharing so many other tiny details about my life so easily. "Marcelo, I'm a Muslim. An American Muslim. I converted to Islam six years ago."

"You're a Muslim?" he asked. "Wow. To be honest, Angela, I don't know much about Muslims. So, how did you become one?"

Although we were famished, our dinner grew cold as our conversation, once again, took center stage. It was a relief to learn that he did not share the anti-Muslim sentiment many Americans had adopted after 9/11. It was this prejudice that had led me to read the Qur'an for the first time. I had defended Muslims based on my personal experience with them through my travels abroad, but I had not felt qualified to debate the topic of terrorism without understanding their beliefs. The Qur'an alone was my sole source of knowledge, and I had begun crying tears of happiness while reading Surah Rahman. I had said to myself, *I believe in one God and all that is written in this holy book. Am I a Muslim?*

Marcelo listened with an open mind and admitted that, just as I was raised Catholic and he Protestant, many of the ideas about God our parents taught us did not add up logically in our personal views. He seemed relieved to know that God could be complete as one being. Given his openness, I couldn't help but wonder: Could he someday become a Muslim, too?

This question played over and over in my mind as Marcelo learned more about Islam in that three-hour conversation than someone might learn in an entire semester. A sudden calm came over me. For the first time, my passion for my inspiring beliefs was not up for debate. Marcelo asked many of the same questions I had asked when I first read the Qur'an, and seemed genuinely interested. Then it occurred to me that the level of trust we had gained was what had allowed this conversation to occur. I then understood why I had held back from sharing all of me during

LOVE IN THE ANDES

our first meeting in the restaurant in Bariloche. Could there be a divine plan for us together?

Once more, we were the last ones remaining in the restaurant. "Oh no, Marcelo—we have only a half hour to catch our bus to Santiago from here," I warned.

We caught our bus just as it was exiting the station. The exhaustion of an overnight trip was completely masked by our conversation about being American and Muslim, and how some people on both sides believe that there is no intersection between the two identities. I divulged my challenges around believing strongly in the revelations of the Qur'an, yet also struggling every day to find how to make my new life a part of my culture. I had found a new belief in God, but did that mean I could no longer be me? Did the way I think, dress, speak, relate to others as an American woman disqualify me from being a Muslim woman at the same time?

I strongly believed that it was because of these traits that I was able to do what so few people ever allow themselves to do: understand God in a way that makes sense to them personally, not just to their families and peers. Marcelo seemed fascinated by my perspective and was empathetic while listening to my personal struggles. He related in a way that very few people could, whether they were from a similar culture or not.

Without hesitating, I dropped my head onto his shoulder and slid my hand around his waist. His hand gripped my arm. My shyness and fear about spending my time in the company of a man evaporated into the fog of the night. Marcelo was no longer just a man I had met—he was the man I was destined to meet.

The ride was bumpy, and the oncoming cars' high beams scorched my eyes repeatedly. Even so, I wished it would never end. When we arrived at our destination, my blissful time with Marcelo would come to an end.

• • •

A European city surrounded by colossal mountains appeared in the windshield.

"Santiago," announced the bus driver.

It was already dark, so we quickly searched for an Internet café to look up the address where I was supposed to meet my girlfriend Coral, but we couldn't find one that was open at that hour. Even though I didn't know where I would rest my head, I was grateful that I was not alone on the streets of an unfamiliar city late at night.

During our walk in a neighborhood known to welcome tourists, we came across an enormous colonial-style mansion that rented out rooms. With each stair I climbed to enter this unique hotel, my heartbeat started to accelerate and panic overcame me. Would we ever see each other again?

"Two rooms, please," Marcelo asked. I took a deep breath and felt relieved that we would at least have the next morning together.

"I'm sorry, sir. We only have one room available. But it's a suite with two beds. Would you like to see it?" the clerk asked.

Marcelo looked at me with exhausted eyes, waiting for my approval.

The suite was enormous. It had two rooms—a living room and a bedroom with two beds—floor-to-ceiling French doors leading onto a balcony, and a bathroom half the size of my apartment back home.

"I get the bed by the window," I exclaimed, to gloss over the awkwardness of the situation.

Despite our exhaustion, we lay in our separate beds and talked about life after death and the feeling that we are not alone, that there are others around us. As we talked more, we felt less and less alone and were very grateful to have each other's company. It was comforting to have a companion and to be able to talk about topics typically reserved for lifelong friends. After all, we had only a few hours to catch up on the lives we'd lived before we had finally met.

Morning arrived, and we finally slept. After we ate a late breakfast and visited a nearby Internet café to retrieve the address where my girlfriend was staying, the thought of parting began to weigh me down. By midday, we had no choice but to reenter our separate lives. We held hands tightly, afraid to let go, as the taxi teetered over the cobblestones of the historic district and arrived at the address where my friend awaited me. Marcelo was like my better half—balanced and comforting. How was I going to let go?

"Here is my card. But I need more than just your nonoperative number in Argentina," Marcelo said, smiling.

"Oh, of course." I quickly wrote down my California phone number and email address for him.

"I will see you again Angela, in-sha-Allah," he said, carefully enunciating the word I had taught him just the night before. "I love you. You are very special."

My eyes filled with tears upon hearing those words. If we tried to be together, a difficult path lay in front of us. How would we integrate two lives in different countries, and different religious beliefs, languages, customs, and professional obligations? I held back what I was feeling so I wouldn't fall to pieces in front of him. I felt the same way about Marcelo but wanted to reserve those words for someone who shared my beliefs in God. If God willed, someday I would say them to Marcelo.

Marcelo embraced me, kissed my forehead, and brushed his hand across my cheek. I waited a moment, until it felt impossible to hold back tears, and then aggressively opened the taxi door. I blew Marcelo a kiss good-bye as the taxi hurried off toward the airport. Once he was out of sight, I collapsed and wept uncontrollably in the street.

Finally, I wiped away my tears and went hesitantly inside the hotel, where my friend Coral was waiting. When I asked to check into her room, the receptionist handed me a note from her.

It read: "I decided not to stay at this hotel. There's this great place on the other side of town. Go to 11 Lindon Street. I'll be waiting for you tomorrow morning. —Coral."

I panicked; 11 Lindon Street was the mansion I had stayed in with Marcelo! Did Coral know? How could I face my fellow Muslim sister if she did?

As the taxi drove me back to the hotel I had just left half an hour before, I prayed that my friend would understand my intentions and know that Marcelo and I had no other option. She was waiting for me out front with a huge smile, by which it was evident that she hadn't seen me in Marcelo's company.

I decided not to speak to her about the experience. After meeting Marcelo, I was terrified to reenter my old life. Would my community judge me harshly if they found out about this? Would they be able to understand the complexity of my experience? And if they could, would they defend me against those who were quick to judge anyone, especially a woman in my position?

I swallowed my fears and hugged my friend as she shared what she had planned for us to do that day.

I had lost his business card.

I realized it on the shuttle from the Los Angeles airport to my apartment in Orange County. Agony set in. Perhaps I would have an email from him waiting for me at home? But when I logged on to my computer, there was no message. I truly believed he was sincere. Had he changed his mind?

With just two weeks to get registration in order for the parents, students, and teachers, I poured all my energy into starting the new school year. My job provided my only comfort in light of the possibility that Marcelo had realized the complexity of our lives and had decided first that there would be no way to grow our relationship.

But when I returned home from work three days later, I had a message from an unidentified caller.

"Hi, Angela, this is Marcelo. I hope you enjoyed your trip with your girlfriend and that you made it back safely. Listen, I can't stop thinking of you, and I can't concentrate on anything but you. I have to know if you feel the same way. If you don't return my call, I will understand that I don't fit into your life back home. I hope you call, because I am sure I love you. Call me."

He didn't leave his number.

I was unable to breathe and felt panic overcome me.

I began searching for the name of the bank he worked for, but I couldn't find his contact information online.

I couldn't lose the only man I had ever met who was compatible with me in every way, and who had the potential to know Islam free from the misperceptions that many Americans had post-9/11.

I lightly washed my face, arms, head, and feet with water in the ritual Islamic ablution, to prepare for prayer. After a heartfelt Maghrib prayer, I begged God for His guidance and help.

"Ya Allah. If we are meant for one another in this life and will become closer to You in the end, please, Allah, encourage him to contact me again. Please, Allah, have him come to know You through Islam. I believe that I could and will be the best wife for him. Please, Allah, if this is Your plan, ease our longing and facilitate our union. I need Your help; I am nothing without Your guidance. Amen."

Two hours later, I received an email from Marcelo in my inbox. I read it with tears rolling down my cheeks. My prayer had been answered.

He wrote: "I just want you to know that I really enjoyed spending time with you. Despite the short time we spent together,

I developed strong feelings for you. You mean so much more to me than you can possibly think. (Maybe I should have not written that.)"

"No, Marcelo, you definitely should have written that," I said out loud as I clicked Reply.

Three months later, on Eid of November 2006, after being inspired by the just nature of Islam, Marcelo took his *shahada* and declared belief in One God and all of his prophets, from Adam to Muhammad.

In January 2007, we were married at my mosque in Orange County. My entire community came together in support to witness our miraculous union.

Latin America decided it wasn't finished with us as a couple just yet. Soon after our second wedding that took place in Brazil the country adopted us and has been our home since 2007. It was in Latin America that our marriage blossomed from a couple destined to meet under the rarest of circumstances into a loving family of four. Our two sons Gabriel and Ryan remind me every day that those in search of love can find their happiness through faith.

Last Night on the Island

Nura Maznavi

I *so* wanted to kiss him.

I could think of nothing else as I stood in Rohan's sparsely furnished, one-room bachelor flat in a beachfront neighborhood of Colombo. Rohan—sweet, ridiculously good-looking Rohan—was standing just inches away from me, patiently, expectantly. Everything within me wanted to lunge, grab his face, and kiss, kiss, kiss!

The cab downstairs honked.

Great, I thought, momentarily distracted from the man in front of me. *I'm spending my last night in Sri Lanka, after a year as a Fulbright scholar, in the apartment of my hot Catholic personal trainer, who happens to also be a* model, *and I'm slinking out the door like a hooker at two in the morning.*

Was this really fitting of a good Muslim girl?

It wasn't supposed to happen this way—not in Sri Lanka, of all places. I had always been completely straitlaced, though I'm not sure why. I grew up in a suburb of Los Angeles in a Sri Lankan American Muslim family, but my parents were never strict. I'd like to say that God was my primary motivation for staying on the straight and narrow, but the truth is that He was merely a member of the audience I assumed was watching—and judging—my life. I was much more concerned with what everyone else thought about me—my family, my friends, and the sprawling South Asian immigrant Muslim community in which I was raised. I wasn't going to be one of *those* girls—the girls who snuck around behind their parents' backs, dating and hooking up. The kind of girls whom everyone talked about.

That wasn't me. I was going to marry a Muslim man, and until then I was saving myself—saving *everything*. No sex, no kissing, no holding hands—my lips, my hands, and all my other body parts were left untouched. Admittedly, this got harder as I got older (the decision not to have romantic, physical contact with men until marriage didn't make me like them any less). But the community I grew up in made it a bit easier—I was dark-skinned, which meant that the South Asian men I met (Indians, Pakistanis, *and* Sri Lankans) didn't like me.

Sri Lanka, of course, was the safest place in the world—the men there liked "fair" women, and as a hijab-wearing American Muslim woman with a Southern California accent, I was much more of a curiosity than a serious marital prospect. When I moved there on my Fulbright scholarship after law school, I never imagined that Sri Lanka would present me with my first serious test. I never imagined Rohan.

I met him halfway through my year there. He was a personal trainer at Colombo's most exclusive gym, where I started working out—alongside fancy Sri Lankan aunties and the overpaid, foreign staff of international NGOs—after outgrowing all the clothes I had brought with me to the island, thanks to the piles of food my relatives heaped on my plate at every meal.

He was standing behind the front desk the first time I walked in. Rohan was everything I was not: light-skinned, Catholic . . . and incredibly fit. His perfectly tanned and chiseled biceps were the kind you wanted to see on a trainer, and his sculpted face and chocolate brown eyes were perfect for his part-time job as a model for one of Sri Lanka's largest cell phone companies. Between the billboards that lined Colombo's congested streets and the time we spent together, in and out of the gym, I came to know that face well.

But when we first met, he was just a guy trying to get a new client. "I'm available for training," he offered, before the yelps of a ruddy German expat, struggling to control runaway dumb-bells, summoned him into the weight room.

He didn't have to try too hard. I signed up for a session that afternoon.

He was a patient but tough trainer, smiling sympathetically when I whined about the oppressive heat of Sri Lanka's premonsoon season while simultaneously turning up the speed of the tread-mill. I chattered on endlessly as he guided me through lunges, squats, and crunches, silenced only when he let out an exasper-ated sigh: "If you don't concentrate on this next set, I'm going to make you do an additional thirty minutes on the bike."

He turned out to be one of the closest friends I made during my year in Sri Lanka. He offered to show me around town on his days off, and we were soon spending all of our free time together. He was the friend I called when I got tired of being on my best behavior in front of my relatives and wanted to curse with reck-less abandon, and the only person I let visit me the day I spent puking up the street food that my coworkers had warned me about eating.

I was amused by the looks we elicited when we went out, particularly at Colombo's hot spots, where he was well known among the children of the Sri Lankan elite who were his clientele. *Is this dark, scarf-wearing woman with a funny accent Rohan's new girl?* they seemed to be wondering, as they greeted him and looked me up and down.

Because he was Sri Lankan, it never crossed my mind that he might be interested in me. Coupled with the fact that he wasn't Muslim—and therefore not a marital prospect—I felt at ease around him, comfortable with being just friends without the pressure of anything more.

But for a man used to women constantly preening in front of him, he found my lack of interest—made obvious by my unrestrained speech and often disheveled appearance—refreshing. And, apparently, alluring.

While we were eating lunch on the terrace of his favorite café one afternoon, he unexpectedly said, "I really like you."

I stopped midbite, taken off guard by his confession. "Thanks," I said, eyebrows raised. "*Why?*"

"Don't look so surprised," he smiled. "You're fun and you're pretty."

"You're pretty, too," I replied reflexively, cringing as the words passed my lips.

He roared with laughter as I sat there, lunch forgotten, flustered and confused.

"But don't you think my skin is too dark?"

"No, I think it's beautiful."

A Sri Lankan man thinks I'm pretty and my skin is beautiful? This was a first.

I suddenly felt too shy to look at him, but couldn't seem to find a place to rest my eyes other than on his pecs, nicely outlined by his snug, navy polo. I became painfully aware of the ratty T-shirt I hadn't bothered to change out of after our morning workout.

I was flattered, but I told myself, and Rohan, that we would have to remain friends. He wasn't Muslim, so the relationship wasn't going anywhere—after all, I wasn't the kind of girl to hook up with a guy I had no intention of marrying. Absolutely nothing physical would happen, even as the attraction between us grew and my days on the island drew to a close.

But then I ended up spending my last night in Sri Lanka at his apartment.

I'd spent the day packing up my place while relatives stopped by to wish me well on my trip home. The last of them left past midnight, promising to be back early the next morning to take me to the airport. Rohan arrived shortly thereafter to bid me farewell, only to find a mountain of stuff by my front door that I couldn't fit into my already overflowing suitcases. "You need any of this?" I asked hopefully, gesturing to a random assortment of pots and pans, electronic gadgets, and clothes. He looked at the pile and shook his head. "Not really, but I can get rid of it for you."

We hauled the stuff back to his apartment, dumping it by his front door and filling up his already small living space. As I looked at him surveying my discarded junk, I realized how much I would miss him. He'd been such a good friend over these past months. And I swear he had added a couple more packs to his already well-defined abs.

It was late, we were alone, and it was the last time I'd ever see him. I was standing less than a foot away from the only South Asian man who had ever liked me. And suddenly, all I could think about was how much I wanted to kiss him. He looked up at me expectantly, and I didn't look away. One little kiss—no one would ever know.

But I would.

It was just a kiss, but I had built up this moment in my mind for years. It was supposed to happen with my future husband—it couldn't happen now. I had to get out of his apartment. Quickly. Before I lunged.

I asked him to call me a cab and, while he did, moved to the other side of the room and busied myself with the mechanics of the small glass vase on his coffee table.

As we waited for the cab to arrive—I'd now moved on to studying the coffee table itself (Was it oak? Or bamboo?)—he told me that he couldn't believe I was leaving and made me promise that we would keep in touch. He said some other stuff, too, that I can't remember—I was too busy panicking as he made his way across the room until we were face-to-face.

Oh God. I balled up my fists to keep them from grabbing him.

There was a honk outside.

My heart was pounding as he leaned his face close to mine. I managed to hold up a shaky hand when he was just an inch away.

"Stop. Don't kiss me."

He sighed and straightened up.

I gave him a quick hug, grabbed my bag, and ran downstairs, into the backseat of the waiting cab. With a disapproving glance in the rearview mirror—it was not appropriate for a woman to be leaving an apartment alone so late at night—the cabbie backed out of the driveway just as Rohan came out onto his balcony to watch me leave. I didn't turn around as we drove away. I was exhausted—it was hard work fending off the advances of a hot man.

As the cab took me back to my barren apartment, I believed I had done the right thing. I had maintained my chastity and preserved my reputation, even though no one was around to appreciate the extent of my sacrifice. I had succeeded in saving *everything* for the perfect Muslim man whom I would someday marry. But if there's one thing I should have learned from Rohan—the Catholic, Sri Lankan personal trainer with a crush on a dark-skinned, hijab-wearing, sweaty American—it is that we can never be certain what the future holds. As the years passed and I remained single into my thirties, with no Muslim man in sight—my lips, hands, and other body parts also alone—I would come to look back on my last night on the island with regret.

I can't believe I passed up the chance to make out with a model.

Even Muslim Girls Get the Blues

Deonna Kelli Sayed

When I first decided I was ready to get married, a Pakistani friend said, "You'll have too many men wanting to marry you. Go to the mosque. Some will look in one of your eyes and see American dollars. In the other, they will see a green card. Everyone will tell you that you are beautiful."

I wasn't your typical Muslim girl: I was a twenty-six-year-old, blonde American who had embraced Islam five years earlier, after hearing scholar Seyyed Hossein Nasr suggest that faith is a thinking woman's realm that requires both intellect and the heart. Faith is not a passive space for either gender.

My friend's words were a warning, veiled in humor. Perhaps his certainty came from the fact that he had already found his perfect match—a Pakistani-Scottish woman with solid Punjabi family credentials. Another friend was in pursuit of a "wheat-colored" *desi* girl. Nobody told me that I was beautiful or even desirable, despite my green eyes or green-card access; all the well-educated, open-minded practicing Muslims I knew were looking for girls from "back home"—girls from good families in their respective cultures. There were actual print catalogs of available women circulating among certain immigrant communities, and few, if any, of those girls were white Americans.

I knew a few secular Muslim men from abroad who had married non-Muslim American women and had subsequently become more red, white, and blue than their spouses. I had also witnessed American-apple-pie women come into the faith, only to disappear behind an abaya, a hijab, and an Arab name.

No, thank you, I said. *That is not the story I want to tell; that story is not mine.*

Adopting Palestinian activism and socializing mostly with Muslims in college was a departure from my intended path. I grew up in the rural South as a Southern Baptist, and any global awareness I had came from Holy Land pictures in the Bible. "Those people"— the Orientalist version of the "exotic other"—fascinated me, as the Holy Land is a spiritual compass for so many Americans.

First, let me make something clear: I did not get into all "this" by dating a Muslim man. Many people assume that any white woman who stumbles into Islam does so through a man. I was intrigued by cultural hybridity before I had learned the phrase in a social-theory class. Let me also say that I was not a casual observer regarding the intricate intersections of immigrant, American, and Muslim identities, but experienced them personally. My best friends in college were Muslim women from VIP Arab families. I taught my Lebanese friend, pursuing her PhD in English at the time, how to drive after her American husband died unexpectedly. She had kept her marriage hidden from her relatives in Lebanon for fourteen years, for fear of their reaction. I cruised *shisha* joints in New York City with another friend, a Syrian-Canadian fashion designer, as she bemoaned the complexities of dating post-divorce from her white, American husband.

My friends lamented the challenges of finding a good Muslim man who appreciated smart women. These were beautiful girls with refined tastes from respectable, upper-class families who could not find husbands, in spite of their affiliations with cultural institutions and worldwide networks. My fashion-designer friend summed it up while we were waiting at the 110th Street subway: "We aren't considered good Muslim girls."

I sighed. "I don't understand. We don't sleep around, don't drink; we're smart, intellectually invested, and interested in Islam. Why aren't we good Muslim girls?"

The subway train approached, and her black hair bellowed in the tepid breeze as she explained, "We aren't in hijab. It's 11:00 PM, and we are out on the town. We aren't quiet. We have desires and goals. We are too complicated." Most of my Muslim girlfriends echoed her sentiments.

I had no serious prospects. I was effervescently white, with ample, fertile hips. I was a practicing, educated, intellectually curious American Muslim woman. I wanted a man who was the same, but probably not the average American. After years of spending time with Muslim girls, I had a taste for ethnic food, crossbred ideologies, and complicated expectations. I wanted a man who knew something about crossing boundaries. I was an American, but not just.

Being a Muslim can do that to a girl. Your faith connects you to the world in mysterious ways. When you live between cultures and boundaries, invisible appendages take root. Tandoori chicken with macaroni and cheese is more than fusion food—it is the zoom lens with which one experiences the world. There are pauses and uncertainties from this vantage point as a new culture emerges.

I didn't know all of that yet, and I was still searching for a co-conspirator, a fellow traveler, in my boundary crossing. Someone suggested I put an ad in the magazine published by the

Islamic Society of North America, *Islamic Horizons*, which has a matrimonial page. I considered the idea, but the only advertisements I saw from women were from middle-aged American Muslims. Even more intimidating were the ads placed by parents inviting "correspondence" for their doctor/lawyer/engineer son from "slim, fair, beautiful, highly educated girl of [fill in the blank] heritage, age 21–30." In those days, I never saw anything suggesting that someone like me would be seriously entertained as a spousal possibility.

I hate to perpetuate stereotypes, but a few Muslim men did want to marry me for a green card. One offered to pay $20,000 to be married *just long enough* to become a resident, and then we could divorce. It was an act of desperation on his part, not a lack of ethics. I understood that, but I was not interested in such an offer.

I met Sayed in a church and thanks to bombs. This is not a joke. Muslims do not joke about such things.

I was working at the General Board of Global Ministries for the United Methodist Church (GBGM), headquartered across from Columbia University on Riverside Drive. Manhattan was not the glamorous *Sex in the City* experience for a single, Muslim, twenty-six-year-old woman in 1999. Sayed, based in Washington, D.C., at the time, was an internationally recognized land mine expert—a Nobel Peace Prize laureate, to be precise—who had accepted the award in 1997 on behalf of the International Campaign to Ban Landmines. He also had five children—an overwhelming number to me at the time—from a previous marriage.

Oh, my.

I met him over dinner the night before an official Methodist Church meeting on land mine awareness. I first noticed his long legs as he emerged from the cab. I did not like the blue of the shirt he was wearing. I thought a man so accomplished would be much older, but he was just nine years my senior. He was nice, but did not take hold in my mind. He spoke of his children in Pakistan and ongoing issues related to the Taliban. Other Afghan men were present, so I retracted from the conversation. I went to bed and thought nothing more of him.

Until, that is, I awoke to catch a Metro North train to Connecticut for our meeting the next day. Sometime during my slumber, fate had cracked open an alternative dimension and thrust a new probability into my life. He was all I thought about in the limo to Grand Central and on the train to Stamford. To this day, the sudden force with which he occupied my mind remains a mystery.

During the meeting, I noticed the extraordinary length of his eyelashes. He did not look at me beyond formal, polite exchanges. Had he not called me later that day to discuss Afghan politics, I would have returned from whatever parallel universe I had woken into that morning.

We kept in touch, and I moved to Washington, D.C., a few months later. I did not pry into his private life, but I intuitively understood that something was amiss. We talked often and met occasionally to have dinner. He was *shariah*-compliant in his demeanor—gentlemanly, that is—and I was soon smitten by his attention and his respectful manner. Oh, but my being smitten was not pretty. I had horrible indigestion because of the potential outcome of my secret infatuation. Here was a kind, handsome man, honorable and accomplished, who appeared to enjoy spending time with me. I had never experienced such a dynamic. Surely, I thought, there was no way such a person would ever have feelings for me. But I needed to be loved. It was time to take a chance.

My luck with relationships was pitiful, and I assumed this one would meet a similar fate. So I figured, *He's leaving the country— tell him how you feel, and then you'll have his three weeks away to mourn the loss.*

The conversation started in the car on Sixteenth Street as we made our way out of D.C. into Maryland.

"You know," I said, "I don't just hang out with guys."

There was a pause.

"Yes," he said.

"And I know that you don't just hang out with women," I said.

"No, I don't."

"So," I continued, "what is going on here?"

"Um, I don't know,' he said. But he was smiling, and it was nice.

The conversation expanded over tea in his apartment. *What the hell*, I thought, and stated simply, "I want to marry you."

He informed me that he was not looking for a cheap relationship, nor did he desire an American woman just to pass the time with.

That was when he told me that he was looking for a wife. I wanted it to be me.

Risking my emotional well-being to tell Sayed of my love was one of the most important decisions I ever made in my life. The lack of male attention I had gotten before Sayed had me convinced that I was a metaphysical mistake. Being overweight did not counteract that assumption. I felt that I was not good enough for thinness-obsessed American men, or, it appeared, for anybody else. After multiple experiences of not being accepted by someone I had feelings for, it was unthinkable that my affections for an accomplished, kind man would be reciprocated. But I had a decision to make: I could live in fear of rejection and the not-ever-knowing, or I could go ahead and get rejected and then move on.

So I took that grand leap and proposed. It was not easy. I was a twenty-seven-year-old, smart, fat, insecure American woman. Sayed was a land mine expert from Afghanistan, a Nobel Peace Prize winner, and the father of five children, aged five to nine.

But he was already in line for a green card for "extraordinary skills," and when he looked into my green eyes, he saw a partner.

We dated over the next few months. There was a trip to Delaware. There were strenuous hours of conversation. He cooked a full Afghan meal for me at his apartment. We were alone together, but did not consummate our relationship before marriage. About the marriage, he had reservations. He was responsible for a large extended family, as well as for his children. "What if," he wondered in an email to me one day, "we have to move to a village in Afghanistan?"

"Not likely," I mused, "because the political situation in Afghanistan is going to suck for a long time."

I was too naive to fully understand the momentous nature of this decision. In truth, I had no solid career plans at that point in my life. I was emotionally exhausted and ready for marriage, and here was a very kind man who was willing to take a chance with me. I sensed I was at a point in my life that made me vulnerable to less-than-stellar options, and I knew this choice was far better than anything else I might bump up against even in the best of circumstances.

No one knew how this cross-cultural, mixed-family arrangement would work. My mother was worried about many things—the demons and misconceptions that plague so many American minds regarding Muslims. She feared that that Sayed would take me "over there" and I'd never be seen again. She was afraid that I'd turn into Sally Field in *Not Without My Daughter*. She worried that Sayed would make me walk behind him in public.

"Of course she will walk behind me," he said, smiling, "if we should ever stroll in a minefield."

Sayed then told my mother that he had traveled all over the world and had not met anyone he felt comfortable with until he found me. The largeness of his life—and his love—loomed before me with a promise that calmed my mother's apprehensions.

We married in November 2000. We had three ceremonies. The first, outside Washington, D.C., involved the *nikah*, the Islamic wedding contract. He wanted me to learn a Qur'anic verse in Arabic by heart before we consummated the marriage, as a blessing on the start of our life together. And while that was a meaningful gesture, I felt the consummation part was the more pressing issue at the time.

A few months later we had a larger ceremony, at an Afghan restaurant in Washington, D.C. My divorced parents attended, as well as some relatives and well-established members of the American Muslim community. Some of my relatives hadn't known I was Muslim until that moment. My accomplished husband softened the blow a little—he wasn't their stereotypical convenience-store-owning Muslim.

A few months later, we went to Pakistan, where we married for a third time. I wore a purple dress and way too much makeup. The Afghan girls at the salon in Islamabad took my picture—it was rare for an American woman to come in for a bridal updo. Before I got into the car, Sayed's relatives threw a chador over my entire head to help me avoid the prying eyes of curious onlookers. I couldn't see where I was going, and promptly fell on my face en route to the car. Looking back, I realize that moment was a great metaphor for marriage: You can't really see what lies ahead. You know that you are going to fall—many times—but you just stand up again, get your ass in gear, and run forward.

Shortly after our nuptials, my husband joined the United Nations and became a diplomat. With varying combinations of children, we traveled in Maryland, then central Asia (where I gave birth to a son), the Middle East, and finally back to America.

No one prepared me for this matrimonial journey. The children, three ceremonies, the moving back and forth around the world with what were now six kids—it all became a delirium. Few wives are flexible enough to fluctuate with such dramatic, global family dynamics, and I became an unimpressive, obese housewife.

The turning point in our marriage and for me came when we moved to Bahrain. Sayed became the UN's resident representative for the country, and I was "Her Excellency," surrounded by drivers and live-in maids and having tea with the royal family. As an ambassador's wife, I organized luncheons for the *shaikhas*, helped form a creative-arts group and writing workshops, and started writing for local English-language magazines. In one, I launched a very public weight-loss column. I arrived on the tiny island as my husband's appendage, and I left as an emerging writer who was fifty pounds thinner.

Together we decided that I would return to the United States with all six children to settle the older ones into high school. I went from being a diplomat's wife to being a single parent with six children, including three teenagers who could not drive. By this point, I was eight years into the marriage and we had moved five times, three of those relocations international. A psychologist friend told me that—in terms of stress—the issues I was dealing with were off the charts. For the first time in my marriage, the role of woman-wife completely disappeared as the demands of being only-a-mother took over.

I have not been the wife or mother I wanted to be. After six kids and moving every few years, I have realized that mothering is more emotionally exhausting than anything else. It took me years to realize it is something that I do not do exceptionally well.

My husband, bless him, has been patient.

I'm older now, almost forty. I married with no substantial career and am now an emerging writer. I have pondered what it would be like to be back in culturally familiar territory. To be married to a non-Muslim American would mean experiencing a sort of certainty I grew up with: traditional Friday-night high school football games, family reunions at the river, and Christmas traditions (yes, I do miss those). In my imagination, the rules and expectations would be very clear, the boundaries neatly drawn. In reality, I know that all marriages are wildly complex.

But through my love for Sayed, I've confirmed that I am American, but not just. There are parts of me that fit only in a cross-cultural relationship, from food to faith. I may not know how to be a stereotypically American wife, but I do know how to be a complicated, *fee wasat*—"in the middle"—wife. Being a world citizen is the America of the future, something I understand well, as my marriage, spirituality, and identity have all been negotiated at global intersections.

So, this story is mine; this is the one I tell.

Rerouting

Leila N. Khan

I crossed off the last few items on my to-do list. I had given my landlord notice, canceled my utilities, scheduled movers, and booked my flight to Luxembourg. I sat back in my chair and surveyed my apartment: stacks of cardboard boxes, neatly taped up and labeled, my favorite rugs from Pakistan and Bosnia rolled up and standing in a corner, my bubble-wrapped paintings leaning against the wall, and my bare shelves. There wasn't much left to pack. Everything was falling into place.

After nearly three years of having a long-distance relationship, Luca and I would finally be living in the same city together. We first met in Strasbourg, France. I was there on a yearlong fellowship, researching human rights and refugee law at the European Court of Human Rights, and Luca was interning in the court's Italian section.

We met in the court cafeteria and connected immediately over our field experience in the former Yugoslavia. Slim and stylish in his tailored gray suit, with wavy dark hair, large hazel eyes, and dimples when he smiled, Luca radiated a warm but serious energy. He had come to the court after spending nearly two years in Kosovo for the United Nations, and I had spent a summer in Sarajevo, also with the UN. We stayed in the cafeteria all afternoon, discussing the fate of the Balkans, the work of the UN, and democracy in East Timor over espressos and cigarettes.

We started dating less than two weeks after we first met. Within a month, Luca invited me to a family wedding in the south of Italy, where several of his relatives lived. Communication was stilted, as most of his relatives did not speak English and I did not speak much Italian. But we all smiled a lot, nodded frequently— "*Sì, ah, sì. Sì, sì!*"—and pointed to Luca as a common reference. At the end of the weekend, Luca's mother hugged me closely and invited me to Milan, where she and Luca's father lived. I beamed as I deciphered her invitation, basking in her approval.

As Luca's three-month internship neared its end, he sought to obtain employment at the court in Strasbourg, but did not succeed. We glumly accepted that he would return to Milan and I would stay in Strasbourg.

"*Amore*, I'm willing to take the train every weekend to see you," he said softly. I turned to him, tears in my eyes. I had prepared myself for the relationship to fade when Luca left. I absorbed the intensity of his offer, feeling the love shining from him.

"Oh, *amore*, me too." I took his hand. "We'll make it work."

The day Luca left, I accompanied him to the train station. We hugged and kissed even after the conductor blew his whistle, signaling the train's departure. I stood waving until the train became only a small black spot. As I walked back to my studio, the city felt bleak, despite all the Christmas lights, tinsel, and VIN CHAUD signs. I just had to survive one week until I would see him again.

Before I had come to Strasbourg, I had accepted an offer with a law firm in New York. The firm had encouraged me to complete my fellowship and had agreed to hold my position until I returned. As my year in Strasbourg came to an end, Luca and I brainstormed about how we could live in the same city. He had started working for a nongovernmental organization in Milan that focused on development projects in Africa, and was thinking of ways he could work in the United States for this NGO. We briefly considered my moving to Milan instead of New York, but that plan was replete with logistical hurdles, namely, my inability to speak Italian and my significant student loans.

"Luca, I owe over one hundred thousand dollars in student loans; I have to work at a firm for a few years," I explained to him.

"A few *years*? What do you mean? You'll be in New York for at least a few years?"

"Well, I have to repay some of it. I feel so stressed when I think about how much I owe."

"But what about us?" he implored.

"Well, didn't you want to study law in the U.S.? Maybe you could apply for a law degree at a university here," I suggested.

"Yes, it's true. Every lawyer at the UN had degrees from the U.S."

That summer, as I transitioned from the idyllic life of a researcher in Strasbourg to the demands of a junior associate at a Manhattan law firm, Luca came to New York and stayed with me for two months, working on translation projects for the Italian NGO and researching law programs.

He left one week before 9/11. When the city was attacked, the phone lines went dead and I couldn't call anyone—not my family in California, not Luca, no one. I felt terrified and alone as I walked from my office in midtown Manhattan to my apartment on the Upper East Side. I couldn't bear to watch the images playing on the television, so I lay on my sofa, staring into space. It finally occurred to me to send emails, and that was how my family and Luca learned that I was fine. Luca wrote back immediately,

insisting on taking the next possible flight to New York, but I told
him not to worry and that I still planned on coming to Milan for
a holiday in a few weeks.

Luca spent several months working on his law school applications. But because of the economic crisis that followed the 9/11
attacks, graduate programs received record numbers of applications, and Luca was not accepted anywhere.

"Why did I put myself through this? It was for you. I just wanted
to be near you," he said bitterly. My heart ached as I watched him
suffer through the disappointment. I wanted to tell him that I was
disappointed, too, that I was working hard to repay my student
loans not just for myself, but for us, so that we could have greater
freedom soon.

With so few employment prospects in New York for an Italian
lawyer after 9/11, Luca and I settled into a holding pattern of
sorts. We scrimped and we saved, and we used every vacation
day possible to meet each other in New York or in Europe nearly
every month.

On several occasions, we broke up. He accused me of being
selfish and too focused on my career. I cried that he didn't understand how debilitating my loans were and that, despite my Italian
lessons, I could not speak well enough to work as a lawyer in
Italy. We always reached an impasse when I insisted on wanting
to work.

"But I can take care of us. You won't need to work," he assured me.

"What do you mean? I've studied so hard to be a lawyer,
borrowed all this money for my education. I want to work as
a lawyer," I responded testily. "Your mother is a well-known
attorney; your sister is a professor at a big university—why
should I be the housewife?"

By this point in the conversation, I knew Luca would pull his
trump card.

"You still haven't told them about me," he accused softly. There it was—the blow that reduced me to a heap of shame and guilt.

"Luca, I just need to find the right time," I whispered.

"*Amore*, it has been nearly two years. You've spent the holidays with my family. You stay with my family when you visit. They all ask about you. When do I get to meet your parents? Your sister and brother?"

"Babe, my brother and sister know about you. But with my sister getting married, I just can't tell my parents right now." I felt frantic as I thought about my sister's "perfect" situation. She had met her fiancé at her local mosque's youth group. He was Pakistani, a practicing Muslim, and fluent in Urdu. Check, check, and check. And he was an engineer. Yet another check. My Pakistani, Muslim, Urdu-speaking parents were thrilled. The only wrinkle was me, the unmarried older sister. My parents initially contemplated holding off on my sister's wedding until someone could be found for me, but, given my track record of refusing suitors, they decided to move forward with her wedding.

"You know I'd like to go to the wedding with you," he said. My stomach sank. My parents were devout, practicing Muslims. My entire extended family was. How could I show up with my Italian, Catholic boyfriend to a wedding full of Pakistanis and religious ritual? How would he react to the significant number of women who wore head scarves and the few who were covered in the chador? How would they respond to him? Luca's appearance at this wedding would be uncomfortable for everyone.

"Luca, I would love to share this wedding with you, but you don't understand how strict my relatives are. It would be culture shock for everyone. I promise I'll send you photos and I'll call you every day, but my sister's wedding is not the time to introduce you to my family. I'm really, really sorry."

A long, tense silence ensued. "Why, why are we doing this? How did I end up in this situation?" he wondered aloud.

These conversations haunted me. How had we ended up in this situation? Why was I still so afraid of acting on my commitment to him? When would I be ready to tell my parents about him? My reluctance revealed depressing truths about how I felt about our relationship. But each time I thought about letting him go, sparkling memories surfaced: the two of us whizzing around Milan on the back of Luca's Vespa, sharing a thick hot chocolate in wintry Paris, holding hands as we walked around the shimmering reservoir in Central Park. I was in love with him, but the consequences were paralyzing.

In the months after my sister's wedding, my family's efforts to marry me off intensified. I couldn't come up with excuses fast enough. Even after a decade of pushing back against my parents' attempts to arrange my marriage, I still felt pangs of guilt for not doing what they wanted, and they still hadn't given up hope. My parents expected me to marry a Muslim man, preferably Pakistani. That's what good Muslim girls did, right? Sometimes their disappointment and frustration were so severe that my mother would threaten to disown me and wouldn't speak to me for months.

I tried to placate them, sharing with them whenever I met a promising Muslim man—Nabil, the Algerian-French lawyer I met in Sarajevo, or Karim, the half-Tunisian, half-British man I dated when I was studying Arabic in Tunisia—but I knew they wanted to participate in the selection process, and they wanted someone more culturally familiar. So telling them that I had a boyfriend who was neither Muslim nor Pakistani likely meant losing them. Each time I worked up the courage to tell them, Luca and I would have a fight and I would retreat. Was he worth devastating my parents?

My hands felt clammy as I dialed my father's home office. We exchanged pleasantries, and then my throat went dry.

"Papa, I have to ask you something."

"Yes, *beta*, anything," my father said cheerfully. I took a deep breath.

"What if you had met someone before Mummy, when you were studying in St. Louis? What if she was *gori* and not Muslim?" I heard silence on the other end. He cleared his throat a few times. I imagined him holding the receiver and looking out at his beloved plants on the patio.

"Well, I don't know. I never met anyone."

"But what if you had?" I insisted.

"Well, let's see . . . I guess if I loved her, then that's all that matters." My father's heartfelt response surprised me.

"What if I met someone I loved?"

"Well . . . " He coughed and then was quiet. "Uh, well, then, that's all that matters." I looked into the phone, astonished.

"Really, Papa? Really?" I paused. *Come on, just tell him.* "Because I have."

"I see. When did this happen?" he asked gently.

"Two years ago."

"Oh, *beta*, two years? It must be serious."

"Yes, it is, Papa. It is." I nodded vigorously into the phone.

"So, what's his name?"

"Luca. He's Italian. He lives in Milan."

"Milan—what a beautiful city. I went there once for work." We both sat quietly on the phone. Finally, he asked, "Do you think he'll convert?"

"I've never asked him."

"Well, you know our religion does not accept a woman marrying a man outside Islam."

"It doesn't make sense why a Muslim man can, but a woman can't."

"It's because a woman is more likely to convert for her husband than a man for his wife," he returned evenly.

"But I don't feel like religion is a big part of my life, so why have him convert?"

"Because it's a big part of your family, and he won't fit in if he's not Muslim."

"Shit, Dad, *I* barely fit in with all our *fundo* cousins and relatives." I sighed.

"Watch the language, *beta*. You'll fit in even less with a husband who is not Muslim." I exhaled loudly.

"Just ask him, *beta*. Do that for me."

Even though my relationship with my faith had shifted after 9/11, I still couldn't bring myself to ask Luca to convert. Following the attacks, Muslims in America were vilified. Under increasing scrutiny, and whether willingly or not, we each became an ambassador of our faith. In the face of tremendous fearmongering, I found myself describing the virtues of Islam, its inherent peacefulness, and its similarity to Judaism and Christianity to my friends, my coworkers, and even the West Indian lady at the organic market down the block.

But even though I talked about Islam more openly and often, I didn't practice my faith. I had largely shed those rituals when I had left home for university, a decade earlier. Some habits remained: refusing to eat pork or bacon, greeting a Muslim with "salaam," and attending Eid prayer once a year. There were moments when I collapsed into the familiarity of prayer, the only spiritual language I knew to access serenity. But, on the whole, Islam's daily practice did not return.

Luca and I often discussed the shifting political landscape after 9/11, the senseless war in Iraq, and the crazy things happening to Muslims in America. We talked generally about the misperception of Muslims in the world, but I never probed him about his feelings about Islam or how he felt about my being Muslim. I just assumed that he accepted me for who I was.

My mother didn't believe that Luca and I would work. When I finally told her about our relationship and how he would like to meet her, she snapped, "How do you see this working out? You're Muslim, Leila. Pakistani. It's in your blood, your name, your family. He's Italian. Catholic. This will never work unless one of you converts. I don't care how much he loves you—marriage takes more than love to work." She was adamant. "I'll meet him—if he converts."

"Ma, I don't feel comfortable asking someone to convert. *I* would never convert."

"But for the sake of the children, the same religion is important. Listen to me, Leila. You're almost thirty years old. You've got to get serious and settle down. Enough with all this nonsense. Enough."

"Ma, please, just meet him. He's a really good man—smart, hardworking, and very loving."

"Leila, I told you, I'll meet him if he converts. Otherwise, it's a waste of time. I will not accept a son-in-law who is not Muslim. Is that clear?"

I was typing up a memo to a client when Luca called. He spoke excitedly, telling me that he had just been offered a position as a lawyer for the European Union in Luxembourg. He described the job, the salary, and all the benefits.

"I think now is the time, *amore*. Come live with me. We can have a really good life in Luxembourg."

"Luxembourg?" I grinned into the phone. I knew that I had more employment options there than in Milan. "Luca, I've never been to Luxembourg, but I believe you."

I visited him there, and we strolled along the canal, shopped at the local farmers' market for cheeses, eggs, and fruit, and enjoyed meals at restaurants with mossy stone walls. We also hammered out the details of my move, including all the ways in which I could freelance. I was feeling more financially stable with some savings in the bank, a chunk of my student loans repaid, and no credit card debt. Yes, Luca was right: The time had come.

We also decided that Luca should meet my parents in California before I moved. I told him that they now knew about him, and that this would be my first time introducing a boyfriend to them. His eyes glistened as I spoke. I didn't mention his converting or my mother's possible absence from the gathering.

At the end of my visit to Luxembourg, when I boarded my flight to New York, I looked around and imagined my return a few months later. This was going to be my new home. As I stared out the window at the bucolic landscape, I felt relieved. Finally, Luca and I could be together.

I stood anxiously in the arrival hall of San Francisco International Airport. When I saw Luca walk through the gate, I beamed and let out a small squeal.

"*Amore!*" I waved excitedly and rushed to him. "Welcome to California!" I hugged and kissed him and then wrapped my arm around him. "How was your flight? Are you tired? *T'as faim?*"

We drove down to Southern California the next day with my brother, a student at Berkeley. When we reached Orange County, where my parents lived, we dropped Luca off at his hotel so he could freshen up and change. My parents were not ready to have my white boyfriend stay under their roof. When I first told Luca I had booked a hotel room for him, he was slightly taken aback. "Oh, a hotel? And where will you stay?"

"Uh, at my parents' place," I stammered. "Luca, come on— this is not easy for them. I can't expect them to let you stay the night. They probably hope I'm still a virgin!"

"Fine, Leila, fine. I understand," he said wearily.

After escorting Luca up to his hotel room, my brother and I headed to my parents' home. I held on tightly to the sides of my seat and breathed deeply.

"Hey, chill out. It'll be fine," my brother said, laughing.

"Yeah, sure, try telling *your* girlfriend that Mom refuses to meet her," I countered through clenched teeth.

When my brother and I opened the front door of my parents' home, the mouthwatering smell of cumin and fried onions greeted us.

"Papa? Mummy? We're home!" I shouted, as I placed my shoes in the hallway closet and walked toward the kitchen. My mother was listening to an Urdu translation of the Qur'an on her cassette player and preparing little balls of minced meat for kebobs. I leaned against the kitchen's island.

"*As-salaam-alaikum*, Ma," I greeted her hesitantly. She had prepared so much food; platters of *biryani*, *raita*, naan, and kebobs were lined up on the counter. The table was set, but when I counted the place settings, I felt stung. Why had she made all this food when she had no intention of eating with us? I figured part of it was her pride. She often emphasized our culture of hospitality and serving guests properly. But so much effort to insist on these values? I was at a loss, unable to decipher the full extent of her intentions. "Ma, how are you? The food smells incredible."

"*Wa-alaikum-asalaam*," she answered, keeping her gaze fixed on the crackling frying pan. "Ma, I think Luca would love to meet the person who made all this delicious food," I said.

"Leila." She put down the spatula and turned to me. "I never imagined that my grown daughter would bring her *gora* boyfriend to my house. Never. Every single one of your cousins has married a Pakistani Muslim. Your sister is married to a Pakistani Muslim. Why are you doing this to me? To our family?" The veins in her neck bulged. My face reddened. She was right. Even I had to admit that I had never seen myself bringing a white, Catholic guy home to meet my parents. I sometimes wished that I had found a Muslim man who would help me embrace my roots. But I hadn't.

"Ma, I'm sorry it didn't go according to plan, but I have been with this person almost three years now, and it's serious. You know I tried meeting Muslim men."

"You mean the ones you met in Tunisia?" she asked derisively.

"Yes, I met someone there. Don't you remember?"

My mother picked up her spatula and started flipping the kebobs. "I don't know what I did to end up with a daughter like you. What did I do wrong, other than bringing you to this country?" she muttered, jabbing at the food. A hard lump rose in my throat.

"Ma, all I can say is that Luca has flown from Luxembourg to meet you and Dad." I shrugged my shoulders and went upstairs.

My mother never met Luca. She went to a friend's house that evening as the rest of us ate the dinner she prepared. At the beginning of the evening, when Luca learned that my mother would not join us, he became anxious. "What? Why?" His face went ashen; his eyes darted around the room. He looked around the house, peppered with framed pictures of the Kaaba in Mecca and gilded Qur'anic verses, and *tasbih* beads in every corner.

My father was stiff and awkward around Luca at first. And Luca had trouble understanding my father's accented English, and kept looking at my brother and me for help. But after Luca helped himself to a third serving of my mother's *biryani*, exclaiming repeatedly how much better her cooking was than that of any Indian restaurant he had ever visited, my father beamed and began explaining the differences between Pakistani and Indian culture. I'm not sure how the conversation turned to politics, but suddenly the men at the table were animated, each one impatient to express his viewpoint on how to deal with Al Qaeda, Kashmir, and Iran.

Toward the end of the evening, my father suggested I make some tea and then beckoned Luca over.

"Why don't we sit outside in the garden?" he asked. Luca's eyes widened, and he glanced at me. I nodded reassuringly. He followed my father out to the patio, and I watched them sit down on my father's large swing.

"Okay, Papa, I'll make tea for you guys," I called out. I filled the kettle with water and then looked over at my brother. "Shit, what do you think? You think it's okay for me to leave him alone with Dad?"

"Yeah, don't worry, Leila. Dad's harmless," my brother said.

Once the tea was ready, I placed the saucer and cups on a tray with a few almond biscuits and walked outside. When he heard the clinking tray, my father looked up and smiled at me. "There she is," he said jovially. "I need my tea every night. It's my drink." He winked at Luca. "You know, we Muslims don't drink alcohol, but tea is like my alcohol." He reached for the cup and took a noisy slurp. "Ahh, very tasty, Leila. Even though she doesn't live at home anymore, she remembers how to make her father's tea, right, *beta*?"

I smiled. "Of course, Papa."

"Come sit, *beta*." He patted the empty space on his other side. The three of us sipped tea, rocking slightly back and forth on the swing as the crickets chirped and the scent from my father's jasmine plant enveloped us.

When I dropped Luca off at his hotel that night, he asked, "So, am I going to get to meet your mother?"

I sighed. Other than my mother's absence, the evening had passed smoothly. "I don't know, Luca. Does it matter?"

"Of course it matters. She's your mother," he responded. I tried not to get upset at his answer. He knew about the long periods of estrangement in my relationship with my mother. Even when we were on speaking terms, our conversations throbbed with unspoken resentments, disappointments, and anger. She factored so little into my daily life, why did it matter that Luca had not met her?

"Look, Luca, you have met the important people in my life. You know that my mother and I don't get along, and that she decided not to come tonight." I uncurled my fists and shook my hands out. *You know why she wasn't there. Don't make me say it.* "But look at all the food she made for you," I offered placatingly.

"I want to see you happy in your family, Leila. That's all," he said gently.

"Well." I put my arms around his neck and smiled at him. "I'm hoping to have my own family soon." I paused and lowered my eyes. "With you, and I'm sure I'll be very happy there."

With three weeks left until my move, Luca flew to New York for one last visit. Even after three years, I still got butterflies in my stomach before our reunions.

When I look back now, I wonder how the conversation started. Each time, it hurts to remember.

We had just come back from dinner with friends in the West Village. Luca was sitting with his legs resting on a box. I was at the kitchen sink, rinsing mugs for tea. We were talking about our life in Luxembourg and having children.

"Well, Italy should definitely be our home base," Luca said.

"What do you mean?" I asked from the kitchen, over the sound of running water.

"My parents are there, and Italy's my home. It should be our home base."

"But it's not my home, and I don't speak the language." I laughed. "Why don't we choose another place for our home base?" I came into the living room, wiping my hands on a striped dishcloth.

"Like where?"

"Like, I don't know, but something we decide together. Maybe London? You like London, and I lived there as a kid. I have family there," I offered.

"Family that you never visit when we go there?" he asked with a snort. He was right. I didn't particularly like my banker-wanker cousins in London, and dreaded seeing them.

"I don't know, but I know that we should agree on something together. Italy's not right for me. I feel so foreign there."

"But our kids need a stable home. Italy would be good for them," he insisted.

"Hey, I lived in five different countries growing up. I never had a 'home base,' and I'm perfectly fine," I replied.

"I don't know—you seem so unstable most of the time, never feeling comfortable anywhere, running from one country to the next," he said, looking me straight in the eye.

"You think I'm 'unstable'?" I repeated slowly.

"I mean, confused. You're always confused about where you belong. I don't want my kids to have the same upbringing as you did."

"Your kids? What are you talking about? What's wrong with my upbringing?" I trembled.

"Well, your religion. It's so strict and severe. We can't raise our children Muslim," he said firmly.

What was going on? How had this never come up before? I had not planned on raising our children Muslim, but I wanted them to be exposed to all aspects of their heritage, including Islam. Yet the way Luca spoke, it was as if he wanted our children to have nothing to do with my religion. Part of me felt betrayed; I had spoken with him honestly about my upbringing, in order to share why I was so opposed to a strict religious life.

"What do you mean, we can't raise our children Muslim? What are you trying to say?"

"I'm trying to say that our children should be raised with one culture and one religion so they aren't so confused. They should be raised Italian Catholic."

"Wait a minute, how can you say that? They are going to be my children, too! And you want them to be something so foreign to me? Italian, Catholic—this is not me. I'd feel so distant from my children."

"So, how do you want to raise them?" he asked, his lips tightening.

"I guess with both our cultures, both our religions. Or how about just secular? No religion," I stammered.

"No religion? Our kids need to have morals and values. We can't raise them with no religion," he replied angrily.

"Well, then, let's raise them with both religions. We can teach them about Catholicism and Islam," I said, giving him a small, conciliatory smile.

"Okay, and how do you see that working?" He folded his arms across his chest and sighed impatiently.

"We could celebrate Christmas and Eid. We could take them to church and to the mosque."

"The mosque? You want to take our kids to the mosque in Milan? Where all the terrorists hang out?"

I sat in stunned silence. "Where all the terrorists hang out," I repeated slowly, shaking my head. We looked silently at each other for several long minutes. "What's happened to you, Luca? You sound like your fascist leader Berlusconi."

"We need to think carefully about these things, Leila."

"I don't understand what's going on with you, Luca. The whole world out there is saying awful things about Muslims, and now the person with whom I will share a home, have a family, is saying the same things. You should know better. I should feel safe with you, understood by you, but instead you're saying crazy things about my religion and my upbringing, telling me I'm unstable, confused." My voice cracked. "I don't understand." I fell into a chair because I could no longer stand. I covered my face with my hands, trying to steady my breath and body.

He stood up and came over to me. He knelt down and tried to move my hands from my face. "Look, *amore*, I need to be able to speak honestly with you. I want my kids raised Italian and

Catholic. They need that structure and stability. I don't want them growing up Muslim in Italy or London or anywhere else in Europe. They won't fit in and will have a lot of difficulty in life. Eh, *amore*," he said softly, "please look at me."

I sat there with my face covered for a long while. *Who are you? Have you always been like this and I just never noticed?* I waited for the shaking in my hands and my legs to subside, for the hot white rage churning in my stomach to slow down, for the tears spilling through my fingers to stop. When he tried to touch me, I shook him off, keeping my palms glued to my face, my fingers locked together in front of my eyes. *How can you feel this way about Muslims and say you love me?* Finally, I took a deep breath, placed my hands on my knees, and looked up.

"Get out of here," I said quietly, staring straight ahead.

He stood up, gathered his belongings, zipped up his bag, and left.

When I heard the door close, I lay down on the floor with my eyes shut and my hands by my sides. I felt so terribly afraid about what had just happened. It felt irreversible. Still, I waited for him to come back, hoping that it had been a moment of hubris and that we would be fine, that our life together in Luxembourg still awaited us.

I never saw Luca again.

So I Married a Farangi

Nour Gamal

My entire life reads like a transatlantic tennis match—Egypt–America; Bahrain–America; Kuwait–America; Egypt–Ireland; Egypt–England. When I was a child, my family moved between the Middle East and America whenever my parents relocated for work. As an adult who felt as if she belonged everywhere and nowhere, I kept moving because it was the only real mode of life I'd ever known. As a result, the most difficult question anyone could ever ask me was "So, where are you from?"

Despite this deep-seated identity crisis, there was one thing I was always sure of: I would grow up to marry a nice Muslim boy of (any) Arab origin and make my parents happy.

The signs that I was a Farangiphile appeared at a very young age, but I ignored them—just as I chose to spend my first year at university as an engineering student, despite the signs that I belonged in the humanities.

It began with Neil Fields in the second grade at the international school I attended in Bahrain. Neil was a wild one and, in retrospect, most certainly had ADHD. But dear lord, did I love him. He was always trying to emulate Chuck Norris by climbing up the walls or throwing paint around or knocking a desk over. What was there for a chubby tomboy like me *not* to love? Alas, it was not meant to be, as he only had eyes for Dutch Barbara and her stupid stick-straight, honey-blond hair. Also, we were seven.

We moved back to New Jersey in 1988. Fourth grade brought Jonny, who set the tone for all future Farangi crushes. Jonny and I were the best of friends. He was like my white, Coke bottle lens–spectacled, silky-straight-haired brother from another mother. He was also the first in a long line of boys I would insist were "just friends—no, really," but about whom I had some very unfriendlike feelings. This was my coping mechanism.

My parents are observant Muslims who would take us to the mosque in central Jersey every Sunday for religion and Arabic classes. Starting when I was very young, they drilled into me that dating is haram and that interactions with the opposite sex are to be undertaken with that in mind. But they were pretty accepting of my having boys as good friends. I came to understand that my interactions with boys (and, later, young men) would not be criticized as long as they took place within the context of friendship. And boys didn't really find me attractive as more than a friend until I was sixteen, anyway. Though I had many crushes, I only ever behaved towards them in a manner that could be explained away as something one friend would do for another friend. If I gave a crush a Valentine's card, he would get the same one that all my other friends got. If I gave him a mix tape–that early 1990s symbol of devotion—I would be sure to qualify the gift by claiming that I'd made the tape for myself and just thought he might like to check out the songs. If one of my girlfriends happened to ask me if I thought my secret crush (they were always secret, as I was never outwardly boycrazy) was cute, I'd respond nonchalantly, "Oh, him? Um, I guess he's alright. We're just such good friends that I can't think of him that way."

During the entire fourth grade, Jonny and I sat next to each other on the bus to and from our private elementary school in New Jersey, and generally did everything together. We partnered in class and spent most of our time at recess together, and he was the first guest on my birthday party invite list. The only time there was any indication of something "more" between us was when our bus would pass Lovers' Lane and we'd both momentarily jump to different seats because, ew, cooties.

Jonny was followed by a string of blond-haired, blue-eyed biker/skater boys: Griffin, with his scientist parents who wouldn't allow him to eat tuna because of the dolphins; Ivan, who had the raddest skater-boy haircut and whose parents were Eastern European exiles; Brian, the seemingly all-American son of an abusive alcoholic; Seamus, the son of a recovering alcoholic, who had been sexually abused as a youngster.

Did I mention my penchant is not just for white boys, but for *tragically damaged* white boys? After all, what better excuse is there to be close to a guy "only as friends, Mama and Baba" than to claim you're spending so much time on the phone and after school with him because you're helping him out?

The list goes on. Despite spending my middle- and high-school years in post–Desert Storm Kuwait, I somehow managed to limit the scope of my crushes to the troubled-white-boy contingent, with almost no exceptions. In fact, until I started college, there were only two blips on my white-boy-loving radar—most memorably, Mohammed.

Mohammed was, if we're to be honest, much more than a blip. He was my first love. Our relationship was kindled over his ability to use this newfangled thing called the Internet to find

Kurt Cobain's suicide note, which he read to me over the phone that first heady summer of '96. From that point on, we began writing each other passionate love letters (one of which he even wrote in his own blood to convey the depth of his affection).

I was sixteen going on seventeen, and this was real love, man—whether or not I admitted it to myself at the time.

But despite his name (and actually, most people knew him by his decidedly non-Arabic nickname, Freddie) and his chocolaty-brown complexion, Mohammed's soul was white as the driven snow. He played lead guitar in a band. He wore his hair long and lived in plaid flannel shirts. He wanted to be a rock star (alongside being a dentist, of course) and live the life when he went off to college in Canada later that year. My point is, Freddie was as Farangi as you could get without actually being a Farangi.

My relationship with Mohammed/Freddie ended—as so many tragic first-love stories seem to—when my parents found one of the notes he'd written me. This commenced a three-month period of hand wringing, head shaking, and fierce under-the-breath yelling (is this a particular specialty of Arab parents?) about how ashamed they were that I was carrying on in this manner with someone whose parents they were friends with. They then grounded me for two months and told me to never speak to him again. Despite the fact that I had to see Mohammed every day in school, I dutifully did as I was told. I refused to be sad or sorry about the breakup, and resolved to forget about it. I would not let something as silly as love or affection conquer me or compromise my relationship with my parents or my faith.

My mother often lamented that her children's upbringing in a generally Western, non-Islamic environment meant that many of Islam's teachings were lost on us. But they certainly instilled in me the idea that Allah is all-knowing and parents are His eyes on Earth. My first year in college on the East Coast of the United States, with my parents still in Kuwait, I would be back in my dorm room every night for the 10:00 PM curfew my parents had "suggested" to me before I left for college. I was always sure that somehow they would know if I wasn't home at the allotted time.

It was only after I'd been in college for three years that I started to recognize realities I had denied about myself—namely, my long history of white-boy loving. I set out on a mission to deprogram myself. I wouldn't ever end up with a white guy—because my mother had made clear to me in no uncertain terms that she would not accept my rewarding her leniency in allowing me to live in the United States alone with bringing home a perfectly nice, intelligent, and decent non-Muslim man. So I focused on getting clean.

Of course, I did this by becoming entangled with the smartest, kindest, most helpful—and whitest—Jersey boy ever. I followed that with a relationship with the most devastatingly intelligent, musically talented Midwestern white boy ever. Followed by . . . well, you get the idea.

But I persevered, and after six years in the States, I packed up my things and hauled ass back to Egypt—where my parents were now living—giving myself one last-ditch chance to kick the whitey habit.

But Allah has a wicked sense of humor, y'all.

I met Gabriel in May 2004, just six months after I moved to Cairo. Our first meeting, through my best friend, was unremarkable. Gabriel had just arrived from England to finish up his research for his master's degree dissertation on governance in Egypt. His uncle was my best friend's master's thesis advisor, and had asked her to show Gabriel around as a favor to him. He seemed like a lovely guy—which explains my lack of immediate attraction to him. (Remember, I like 'em damaged.) So we became friends—*really* just friends.

Then one day a few years into our comfortable, close friendship, I started to think that maybe there could be something more between us—a thought that I promptly shut down when Gabriel started seeing an acquaintance of mine. Sloppy seconds were not my style.

But a few weeks later, they called it quits and I became Gabriel's go-to girl. We started hanging out like never before, and he began calling me late at night to check that I had arrived home safely from whatever outing I had been on. It was during this time that he told me, "If you were my type, you'd have to get a restraining order to keep me away from you, because we get along so well otherwise." Just the sort of lukewarm praise every girl wants to hear. I was finally at peace in my relationship with my parents, with Islam, and with my heritage. I didn't want to risk shaking that up by taking a chance on a Greek Brit, even though he had surprisingly nice teeth for a Brit and a wickedly wry sense of humor.

The few friends I consulted all said the same thing: "He's a *wonderful* guy, but why do that to yourself? Just choose not to feel this way about him." They said I was too old (a decrepit twenty-seven) to embark on a relationship that was destined to end because he was not Muslim and I would not marry a non-Muslim.

I am the sort of person who believes one can and does choose love. I can put the lid on my feelings better than Don Draper, so that's what I did for a while.

But every so often, questions would enter my head: *Why am I rejecting this good, decent man who has been nothing but a great friend and upstanding human being in all the time I've known him? Why am I turning down the chance to be with someone who has lived like me— all over the world, straddling two cultures, never quite feeling like he belonged but never too bothered about it, either?*

The whole situation reminded me of a verse from the forty-ninth chapter of the Qur'an, Al-Hujurat:

"O mankind, We created you from a male and female, and We made you into nations and tribes, that you may know one another."

I would find myself muttering this verse under my breath like a sort of mantra, and like any good mantra, it led to an epiphany: I was finally ready to really take a chance on love and a white boy.

So I set about doing what any woman does in such a situation. Over the course of several late-night phone calls with Gabriel, I started letting it slip that I might be interested in advancing our relationship. But then, the day after Gabriel finally got the hint, I announced to him that I was "over it" and that my feelings for a previous crush, who had just blown back into town after a couple of years in Japan, had been rekindled. I am not very good at being emotionally vulnerable, and I was embarrassed and worried that he didn't feel the same way. So I backtracked like an emotional coward.

Gabriel, understandably, did not take this very well. After getting me to 'fess up to the fact that I had said that thing about that other guy purely out of fear of screwing up our wonderful friendship, he spent the next week convincing me that we should give it a go.

So like any red-blooded woman in the throes of a budding romance, I came up with a contract. I made Gabriel promise that no matter what happened, we would always remain friends. That there would be no bitterness if (when) our romantic relationship ended. And that in the unlikely event that we did decide to really make a go of it and get married, he would convert to Islam. Not for the sake of convenience, but out of conviction. He would take the time to educate himself, and then—without any prodding or help from me, and preferably without my knowledge at all—he would convert.

I figured if he could accept such nonsense, he was a definite keeper.

Gabriel did accept—the first of many harebrained schemes I cooked up that he would go along with. Our relationship didn't so much change as deepen. Over the next few months, Gabriel went from being a good friend to being my best friend and my biggest champion. When I was frustrated and fed up with the intensity of life in Cairo, he was the first one there with a smile and a funny story. When he went on one of his many scuba diving trips, I was the first one he called to describe the giant sea turtle he'd seen. When I was hesitant about leaving my job and pursuing a master's degree, he encouraged me to do it and, a year later, slogged through my dissertation, editing it and making suggestions.

I came to realize that his particular brand of sweetness, which I had often taken for softness or weakness, was in fact a generosity of spirit the likes of which it is rare to encounter. His ability to laugh at himself was equaled only by his self-respect and respect for others. Things fell into place for us in a way that allayed all the fears I'd ever had about being with a Farangi, especially this particular one.

A year and a half later, on Valentine's Day 2009, Gabriel sat me down and said, "I have something I've been preparing." He proceeded to recite the Fatiha, the opening chapter of the Qur'an. He made me turn away from him as he haltingly made his way through it. It was the loveliest thing I'd ever heard. Two months later, while I was out of Egypt on a work trip, he took two friends of ours down to Al-Azhar to act as witnesses to his conversion to Islam. Though I knew he was planning to convert while I was out of the country, I tried not to get my hopes too high, telling myself I'd believe it when I saw it. But when my plane landed in Cairo and I turned on my cell phone, there was a text from Gabriel: "It is done." A huge smile briefly spread across my face, before the realization that it was now time for the really hard part—telling our respective families that we wanted to get married.

Two months after Gabriel converted, I told my parents about us. It went about as well as I could have expected. The five stages of grief unfolded in our household over the next three months. It was not easy, but it was not as difficult as I had always (deep down inside, you know, where I'd buried my Farangi love) anticipated it would be.

When we had our *katb kitab* several months later, Gabriel and I chose to have *el-maktoub*—Arabic for "it is written"—inscribed on the inside of our wedding bands. Despite obstacles of culture, religion, timing, and good old human pride, he and I eventually found our way to each other. As we discover what other things have been written for us, I am forever grateful that I put my faith in a higher power—be it love or God or the chaotic order of the universe—and allowed myself to read what was being written all along.

Third Time's the Naseeb:

Loving After Loss

Three

Asiila Imani

In 1979, the Iranian Revolution erupted.

Ayatollah Ruhollah Khomeini replaced the dethroned Shah in the newly formed Islamic Republic of Iran. Each weekday night, U.S. households were riveted to Ted Koppel's *Nightline* as the American hostage situation unfolded. Iran's revolution also triggered a renewed sense of pride and religious fervor in the rest of the Muslim world. For the first time, the immigrant American Muslim population appeared wearing their *khimars*, *kufis*, *jilbabs*, and *thobes* in public.

At the time, I was the secretary of the Black Studies department at Washington State University (WSU)—my first job after graduating from the same institution six months prior. Like most WSU students and faculty, I was curious about what was going on in Iran. The late '70s were a time of political disillusionment. On campus, moments of silence and marches against South African apartheid or the treatment of Palestinians were regular occurrences. Many of us did not doubt Iran's claim, which came

not too long after the end of the Vietnam War and Nixon's resig-
nation, that the American embassy was a "den of CIA spies." We
were impressed with a real-life "power to the people" revolution
against yet another oppressive regime.

My boyfriend, Talib, was Muslim, as was my closest friend,
Asma. As the world's eyes turned to Islam, Asma and Talib shared
their faith with me. Asma introduced me to the newly formed
Muslim Students' Association (MSA), and we attended sisters'
meetings and Islamic conferences. I was impressed with the
incredibly kind and cultured female students and wives of students from Asia, Africa, and the Middle East. They welcomed me
into their fold, and I quickly felt at home in their company and
with the teachings of Islam. After a few months, I converted, my
new sisters witnessing my *shahada*. In 2011, after being Muslim
for thirty-two years now, I have rarely experienced as much of a
true united *ummah* as I did then.

Talib and I had previously discussed the "what ifs" of our relationship, realizing that Islamically we should either marry or
break up. Since we were no longer on the best of terms, the latter
choice was imminent, until a positive pregnancy test changed
our minds. We made halfhearted preparations to marry, never
committing to a solid date.

Three months later, I miscarried a girl I named Turiya.

This was an opportunity to go our separate ways, but we married anyway, brought together by grief. We rationalized that we
had already been together for nearly three years and that perhaps the miscarriage was a punishment for our sexual transgressions. Three years later, two more babies had passed: Jihad died
in utero; Amina, born prematurely, lived for just two hours.

In a fog of intense emotion, we were determined to have a
child. A year and a half after we lost Amina, Raheem was born.
Our mission complete, it seemed that our marriage was, too.
But by the time Raheem was fifteen months old, our union of

six years was in shambles. I packed my things and moved into my parents' home in Hawaii.

Oahu's Muslim population was sparse. Sparser still was the number of single Muslim men: four. One was certifiably insane, and two were half my age. The last, Ali, was the one whom friends kept insisting I meet. We eventually made phone contact. I don't remember much of our two or three conversations, except that he wanted to get married right away and I was still reeling from my divorce.

Ali also wanted a wife who wore the full head covering and practiced more of the *Sunna*. Living the Prophetic lifestyle was easier to do when husband and wife helped each other, he said. But I was barely able to wake up in time for Fajr and didn't eat ritually slaughtered *zabiha* meat, and I wasn't about to start looking like an Arab with my neck and ears all wrapped up, when my "American hijab" (a West African–style *gele*) was good enough.

Ali also spoke of homeschooling, gardening, learning Arabic, giving *dawah*, and making *tahajjud* prayers regularly. It sounded lovely—for someone else. I was content with my nine-to-five workday and prime-time-TV nights. Our courtship ended quickly, but, both seeking friendship within Oahu's small Muslim community, we kept in touch.

A year passed. My son was getting older, attending a Catholic preschool, giving out candy for Halloween, and helping my mom decorate the Christmas tree. I wanted to raise him in more Islamic surroundings. I was also lonely, and celibacy was beginning to take its toll. I needed a husband, and this time I was going to do it right. The Internet, online social networks, and cell phones were a decade in the future. Instead, there were "marital services" provided by *Islamic Horizons* and other Muslim magazines.

The courting process required filling out a data sheet with name, ethnicity, age, height, weight, looks (below average, average, or above average), likes, and dislikes.

> African American female, 30, 5'3", 138 lbs., previously
> married with one child, average looks. I like reading,
> writing, exercising, spending time with my son. I am
> looking for a practicing Muslim brother, 32–42, who
> is kind, knowledgeable, has a sense of humor, and will
> be a good stepfather to my 2-year-old son. Ethnicity
> unimportant.

The information was then printed on a sheet with that of other candidates and mailed to male members; vice versa for the women. Participants then chose whom they wanted to meet and wrote an introductory letter with more information and questions. Admittedly, it was thrilling to read letters from so many brothers vying to impress me. The only problem was that 99.7 percent of them were unhinged.

I had the "pleasure" of meeting the American who thought it a sin for men and women to speak on the phone; another American, who wanted to collect as many concubines as was humanly possible; a Sudanese who demanded I be circumcised and wear the face veil; a Moroccan who wanted to marry for the green card; the double-murder inmate looking for his queen; the 5-percenter searching for his black goddess; the Egyptian who demanded I send him a picture of my hair because he didn't want kinky-haired kids; and the seventeen-year-old who was ready to marry because he had a paper route and a bike.

The next profile was a breath of fresh air:

> African American male, 39, 6', 180 lbs., practicing
> Muslim for over 20 years, traveled throughout the Middle
> East and Africa, one or two children OK, looking for an
> American sister willing to relocate. I love jogging and
> exercise.

Ishaq was friendly and conversant during our weekly phone calls; his letters were long and amusing. He had a great sense of humor and an infectious laugh. He was a former merchant marine and regaled me with tales of his many travels. We became friends.

We had been courting a year when Ishaq flew to Hawaii. "*As-salaam-alaikum!*" he greeted me at my *wali*'s house, wearing the blue *shalwar kamiz* I had sent him for his birthday. We picked up where we had left off on the phone, gabbing like the friends we had become. He made it a point to interact with Raheem, sitting on the floor building Lego castles, which impressed both my son and me. I picked him up from my *wali*'s house every morning for a week and we toured the island together, relaxing on beaches and spending time with my parents and Raheem.

Our long-distance courtship lasted for nearly two years. Ishaq was divorced, too, and we both felt cautious moving toward our next *nikah*, but we liked each other and felt comfortable together. The more we talked, the more certain we became that we were ready to commit ourselves to each other. Marriage was the logical next step. It would take a couple of months to get things ready, and then we'd marry in Hawaii before moving to Oakland, California.

One day, Ali called. He was also about to marry and relocate to Oakland and wanted to find out how I was doing. I told him about Ishaq and our plans. We laughed at the coincidence of ending up in the same city and congratulated each other on our upcoming nuptials, promising we'd get our two families together.

Unlike with my first wedding, I planned the day cheerfully, inviting my family and friends to share in our happiness. But when Ishaq returned to the island, the easy energy between us had changed. There wasn't any obvious problem; it was as if we had fallen out of sync. When we hugged and gave *salaam*s, my heart said, *Uh-oh*. My head countered with, *It's just nerves*. Still, we had our *nikah* ceremony at the *masjid*. It felt like an obligation then—no longer the day we had been looking forward to. We barely smiled in our wedding photos and coolly received congratulations from our loved ones. Boarding the plane to Oakland, I hoped the disappointment of the wedding would subside once we settled into our life together. It did not.

By the fourth week, the cracks were apparent. We were getting on each other's last nerve, and Ishaq broke out in hives. By the sixth week, we were divorced. It was a mutual decision. We realized forcing something that neither of us wanted anymore was useless. As soon as the binds of our marriage were lifted, the ease of our friendship returned. I moved to my brother's apartment in Fort Bragg, North Carolina.

There I was, a thirty-four-year-old, twice-divorced black woman with a five-year-old son. Given my two marriages of six years and six weeks, respectively, if I could have found another husband, it would probably have lasted only six days. I now lived in a part of the country that was chock full of *masjids* and Muslims. There were plenty of single men. The problem was that everyone I was introduced to reminded me of either one or the other ex-husband. I was also considered too dark and too old for the nonblack immigrant brothers looking for wives. I began to feel that I wasn't meant to marry. I was tired of being introduced to men who were incompatible. I was tired of investing time and energy in relationships that seemed destined to fail, and I couldn't stand the idea of dragging my son through yet another divorce.

Still, I was willing to give it one more try. I didn't want to be a single mother or alone for the rest of my life. I was raised in an intact family and wanted the same for my son. I liked being married. I just had to find the right man.

I enrolled in another marital service to widen the net. Right away, I noticed a profile that looked very familiar:

44-year-old African American, 6', 180 lbs., practicing
Muslim for over 20 years . . . I love jogging and exercise.

Ishaq!

I called him.

"Brother, you need to stop lying about loving to jog."

"Asiila?! What you doing in my network?"

"I'm searching for what is starting to seem like the impossible
dream, and you?"

"Same here. I've been married and divorced twice since you
and I divorced."

"Ishaq, what are you doing to these women?"

He laughed. "It's more like, what y'all doing to me!"

We wished each other good luck and hung up. And I disen-
rolled from the matrimonial service.

That was it. Only God could do this. I prayed halfheartedly,
asking Him to send me my match, doubting it would happen.
I got involved with my sister friends, enrolled in prenursing
classes, and concentrated on my studies and my son. It was time
for Plan B: living single, happily ever after.

One Friday evening, three months after my new resolution
and six months after my divorce, Ali called. He had heard Ishaq
and I had separated and was calling to check on me. We spoke for
a while, and he asked if I planned to marry again.

"I don't know. I won't marry just to be married this time," I
told him.

"That's good," he replied. "I just worry about my sisters living
alone, raising their children by themselves. It's not what God
wants. My wife Hajar and I will keep an eye out for men for you."

I thanked him, but, just as when I prayed for God's help, I
felt nothing would come of their efforts. It wasn't just the failed
marriages that bothered me; it was a deeper feeling of numb

discontent and a deadness of spirit. Even if I found a man I could stay married to, what of my soul, my own path in this life? Marriage is half the *deen*, but not all of it. What of the other half, my personal relationship with God?

As promised, Ali called to check on my progress and became my sounding board as I bounced these concerns off him. He was a great listener. His insights were poetic and wise and his advice spiritually based, guiding me back to Allah.

Nearly every time we spoke, he asked, "What do you want?" I responded with an ever-growing list: to leave North Carolina, to make more money, to have a Muslim family, to pass Chemistry . . .

"Okay, is that it?" He was obviously trying to get me to go more deeply into myself, to find the root of the problem, not its many stems. It soon became clear: I wanted to please God.

Once I realized my bottom line, it became easy to wake up for Fajr and refuse non-*zabiha* meat. Instead of feeling sorry for myself, I felt gratitude for God's innumerable graces. Ali became my spiritual advisor. He sent me books on the Prophet and the Prophet's family and encouraged and helped my Arabic and Qur'anic studies. I read everything he sent me, which solidified my beliefs once again. I began to wear the *khimar* and identified myself with the Shi'a school of thought. Ali's letters and phone calls came whenever I felt myself slipping back into doubt, and my faith in him grew alongside my faith in God.

We conversed about my son and about my plans to become a midwife; he told me about the communal business he ran with the brothers of his *jamah*, and their desire to live self-sufficiently. Within the year, talk turned to marriage, both a hopeful prospect and a dreadful thought. Was I ready to do this again? Ali believed that both of my previous marriages had failed because he was my match. God meant for us to be together, he said. Our paths certainly had crossed many times, and we seemed to fit together perfectly, but for one thing—Ali was already married.

Even though I had heard that polygyny always ended in broken hearts, mayhem, and dismemberment, the idea of sharing a husband had never bothered me. I had never understood why women fought so much over men. If a man loved two women, the women could either leave or share him. I believed women should be confident enough in themselves that they wouldn't need to be the sole object of a man's affections. I knew there were men who loved and supported two families with equal devotion. To me, husband sharing sounded like the perfect blend of being married and single at the same time. I would have a loving partner to care for me, and time alone to care for myself. In every holy book I'd read, God was clear that love, unlike money, is infinite; it's a metaphysical commodity that grows when shared. In short, polygyny seemed not an unholy aberration, but a sacrosanct communion between a family and God.

I realized that most other women did not share my philosophy, and I had already decided that I'd never marry a man whose wife did not agree with having a co-wife. Ali said his wife, Hajar, was an exception. He said she was fully aware of our relationship and supported it openly. Learning that eased my worries some, but I still had to hear it from Hajar herself.

Hajar and I had spoken many times before, and so, during our next conversation, I asked her what she felt about the idea of our sharing Ali. I began uncomfortably, unsure of what to say, but Hajar was quick to put me at ease. She told me that she had traveled to Africa when she was younger and lived with a polygynous family. Seeing the community they had together, she knew that she wanted a marriage like theirs. Ali had told her soon after they met that he felt obligated to marry more than one woman; there were too many single women in the *ummah* for him to care for just one. Hajar agreed, and said she believed that I was the right woman to join their family. She invited me to visit them in San Diego, to see their home, meet the rest of the family, and feel what it would be like for it to be mine, too.

I bought a ticket and scheduled a two-week visit to San Diego.

Ali—nine years my senior, tall, fat, with a beautiful obsidian complexion—picked me up from the airport. Seeing each other in person for the first time ever, we both felt we were greeting someone we had known our whole life. He even claimed that for decades he had dreamed of someone who looked just like me. It sounded like a seriously lame line, but Ali was not one for lines.

I met Hajar and some of the men in the community that night. We prayed Maghrib and Isha in congregation. My room was a cozy sanctuary: olive green walls peppered with framed Qur'anic calligraphy, *hadith*, and God-focused poems Ali had written. I slept on the floor on a comfortable futon.

The next day, Hajar took me out. We sat alone together and talked. When I looked into her eyes and asked her if she was really willing to share her husband, she told me she was, and I knew she was speaking truthfully. She had married Ali after twenty-five years of being single. She liked being married, but after five years of being the sole spouse, she was ready for a sister wife.

The decision to share was solely mine. I had to decide if this was the right life for Raheem and me. It seemed so. I loved Ali and the feeling of his home; it was very much like the warmth of community I had felt when I first converted, and that I hadn't found since. I woke up every day to the *adhan* and the Southern California sun. The extended family prayed in congregation. We ate dinners together each night: salads with homemade dressing, whole-grain bread, fresh vegetables and fish, or *zabiha* chicken on the weekends.

I had been in San Diego for six days when Ali asked me again to marry him and Hajar asked me to join their family. As perfect as everything seemed, I was afraid to make the decision. I recalled that my engagement to Ishaq had seemed "perfect," too.

I no longer trusted myself to make up my mind. It wasn't just about me, either—Raheem had never met Ali. Interviews of traumatized stepchildren on *Oprah* flashed through my mind. I also had no idea if sharing a husband would actually work. Now that it was time to commit to a polygynous life, my faith in its success was greatly shaken. Additionally, I had received a scholarship to attend nursing school in Durham, and classes would begin soon. My return flight to North Carolina was in eight days; I had to resolve this before then. Hoping to clear my heart, I sought out the Knower and Source of all Outcomes to tell me what He wanted for me. I did the only thing I could do: I took out a prayer rug and made *istikharah*, a special supplication to God to clarify a difficult decision.

Istikharah literally means "to seek goodness from Allah." The answer sometimes comes in a dream by the end of the seventh day of prayer. For the first four nights after I began to do *istikharah*, I felt just as frightened and confused as I had before. On the fifth day, I read extra passages from the Qur'an, taking my time. Day six heralded nothing new. I felt lost and worried. God was not going to answer me!

That night, I carefully pronounced each word of the prayer in Arabic and in English. I woke feeling the same. This coming night would be the last. Distressed, I stayed in my room the entire day. I didn't want to pretend everything was okay when nothing was. This was a pivotal moment in my life, and I didn't know what to do. I cried for the first time in years, begging Allah to send me a sign. I tossed and turned on my bed, falling asleep two hours later.

And I dreamed.

It was a sunny, cloudless day with deep-blue skies. Ali, Raheem, and I were standing on a hilltop covered with huge white daisies. Ali wore a white prayer robe, Raheem was in a white *shalwar kamiz*, and I had on a white gown and scarf. My son and I ran playfully down the hill, laughing. Ali gave chase close behind. Just before we all reached the bottom of the hill, Ali grabbed me by the waist with his right arm, and Raheem with his left. He swung us around, holding us tightly to him.

I sat straight up. God's message was clear: Ali was, literally, the man of my dreams. The next morning I told Ali and Hajar I would absolutely love to join their family.

I returned to North Carolina to wait for my brother's return from the Gulf War, quit school, and pack. It took five more months to relocate, and Shaytan did his damnedest to get me to renege on my intentions. He murmured his fear of poverty if the family business failed. He whispered that I might regret giving up an educational grant. He mumbled that Raheem was already emotionally bruised and I was putting him at risk for more. He screamed doubt into my heart about the possibility of co-wives' ever getting along. He conspired with my vanity: Ali was not handsome like Talib, nor as wealthy as Ishaq, and was very over-weight. Above all, he tried to make me forget the signed, sealed, and delivered message God had sent me directly.

Ultimately, Shaytan failed. The dream remained as vivid in my mind as the night I'd had it. Ali, my long-distance empath, always called right on time. His voice was all I needed to reassure me that I was doing what Allah willed.

Raheem and I moved across the country to our new life. At first, I stayed in one of the two houses the *jamah* rented; Hajar stayed in another. Ali alternated spending three nights with each of us. Our village helped me raise Raheem and the other children born to the *jamah*. We prayed Fajr, Maghrib, and Isha together every day. The sisters took turns preparing dinner. We all lived off the profits we made from our carpet-cleaning business. There was more time to pursue our own interests. Hajar was able to work full-time, and I became a doula-midwife and homeschooled Raheem. As living arrangements and economics changed, we adapted by working together, relying on Allah to go forward.

We've been a family for twenty years now, living together in one house for the past fourteen. Hajar and I are like sisters, and she is Raheem's "Mama Two." I've felt at home with her and Ali since we first moved in. Muhammad, my surprise "*subhanAllah* baby*,*" was born four years later.

The interplay of free will and fate is interesting. Although God does not make mistakes, people often do. I've wondered if my former marriages were errors, or what I needed to go through to prepare me for my marriage to Ali. Allah, in His infinite mercy, answered my *dua* and delivered my soul mate, complete with a Technicolor dream to make sure I got the message, *alhamdulillah*.

We never expected everything to be perfect, and it never will be. We've learned to compromise and be patient with one another as needed, and to cherish the good times, which far outnumber the bad. That's all it takes for us to be content. For the first time in my life, I feel whole, in myself, in my family, and in my faith.

A Journey of Two Hearts

J. Samia Mair

My parents made a conscious decision to raise me as a boy. Instead of learning how to cook and clean, I mowed the grass and shoveled snow with my father. Every fall Sunday, I sat next to my father on the couch, watching the Pittsburgh Steelers play football. In sixth grade, I could beat every boy in my class in the mile run. I was the son my father never had, and it was a role I embraced.

Surprisingly, my parents had a traditional relationship themselves. My father worked to support the family, and my mother stayed at home. But I grew up in the '60s and '70s, and even my parents got caught up in the hippie and feminism movements that swept the country. I can still remember my mother's silver paper minidress that was far too revealing for her hourglass figure. By wearing it, she told the world that she was a liberated "womon."

Unlike my mother, I was expected to get a doctoral degree and support myself. Depending upon a man was out of the question.

My parents wanted me to be fiercely independent and think for myself.

For the most part, I met their expectations. I graduated with a degree in geology from Smith College, where I was surrounded by high-achieving, goal-oriented women. My father was an attorney, and I decided to follow the same path, even attending his alma mater, the University of Pennsylvania Law School. I did well there and eventually ended up working as a prosecutor in the appeals unit of the Philadelphia district attorney's office. A prosecutor's office is no place for timid men or women, and I held my own among even the most hardened attorneys.

Although I was a tomboy and raised to be independent, I always wanted to marry my Prince Charming. I dreamed about a handsome man sweeping me off my feet and carrying me away to happily ever after. As I watched my parents' long-standing, unhappy marriage deteriorate into divorce in my early twenties, I vowed not to let that happen to me. But by the time I was in my early thirties, I was divorcing my *second* husband.

I met my first husband in college while I was still dating my high school sweetheart. He was a few years older than I was and had been a corpsman in the Navy but stationed with the Marines. His many adventures around the world intrigued me. He made me laugh, and we had a lot of fun together.

But he turned out to have a drug and alcohol problem and lied incessantly. I learned that most of what he had told me about his past was fabricated, including his stories about his adventures in the service. The more the truth came out, the more I realized that I did not know my husband; I felt like I was married to a stranger. I thought that with my love and support he could turn himself around, but, like so many women who feel this way, I was wrong. Even after he went to rehab to address his addiction, he could not stop lying, and eventually I realized that I did not want to spend the rest of my life with someone whom I could not trust. We separated during my second year of law school, after only a few years of marriage.

Four or so years later, after a few relationships in between, I met my second husband. Although we did not know each other long, I felt that I had finally met my soul mate. He worked for a nonprofit organization, building homes for the poor. He seemed to be civically minded and treated me well. At the time, I was working at a stuffy, corporate law firm and was very unhappy in my work. He would often pick me up at my office on his bicycle and ride me the thirty minutes home on his handlebars. When I quit my job and moved to Brazil for six months to work on indigenous rights, we continued dating. We decided to get married when I returned.

I felt so lucky to have found him. But once again, I ignored the red flags that should have scared me away. He was not nice to his mother and had difficulties with some of his colleagues at work. As soon as we returned home from our honeymoon, he changed. He stopped helping around the house, telling me he was no longer going to cook or clean. He tried to monitor my every move and undermined everything I did. He constantly accused me of being unfaithful. When he got mad at me—which was often—he would not speak to me for weeks. When he started throwing things at me, my friends told me to leave him. He had all the signs of an abusive husband—he just hadn't hit me yet.

Later, he told me that he used the book *The Art of War* to guide our marriage. He wanted to deprive me of everything and then slowly give me back some of my "privileges." We went to counseling, and I spoke to the priest who had married us. You know that your marriage is in trouble when your priest advises you to divorce your husband. I took the advice and moved out, embarrassed and ashamed to be in my early thirties and getting divorced a second time. My priest also told me that I needed to choose a different type of man. I started thinking about my choices and realized that "bad boys" attracted me. I used to like a bit of bravado, bordering on obnoxious. Looking back now, I cannot understand the appeal, but it was there.

Nine months later, I was ready to date again. I was now working in the district attorney's office, and a colleague there suggested that I meet his friend Mike, who was a molecular biologist and, by the way, also modeled. To entice me, my friend showed me Mike's comp card, a collection of photographs on eight-by-eleven-inch card stock that modeling agencies put in display racks for potential clients. Intelligent *and* gorgeous? I was interested.

We met at a bar for our first date and played pool most of the evening. That date led to others, and I soon discovered that, in addition to being good-looking and smart, Mike was kind and funny and loved children. He also was an excellent cook, which was a huge bonus, since I hated to cook. My dinners usually consisted of cold tofu, cut right from the package, and Grape-Nuts cereal.

Not long after we started dating, I realized that Mike thought I was several years younger than I was (I was five and a half years older than him) and that I had been married only once before. I had told my colleague who set us up to tell Mike my age and my divorce status so that he would know my situation up front. But clearly, my colleague had gotten it wrong.

I agonized over what to do. I really liked Mike and did not want to scare him away with the truth. If someone wanted to set me up with a man who had been married twice before, it would give me pause. I could understand his hesitation. All of the women whom I asked for advice told me not to say anything until he got to know me better; presumably, my "winning personality" would eventually overshadow my inglorious past. The one man I asked told me I should say something immediately; otherwise, it would be dishonest, which, he noted, isn't a very good way to begin any relationship. I took his advice and carefully raised the subject with Mike.

"How old do you think I am?" I asked.

"Thirty-one or thirty-two," he replied.

"I'm actually thirty-four."

"That doesn't bother me. I once dated someone eight years older than me."

I continued, "How many times do you think I have been married?"

"Once?"

Okay, here goes, I thought to myself. "It's actually twice."

There was a slight pause before he answered, "Well, my stepfather was married twice before he married my mother, and he's a great guy."

A longer pause ensued; then he asked, "Do you have any children?"

Luckily, the answer was no. If I had had kids, I believe it would have been a deal breaker.

After we had been dating a little over a year, I moved to Baltimore to get a master's in public health from Johns Hopkins. I was disillusioned with the criminal justice system and wanted to learn how to prevent violence. Mike moved in with me about a year later, and we started to plan our life together.

Part of that planning involved discussions about our spiritual beliefs. At the time, I would say, I was spiritual but not religious. Both of my parents were raised Catholic, and I was baptized as a Catholic. Despite my father's upbringing, he was and still is a devout atheist. He taught me that God did not exist and only fools followed a religion. There was no afterlife, and the stories in the Bible were bizarre fairy tales—a crutch for the weak. My mother took my sister and me to a variety of churches off and on when we were young, but by the time I was ten, we stopped going altogether. I cannot recall God or religion ever having been mentioned in our house in a positive manner. Even as a young child being raised as an atheist, though, I always believed that there was something more.

While I was in Brazil, I lived with Christian, mainly Catholic, missionaries from all over the world, in a school to learn Portuguese. They did not seem to be fools or weak, as I was raised to believe. They were dedicating, sometimes risking, their lives to help others. They did not openly proselytize. I respected them and admired the work they did. I wanted to be more like them. When I moved back to the United States to marry my second husband, we started attending a liberal, inner-city Catholic church. I never believed, however, that Jesus, peace be upon him, was the son of God or part of a trinity.

This deep incongruity between my beliefs and the teachings of Christianity encouraged me to explore other religions. I read many books. To my surprise, I already held theological and eschatological beliefs that were similar to those of Islam. The more I read, the more Islam appealed to me. I used to say that if I ever converted to another religion, it would be Islam. However, I did not feel the need to join another organized religion.

While pursuing my public-health degree, I sat next to a man from Bangladesh in my Biostats class. We often spoke about our spiritual beliefs. When I told him what I believed and what I thought of Islam, he responded, "You are Muslim." Eventually, he gave me a translation of the Qur'an to read.

It sat on my desk for months before I decided to look at it. After reading the opening chapter, Surah al-Fatiha, I knew that I was Muslim. I had read verses of the Qur'an in other books, while exploring different religions, but I had never read this particular chapter. The reason it had such a powerful impact on me was that it contained the prayer for guidance that I was always trying to write but could never quite express properly. In just seven short verses, this *surah* addressed all of my spiritual aspirations. I told Mike that when I finished reading the translation, I was going to convert. He replied, "I always thought you would someday."

But there was a problem: Mike and I were about to become engaged, and I vaguely remembered reading that a Muslim woman could not marry a non-Muslim man. Mike had no intention of converting. He was a lapsed Catholic to whom Catholic school had not been kind. We held similar spiritual beliefs, but whereas I felt organized religion was unnecessary, it scared him. I did not want to face the possibility of having to choose between love and religion. I had found my Prince Charming and was far happier than I had ever imagined I could be. And I had finally found the spiritual home that had eluded me my entire life. That these elements of my life could be at odds was devastating.

Before I finished the translation, I decided to speak to an imam about my concerns. I searched through the telephone book and made an appointment with an imam at the largest *masjid* in the city. The meeting was scheduled for Thursday, January 11, 2001. I will never forget that date.

I walked slowly up the steps to the townhouse next to the *masjid* where the imam lived. My hand shook as I knocked on the door; I was dreading the potential answers to my questions. *What will I do if he tells me I cannot marry Mike?* I asked myself. *Is this going to be God's first test of my sincerity? Will I fail?*

The imam answered the door wearing a long white robe. He had a beard, and his head was covered with a small white hat. He looked like some of the Muslim men I had seen on the news— not a particularly comforting sight for me at the time. I extended my hand to shake his, but he quickly informed me that Muslims do not shake hands with members of the opposite sex. I thought that was odd, as the gesture seemed harmless to me.

He asked me to come in and led me to his office. He motioned for me to sit down in the empty chair across from his desk. Another man occupied a chair next to mine, which made me uncomfortable. It was difficult enough to speak to the imam about my concerns, but at least I equated him with a priest, so I felt somewhat at ease divulging personal information. But I did not know this other man and did not want him there. Later, I learned that a Muslim man and woman who could potentially marry should not be alone together.

After the initial pleasantries, I told the imam that I wanted to convert and shared the reasons that had led me to that decision. But first, I had two questions. He told me to go ahead. I hesitated, embarrassed by the first question. Although I had been raised to believe that my current living situation was perfectly acceptable and actually preferable before committing to marriage, I knew that the major religions held otherwise.

I was blunt: "My fiancé and I are living in sin. I tried to find a loophole in the Qur'an, but there is none. Should I wait until we get married to convert?"

"You are living in sin no matter what religion you are in," the imam told me. "If you should die before you are married, it is better that you die a Muslim. So your living arrangement should not prevent you from converting."

I continued, far more worried about his next response. "My second question is that if my fiancé is not Muslim, can I still marry him?" My heart pounded as I braced myself for the answer.

"Does your fiancé believe in one god?" the imam asked me.

"Yes," I replied.

"Does he believe that the Prophet Muhammad, blessings and peace be upon him, is the last Messenger of God?"

"Yes."

"Then, even though he has not taken the *shahada*, we consider him a Muslim and you can marry him."

A huge wave of relief rushed over me, as it sunk in that I did not have to choose between my fiancé and my religion. Suddenly it occurred to me that nothing was holding me back from converting.

"Can I convert now?" I asked.

"Yes," the imam replied.

After some more discussion about Islam, we started to speak about the major beliefs of Islam, my experience with Christianity, and what to expect from my conversion. He told me that converting was a simple process, and that I needed only to make two professions of faith. I then repeated after him in Arabic and then in English, "I testify that there is no god but God, and I testify that Muhammad is the Messenger of God."

After years of searching for guidance and praying on what to do, I found taking the *shahada* to be both momentous and anticlimactic. It was enormously transforming, but over too quickly. I experienced a similar feeling of elation and disappointment later, when I first entered a *masjid* to pray. I was accustomed to large, colorful, stained-glass windows, life-size statues of Jesus on the cross, peace be upon him, and ornately carved, dark-wood pews. The plain walls and the large, empty prayer room in the *masjid* were amazingly peaceful, but seemed to be lacking something as well.

It did not take me long to appreciate, however, that stillness and simplicity offered me the best atmosphere for prayer. I also came to realize that a few words spoken from the heart and for the heart are far more meaningful than any public display and celebration could ever be.

After I took the *shahada*, the imam told me to take a shower when I got home, to purify myself as a new Muslim, and that all of my previous sins had been forgiven. He gave me several pamphlets about Islam, and I bought a long, thick, black hijab to wear during prayers.

Driving home, I realized how grateful I was to be a Muslim. I felt that I had wasted my life until that moment. I could not wait to tell Mike what had happened. I thought about how best to tell him. After all, neither he nor I had thought I was going to convert that day—I was on a fact-finding mission, nothing else. I decided not to call him but to surprise him when he returned home. I would be waiting to greet him, wearing my long black hijab.

After several hours of waiting impatiently, I heard him unlock the door. I stood in the hallway, smiling. As soon as he walked inside, I blurted out, "What do you think of your Muslim fiancée?" He answered with silence, not the reaction I had been expecting.

In fact, his blank expression made my smile disappear. I began to explain clumsily how I had ended up converting. Still, he did not appear pleased. I asked him directly if he was upset. After an uncomfortably long pause, he responded, "No . . . no. I just wasn't expecting this today. The scarf sort of startled me, too."

In retrospect, I should have never sprung such news on him as he walked through the door after a long day at work, while wearing that exceedingly unattractive hijab. The news of my conversion would have been enough of a wallop.

After his initial shock, we discussed my conversion and laughed about his first reaction. But then he said something that made me cry: He told me that we should not be intimate until we were married. He said that he knew that I took my conversion seriously and he did not want me to begin my new life in sin. I had not even considered that as a possibility.

A few months later, we married. He supported me in every decision related to my faith, even agreeing to raise our children Muslim. He always told me, "I don't want to stand between you and the Big Guy." When I decided to wear a head scarf in public and not just for prayers, he supported that decision as well. I was scared that he would find me unattractive, but he told me that I was beautiful. I also was afraid that he would not want to be seen with a wife who was so visibly Muslim—there's nothing inconspicuous about wearing a head scarf in the post-9/11 United States. While I was willing to accept the inevitable flack, it seemed a lot to ask of my non-Muslim husband, but he told me that we had nothing to hide.

We lived in blissful peace for about six years. Then one day, while I was at a Muslim toddler playgroup with our daughters, it somehow came up in conversation with a sister that my husband was not Muslim. I was not prepared for the discussion that followed.

"Really?" the sister asked. "So, you converted after you were married?"

"No, I converted a few months before."

The sister hesitated, clearly not sure if she should continue.

"Do you know that your marriage isn't valid? Muslim women cannot marry non-Muslim men. You are committing *zina*! "

Zina?! How could that be? I asked myself. "But I specifically received permission from an imam that I could marry my husband," I told her. *Surely, he would not have said it was okay if it were not true.*

"I don't know what that imam told you, but you need to talk to your husband about converting. Your marriage isn't lawful."

I left the toddler group in an awful condition. *Zina* is a major sin. I could not ignore what I had just heard. The imam with whom I had converted had moved away long before, so I could not speak with him. I asked my new imam if what the sister had told me was true. He had known that my husband was not Muslim, but erroneously believed that I had converted after we were married and apparently was giving my husband time to convert before speaking with me about my situation. In fact, most of the other Muslims whom I knew thought that was the case. When the imam learned that I had converted before we got married, he confirmed what the sister had said: I should not have married a non-Muslim. My marriage was invalid.

The news was tremendously upsetting. My husband was more supportive of my faith than many Muslim men. He gladly watched our children while I attended lectures on Islam; we celebrated Islamic holidays (he even fasted) and gave up the Christian holidays; he helped to raise our daughters as good Muslims. We had such a wonderful relationship that it was difficult for me to accept that it could be wrong. I wondered what was expected of me now. Some scholars say that a Muslim woman must divorce her non-Muslim husband immediately. It was devastating to even think that was a possibility.

I knew I had to tell my husband what I had learned right away. I did not know how he would react. He had been reading about Islam and attending lectures, but as far as I knew, he was not ready to convert. In fact, I had purposely stopped asking him about it because I thought I was pushing too hard. But when I told him what I had learned about our marriage, his quick response was completely unexpected: "It's time for me to convert."

I had expected him to convert someday, but I had thought it would take longer. Shortly after we were married, I had a dream that my husband was hanging on to the edge of a very high, steep cliff. I fell off the clifftop, and as I passed him, I yanked him off. As we were falling to the ground, he yelled at me, "I was safe where I was. Why did you pull me off? We are both going to die." I told him that if we just prayed to God, we would land safely. He continued yelling as we fell closer and closer to the ground. At the last moment, he prayed to God with me and we both landed safely together. My interpretation of the dream was that he was going to convert eventually, but that it might take a while.

If I had paid more attention to his spiritual progress, though,

I might not have been so surprised that he was ready. Although he had been reading about Islam and attending lectures, the big shift had come when he started reading books and listening to CDs by an American Muslim scholar who was born in the United States and raised Christian. My husband could identify with this scholar, who spoke in familiar terms and references. He became able to separate the religion from its associated cultural and political baggage. He could see organized religion's utility in modern life. In an articulate, logical fashion, this scholar answered many of the questions that had prevented Mike from converting. He believed in One God and that Muhammad, peace be upon him, was a Messenger of God and the Seal of the Prophets. Mike's reasons not to convert had slowly dropped away.

A year or so after he converted, we were attending a weekend-long Islamic seminar in another state. As my husband shaved and I pinned my hijab, I smiled. We had met as non-Muslims in a bar. At the time, we would never have guessed that in the not-so-distant future we would be gladly spending our precious weekends together, learning our *deen*. I am so grateful to Allah, Glorious and Exalted is He, for bringing Islam to me and allowing me to share the journey with someone I love.

Alhamdulillah.

From *Shalom* to *Salaam*

S. E. Jihad Levine

> "So be patient. Verily, the Promise of Allah is true, and ask forgiveness for your fault, and glorify the praises of your Lord . . . "
>
> —QUR'AN, 40:55

After nearly six years of marriage, my husband, Habeeb, divorced me, by Al-Talaq and in the U.S. courts. Nothing that I said or did at the time could convince him to try to make it work. I even requested a meeting with our imam for mediation, but Habeeb told him firmly that he didn't want to be married to me anymore. He said he could no longer cope with the arguments and stress. I was devastated. I had finally become Muslim the year before and was still wobbling on new-*shahada* legs, an infant looking at the world with fresh eyes.

When we married, I was a practicing Jew. Born to a Catholic mother and a Jewish father, my brother and I were raised as Reform Jews until my parents divorced when I was twelve years old. After the divorce, my mom converted us to Catholicism. I remember the whirlwind confusion of receiving baptism, confession, Holy Communion, and confirmation all within a two-year time frame. When I was old enough to choose for myself, I returned to Judaism, but Christianity left its mark by giving me a love and recognition for Jesus, peace on him.

My family didn't react well to my marriage. Even though I remained Jewish initially, my father refused to recognize my husband as his son-in-law. It was hard for me to decipher his real objection: my husband's religion, or—though my dad never came out and said it—my husband's race. My father, of blessed memory, in addition to being a Zionist, was bigoted.

"But, Sharon, those people hate us!" he cried. My efforts to explain the difference between the peaceful religion of Islam and the political struggle between the Palestinians and Israelis fell on deaf ears. Never mind that my father himself was the first in the family to marry outside of Judaism, and that my mother remained Christian throughout their marriage.

Later, when I embraced Islam, my father nearly disowned me. He still accepted an occasional phone call, but his replies were cold, distant, and brief. Because he loved me so much, I don't think he could have brought himself to cut me off completely, but he made it very clear how angry and disappointed he was with me. Our relationship never recovered from what he perceived as parental disobedience and family dishonor. He died in August 2001, and, at my stepmother's request, I was not told of his passing until after the funeral. Did they fear that I would show up at the synagogue dressed in a burqa and accompanied by my black husband?

In the beginning, our marriage was good. Habeeb and I met while we were both working in a treatment center for substance abuse. We had a professional relationship, but we also hit it off personally from the start. In addition to a physical attraction, we shared an interest in books, languages, and travel. We had close friends in common, and he had a great sense of humor. Everyone liked and respected Habeeb. We often found little excuses to talk with each other at work, and soon our relationship transcended the workplace. A few months later, after I returned from a vacation to Puerto Rico, he proposed to me. It didn't matter to me that we had different religions.

After we married and I read Habeeb's books about Islam, everything fell into place for me. I no longer had to be conflicted about Judaism versus Christianity, or Moses and Jesus, because Islam united the most important tenets of both faiths. I was attracted to the Islamic idea of One God and the recognition of all His prophets. I also learned about the Prophet Muhammad.

With this truth in my heart, I said the *shahada* and became a Muslim. I asked friends to stop calling me by my Jewish name, Sharon. I asked to be called instead by my chosen name, Safiyyah, after one of the Jewish wives of the Prophet Muhammad.

I didn't convert to Islam for my husband, nor did I do it in an attempt to save my marriage. I did it for Allah, and for me. My husband never insisted I convert, but, rather, served as a role model. I watched him pray five times a day. I shared his joy in breaking his fast during Ramadan by cooking him nice evening meals. I listened as he recited Qur'an. I was intrigued and drawn to the spiritual peace he had, and wanted that for myself.

Given my estrangement from my family, my divorce was a major spiritual and emotional crisis. There were few Muslims in the small Northeastern town we lived in. My husband was the only Muslim I knew well, and he was my entire support system.

Habeeb had threatened to divorce me once a few months before, but had changed his mind and taken me back before the three-month *iddat* period (after which the divorce would be final) was complete. He'd said it out of frustration and anger. But this time, it was I who was frustrated and angry, and made insecure by his threats to divorce me. I decided to move out of the home we shared and into my own apartment to wait out the *iddat* period. I knew I wasn't supposed to leave our home. According to the religion of Islam, spouses are supposed to live together during the *iddat* period in case there is an opportunity for marital reconciliation to occur. But my faith was new, and I felt weak. I was sick of the arguments and Habeeb's threats of divorce. I couldn't think straight and felt the need to escape. I left.

My new apartment was located a few hours from Philadelphia, and the area was home to a large and diverse Muslim community. I met some sisters with whom I grew close. They were from Pakistan, India, Africa, the Middle East, and Malaysia. I also met American-born Muslims: African American, Caucasian, and Hispanic sisters. They gave me the support and encouragement to cope with my imminent divorce and introduced me to the blessing of sisterhood.

"Don't become disillusioned and lose your *deen*," Sister Myra warned me.

"Keep yourself right, and don't come out of your clothes," Sister Zakiyyah cautioned. Sadly, we all knew convert sisters who had left Islam and taken off their hijabs after divorcing Muslim men.

My sisters counseled me to turn to Allah with my grief, and reminded me that He doesn't give us more than we can handle. They assured me of Allah's promise in the Qur'an that *with every hardship is relief*.

Even though I was happy in my new apartment in the city and grateful for my friendships with Muslim women, I missed my Habeeb terribly. We spoke on the phone a few times, and he occasionally came to my apartment to drop off important mail or things I needed that I had left at our home. We tried to talk during those visits, but our relationship was still very strained and we ended up fighting each time. We didn't see each other at all after that.

From time to time, I returned to the small town where Habeeb lived to run errands and tie up loose ends. One day, I stopped in at our favorite department store. I tormented myself while there, fearing that I would run into him, imagining at the turn of each aisle that I would see him there with a new wife. I nearly had a panic attack, and vowed never to return.

"You're being tested," Sister Mahra explained when she heard the story. "Although you don't like it or know the reason behind it now, be patient. Allah knows best."

I was brokenhearted. I reflected on the early years of our marriage, when we were still happy. I missed my friend and lover and was amazed that our marriage had come to this. I wanted him back. But, sadly, I realized that it might be impossible to work things out.

I tried to be patient during my *iddat*. I prayed for Allah to soften my husband's heart and bring him back to me. I soaked my prayer rug with tears, awakening at night to supplicate Him. I constantly prayed the *istikharah* in search of guidance. I had been sure laying down an ultimatum by moving away would bring Habeeb running back to me, but that manipulation failed. The stress nearly led me to a nervous breakdown, and the sisters were extremely worried about me. Though I prayed not to despair, not to give up, solace escaped me, and occasionally I felt suicidal. Had it not been for my fear of Allah and Judgment Day, I would have ended it all, *astaghfirullah*.

The holy month of fasting, Ramadan, began, and I endured. Each night I went to the *masjid* for *iftar*, the evening meal, and busied myself with serving others and cleaning up afterward. While everyone was happily eating and chatting with friends, I dwelled in the background, picking up dishes and utensils, loading the dishwasher, wiping up, and putting food away.

From the shadows, I eyed my Muslim sisters with envy. Smiling, beautifully dressed and bejeweled women, they were surrounded by their friends, families, and children, with seemingly not a care in the world. They were secure in their beautiful houses with protective husbands who cared for them in the way that Allah commanded. I had no one. I was alone.

Stung by my own diseased thoughts, I felt ashamed. I slipped into the *musallah* and prayed for Allah to remove the bitterness and resentment from my heart. I reminded myself that my situation was a test from Him.

Ya Allah! So many tests! Alienation from my family, marital problems, moving alone to a new city and a small apartment, working two jobs just to survive, health problems, and, now, the threat of divorce.

At the end of my *iddat*, Habeeb didn't take me back. He moved forward with finalizing the divorce legally, and I found myself unmarried and alone.

Although I felt it was premature and still loved Habeeb, the sisters said I needed to be married, and set out to find me a new husband.

"What are you looking for in a husband?" one of them asked.

"Well, it's pretty simple," I responded. "A brother around my age, in his fifties or early sixties at the most. Perhaps a widower. A practicing Sunni Muslim. Since I'm close to retirement, I want to finish out my career."

By then, I was working in a state prison as a substance abuse counselor in a specialized treatment program for Spanish-speaking inmates. I enjoyed combining my clinical skills with my ability to speak Spanish, and had only a few years to go before I retired.

"Anything else?" the sister asked, drawing the pen out of her mouth, poised to write in her notebook again.

"Well, a brother who values family and a calm Muslim life, someone quiet and dignified, a gentle soul. Race and ethnicity aren't important."

"Someone who wants to sit in an easy chair in front of the fireplace with you?" she laughed.

"Yes! A brother willing to be my partner, my friend, and a fellow seeker in Islam."

"Okay, I think I got it!" she said, with an excited smile.

• • •

My closest Muslim sister introduced me to the first candidate. He was a divorced Palestinian gentleman in his mid-sixties, living with his two adult daughters and their families. It was clear from the start that they were not for me. When I arrived at their home, I noticed Easter decorations in the window and a huge bunny on the porch. Neither of his daughters wore the hijab, and when it came time for the afternoon *salat*, the gentleman told me that he'd "do it later."

At my encouragement, we did pray, but no one else in the family joined us. His grandchildren ran around the room, screaming and laughing the whole time we were praying. The oldest grandson, who was about seven, kept pointing at us and squealing, "Look at their butts!" as we went through the motions of the prayer.

The second candidate was a married Egyptian man from New York City. He had a wife "back home" and insisted she didn't want to move to America. He claimed that she understood "his needs" and was amenable to his taking a second wife.

"When will I be able to speak with your wife, brother?" I inquired when we spoke over the telephone. I was clever enough to know that I would be marrying a family, not just a husband, if I agreed to be a co-wife. It was important to build a relationship with her from the start.

"Well, uh . . . that will be difficult," he stammered. "She works most of the time, and it may be hard to coordinate, due to the time difference between Egypt and America."

Likewise, it wasn't convenient for me to move to New York with him after I retired. After all, he had just started a new business and had many expenses. Which came to his next question: Would I be willing to remain in my city and continue working in order to support myself?

"Just until my business gets off the ground?" he pleaded.

Now the red flags were waving like crazy. "Would this be an appropriate arrangement for your daughter?" I exclaimed.

"No," he mumbled.

"Then what makes you think it would be good for me?" I replied. Without giving him an opportunity to respond, I slammed the phone back in its cradle.

There was another Palestinian gentleman, an extremely wealthy widower with a large family. "Would you be willing to sign a prenuptial agreement?" he wanted to know.

"Well, yes, if I get a significant dowry up front." I replied.

I never heard from him again. He was expecting a free wife who wouldn't take a piece of his family's pie.

Then there was the Yemeni brother who informed me that he would have to divorce me if his wife couldn't "get used to" having a co-wife. Not that he'd told her he was searching for a second wife, of course.

And, finally, the Sudanese brother who wanted to know, "What is your bra size, sister?"

Worst of all were the Muslim women, not in my close circle of friends, who lived in my own community. The young wives of husbands expressing a desire for a second wife thought they could control the situation by searching for her themselves. They were hoping that their husbands would accept an older woman, a mature Muslimah, who they perceived wouldn't be a sexual threat or compete for their husband's affection.

Other Muslim women pushed me toward polygyny, citing my age as a factor. "After all, sister, men want to have a lot of children," they rationalized, "and it *is* the Sunna," they added when I came up with any objections.

A woman whose family was facing immigration issues after they had overstayed their visitors' visas also approached me.

"Would you be willing to marry my husband? Please," she begged, "just to help us out?"

I wasn't brought up in a culture where polygyny was accepted, but I wasn't necessarily against it. Plural marriage was common in our community. Although having my own husband was my first preference, I was able to see some benefits in plural marriage. I was willing to "share" a husband with another Muslim sister and not have to deal with a full-time husband under my feet. But it had to be the right situation, one that would work both for me and for a potential co-wife. The search for love and security was paramount in my life. I wanted a husband who would love me and treat me as equal to his other wife. I didn't want to be used, to marry simply for someone else's convenience, and had a difficult time understanding how some Muslim women could suggest such a thing to me.

Other sisters—all married—encouraged me not to worry, assuring me that Allah would give me a husband . . . in the Next Life.

"Why do you want to marry at your age, anyhow?" a sister marveled. "Men are such a bother."

My emotional vulnerability and desire for companionship resulted in two brief marriages, in which both men deceived my *wali* and me. Even though I was a mature Muslimah and didn't necessarily need a *wali* to arrange the details of marriage, I wanted one. I wanted someone to look out for me and for my interests, because my trust in men was tenuous. The first brother told my *wali* and me that he was a businessman. This was true, but he failed to mention not only that his business was not profitable, but also that he was receiving partial government assistance *and* engaging in dishonest financial practices.

My second brother told my *wali* and me that his former wife had left their home and abandoned him with their small children.

"Sister, that's not true," his first wife confided a few months later when I ran into her. "He threw me out of the house in the middle of the night during an argument so he could marry you."

She also revealed that she was pregnant. When I confronted him furiously, he admitted it.

Neither marriage lasted more than six months. My friends lamented that I had been deceived so terribly. But was I really deceived? Or did I agree to these marriages with "eyes wide shut" because I desired companionship and love so desperately? I berated myself for not having checked out these brothers more thoroughly.

I then decided to select a man and do the proposing myself. Why not? It's acceptable in Islam. I chose a very pious brother, the butcher at our local halal store. Every time I went to the store, he was reading the Qur'an. He seemed a gentle soul and had a wonderful reputation. I inquired about him and was told he was not married.

But when I sent someone to him, he said he had two wives and eight children in Niger. He was honest enough to tell me that he didn't feel he could do justice to both me and his family back home.

Next, I tried Muslim marriage websites; they were anonymous, so I could screen the candidates without public humiliation. It quickly became clear, however, that my online profile was a magnet for green-card seekers. I was especially amused by the eighteen- and nineteen-year-old boys who were willing to marry an American convert in her fifties. They gave me what I call the "Khadijah line": "But, sister, the Prophet, peace be upon him, was fifteen years younger than Mother Khadijah when they got married!"

Had I became desperate to have a husband, afraid as I was of being alone?

It was so painful. A family member—on my father's side, Jewish—asked me if I was ready to trade in *salaam* for *shalom*. I was almost ready to give up on marriage, but not on Islam. I knew that the religion was not at fault.

Despairing of a successful marriage, I reflected on my first one. I became painfully aware of my own role in our marital discord. Because I was insecure, I'd been bossy, demanding, and controlling. The more I'd tried to control Habeeb, the more he had moved away from me. He was working a full-time job and studying for a graduate degree at night. Although he loved me, he couldn't handle the stress. Habeeb wanted a peaceful home and a calm and supportive wife. Had that been too much to ask?

I remembered something from the book of Proverbs that my Jewish grandmother once told me: "The wise woman builds her house, but the foolish one tears it down with her own hands."

Oh, Allah! What have I done? How I wished that I had another chance with Habeeb! I loved him so much. I had never stopped loving him.

Feeling very low and depressed, I was starting to feel as if I should just stop searching for happiness.

"Why won't Allah send me a decent husband?" I wailed to my *wali*, Imam Shaheed.

With brutal honesty, he replied, "If Allah wants you to have a husband, He'll send you one!"

I was frustrated by his answer, but recognized the truth in what he said.

When you ask, ask of Allah; and when you seek help, seek help of Allah. Know that if people were to gather to benefit you with anything, they would only benefit you with something that Allah had already prescribed for you; and if they were to gather to harm you with anything, they would only harm you with something that Allah had already prescribed for you.

—Al-Tirmithi

I made a commitment to have patience with whatever Allah had decreed for me, and I asked Him for forgiveness for not trusting Him.

I continued to attend Arabic classes and *halaqas*. I read and learned as much as possible. I worked on my insecurity and self-esteem issues. I got closer to Allah. I knew I had to rely on His power to change people and their destinies at His pleasure.

I developed an inner peace with the fact that He hears the *dua* of each and every one of His beloved creations, but answers them in His own time. I accepted and submitted to this truth and His wisdom. I finally realized that I had all I needed within myself, and in the life I'd been given.

Almost three years after those heartfelt *duas*—and two failed marriages—I finally found peace and resigned myself to the prospect of being alone. I kept in touch with Habeeb, feeling less hurt as time went by. When I was promoted at work, I emailed Habeeb to tell him. Sometimes he called me, and eventually our conversations grew more frequent.

One day, Habeeb said that he had been keeping tabs on me and knew I was unmarried. He said that he still loved me and regretted the way things had turned out between us.

"I'd really like for us to have another chance," I told him.

"I'll give Imam Shaheed a call for some *naseeha*, and, of course, we should both pray *istikharah*," he replied cautiously.

After I hung up, I went directly to my prayer rug, made two *rakat*, and prayed *istikharah*. Then I called my best sisters, shrieked out the news, and asked them to include Habeeb and me in their *duas*.

A few days later, Imam Shaheed telephoned me.

"Safiyyah! Brother Habeeb called me and said he's coming to the *masjid* tonight between Maghrib and Isha to talk with me about remarrying you," he exclaimed.

I don't know who was more excited, Imam Shaheed or me.

My imam truly loved my husband like a son, and our divorce had pained him deeply.

That very day, Habeeb and I talked for hours about our love and our mistakes, and vowed to make it work this time with Allah's help.

My prayer had finally been answered, by Allah! My search for true love was finally over.

You've Got Ayat:

Finding Love Online

Cyberlove

Lena Hassan

My aunt used to say that a woman marries the man of her destiny. She would say it with a sigh, after an hour of trying to talk my sister or me into saying yes to a particular suitor. That we were not from the Damascus of our parents, but American born, did not change the rules. You did not find marriage on some quest for romance, according to my aunt. Rather, marriage found you.

At the time, I was in the beginning of my junior year at a large West Coast university. My main concern was not men, but the two years it would take me to complete my computer science degree. There were men in my life—my department was four-fifths male—but, as most were non-Muslims, I never considered them an option.

The prospects were hardly more promising at our mosque, situated only a few blocks from campus. Portable partitions, improvised out of bedsheets stretched over frames of PVC piping, separated the sexes. If I looked through the gap in between them, I could see the men. Arab men, just like my dad, but younger.

My family had recently begun attending the Friday night study circle at the mosque. At first, I would put my ear against the sheet and listen to them talk about exciting, serious stuff, like the first Gulf War, the Oklahoma City bombings, and the arrest of Omar Abdel-Rahman, the "blind sheikh." These crises always seemed to be someone else's fault, our own community always innocent and helpless.

After I'd been eavesdropping for a few months, nothing had changed. So I rejoined the women huddled together, trading recipes and childcare tips. Elderly Umm Hamza would tell jokes and, to our shock, occasionally light up a cigarette. Fatima, a friendly Moroccan, teased me that she wanted to be invited to a wedding. Newly opened, the mosque hadn't yet attracted many undergraduates, and I was one of the few single women who attended.

Over time, our mosque ceased being an exclusively Arab enclave, and more and more American-born Muslims discovered it as a convenient place to pray between classes, hold study circles, or even take a nap. These young men and women were less eager to use partitions to divide the community. Interacting with the young brothers wasn't quite so awkward as it was with the immigrant men. Still, I never went out of my way to talk to them. I did run into them in class, show up silently for the mixed-gender study circle we held at the mosque, and return the *salaam*s they offered me. Then I'd come home and make flippant remarks to my mother about marrying a convert or a Pakistani American.

But none of them was a real possibility. Maybe these men were too close to me in age, more like kid brothers than romance prospects. Or maybe I took my mother's consternation more seriously than I cared to admit. I knew the type of man my parents expected me to marry: the Arab kind, silhouetted mysteriously against the thin partition of those early years at our mosque.

• • •

In 1994, few people outside the computer industry and academia had heard of the Internet. It was before Web pages prevailed, when you memorized arcane key combinations to navigate your cursor in a world of white text on black. But what really excited me was the people you could meet behind the computer screen. It was another sort of partition, yet one that made communication possible with people thousands of miles beyond my sheltered suburban life.

The Internet was magic to someone like me, shy and burdened, with crippling self-consciousness. All through grade school, I'd suffered the bald and ignorant curiosity, and sometimes outright hostility, that being the only practicing Muslim in my grade generated. Lacking confidence to face the constant judgments, I'd chosen to hide. But I didn't have to hide on the Internet. Online, I forgot that I had a thing so unruly and potentially embarrassing as a tongue or a body. There, I could weigh each word a dozen times before sending it off to its recipient.

Paradoxically, in this world divided by barriers and buffers, I opened myself to people and they opened themselves to me. To my family's eyes, I was hard at work in front of my computer, writing code for my school assignments. In reality, I was crossing swords with Asian men while playing the role of magician in a Multi-User Dungeon. I discovered many interesting people on a pen pal forum: a philosophical Catholic, a suicidal Persian, a Greek trapped in a marriage as arranged as any from the East. They were almost all men; back then, women were newcomers to the Internet. We delved into life philosophies and compared cultures.

In real life, I'd often feared that people judged me as a hijab-wearing Muslim woman before giving me a chance to speak. Online, I presented myself at my own pace, on my own terms. The Internet freed my new friends and me from being intimidated by each other.

Occasionally, late at night as I drifted off to sleep, I imagined that someone out there, still unknown to me in the vast Internet, might capture my heart as well as my mind. But it was never a conscious hope. If I had a goal in my newfound social playground, it wasn't romance, but rather the joy of connecting with other minds.

The previous year, we had visited a downtown mosque and made the acquaintance of a lady from the Syrian city of Aleppo. Her eyes grew round when she saw me, a tall, young, Syrian American girl, and she drew my mother aside to talk. I was hardly aware that an appointment was being set up; apparently, receiving suitors was a matter of course for a young woman my age, and I was notified without being expected to approve.

So the very next day, the Aleppan woman dragged her nephew over to our house for a courtship visit. He was a member of the conservative Tablighi movement and sported a full beard. The aunt requested that the women meet in a separate room. Once we were there, she pulled down my scarf, removed my glasses, and peered into my eyes. Apparently satisfied, she stood up promptly and led us back to where the men were sitting. There, she whispered loudly to her nephew, "Look at her! Did you see her?" He ignored her, whether out of mortification or zealous modesty, I didn't know.

His family proposed the next day.

"Do we decide on marriage after only one visit?" I asked my mother.

"Well, sometimes two," she said, as if admitting an uncomfortable secret.

But my parents and I unanimously agreed to give the Aleppan family a no.

I was too young then to understand that what I had just experienced was closer to a cattle market than to courtship. If my parents recognized the horror of it, they understood it as a clumsily executed variant of a perfectly acceptable ritual—family-facilitated courtship à la Syria. They had married each other in the same way, and, when they discussed marriage at all, presented the ritual to us children as the only way that we might meet our future spouses.

My mother acknowledged that it was a terrifying leap of faith. Years later, my aunt was more blunt. "Marriage is like buying a watermelon," she said. "You don't know what you get until you open it."

I refused to gamble the rest of my life on someone I barely knew. But I had no desire to challenge my parents, either. My solution was to put all thoughts of marriage out of my mind.

The next summer, I began to haunt the Usenet forum soc.culture.arabic, with a sudden interest in all things Arab. College allowed you room to be different, and I was discovering and stretching my cultural muscles. My mother was in Syria until September. From the computer at my summer job, I posted a notice looking for pen pals to practice my written Arabic with. "I am not looking for marriage," I said. Inevitably, most of my respondents misunderstood. One man sent photographs of himself. Another complained of how his correspondence with another woman "hadn't worked out." I threw all their letters away.

One pen pal remained, a man named Adnan. He was a doctoral student in information systems and an authentic *Shami* from the heart of Damascus, though now living on the East Coast. More important, he showed interest solely in correspondence, not in what it might get him.

I took out paper, pen, and a dictionary, and struggled to find the right rhythm for my Arabic words. "Brother Adnan," I addressed him. In two painstaking letters I described myself, my family, and the cast of regulars at our mosque. Spurred by his encouraging responses, I wanted to say more, but my Arabic was too clunky for my impassioned opinions, my urgent questions. So we dove into English—gloriously refreshing!—and continued to correspond through email and an early Unix-based chat program.

Not counting relatives, I had never really talked to an Arab man before. At the mosque, they'd made it easy by turning their backs after one look, in a gruff sort of bashfulness. I wanted to know what they were really like. Did they all think the same? Were they like the men in my family?

One morning while dropping me off at work, my father had made a comment about my plastic lunch bag, whose handle was torn. No respectable woman would carry such a thing, he said. I griped to Adnan that I could walk down my college's main drag wearing rainbow colors and nobody would blink an eye. Why couldn't people look at my spirit, instead of my outward appearance? He gently explained to me how my father's standards made sense in the close-knit world of Damascene society, but Adnan refused to hold me to those principles. He agreed: What sense would they make to an American woman?

Adnan was also looking for self-revelation, to see his innermost thoughts spelled out on the computer screen. Against the advice of his parents and his friends, he had completed a degree in philosophy. He was out to make sense of the world, not just to land a well-paying job, so he respected softer forms of reasoning. "Women are lucky," he said. "They never learn that it's wrong to cry." In between our discussions on culture, we traded recipes for *dawood basha* and hummus.

If anyone had called my relationship with Adnan a "romance," I would have protested angrily. I was not sending him love letters. I did not tell him that I saw him in my dreams, or that I couldn't live without him. I was cautious and pragmatic, and considered myself above throwing myself at any man.

But what was growing between us *was* love, if a particularly cerebral sort of love. A love that found joy in sharing our truest thoughts with each other, one that brought us to ecstasy when we discovered an opinion we held in common. Physical proximity was unnecessary; institutions like marriage, country, and family belonged to another realm. Our souls were electron clouds, dancing together in the unbound ether.

On some level, I must have known we'd have to hit the ground sooner or later, that if our relationship did not fizzle out, it would have to enter our real-world lives. We'd have to consider the M-word at last. But for now, I refused to think about it.

So I passed the summer in front of my computer screen, debugging astronomical data analysis software in one window while in another, Adnan and I kept up a constant flow of conversation.

From: Lena H. <lena@westcoastcollege.edu>

To: adnan@eastcoastcollege.edu (Adnan T.)

Subject: Re: you're quiet today . . .

Date: Tue, 19 Jul 1994 11:28:50-0700 (PDT)

> I am not hearing much from you . . .hope you are being productive!

I suppose so. I dunno, maybe. I'm also thinking . . .oh, how different I feel here, why don't I just go and be a shepherdess and compose poetry to the wind. I wasn't made for companies, ambition, excitement. But I'm too romantic to allow myself to not have a dream at all, it just has to be a quiet one. No fame or ambition for me. If I can't be a shepherdess—well, I can sit in front of my computer in my little corner each day, quiet and unassuming and working steadily, and at NIGHT I will fuse my intense, hazy thoughts into words on paper (or into my computer). I think so far, I've only got the daytime part, and even that's not down perfect.

Are you taking me seriously? :) You should.

Lena

From: Adnan T. <adnan@eastcoastcollege.edu>
To: lena@westcoastcollege.edu
Subject: Re: you're quiet today . . .
Date: Tue, 19 Jul 94 15:22:18-0400

YES, I AM! And very much so!

But if my perception of you is correct (and I surely could be wrong—we haven't even seen each other), I don't think you'd be completely content to be (only) a shepherdess and compose poetry to the wind. I think a person as idealistic and conscientious as you are will not feel satisfied unless they feel they have made some, just some, difference, in their usual quiet, unassuming style, of course, to the "real" world. Lena, there is *so much* that needs to be done; we can't afford to let the wind have all your poetry; we need our share too!

Your brother,
Adnan

From: Lena H. <lena@westcoastcollege.edu>
To: adnan@eastcoastcollege.edu (Adnan T.)
Subject: Re: you're quiet today . . .
Date: Tue, 19 Jul 1994 13:13:35-0700 (PDT)

OK, let me think about that. *sigh* Life's too hard. So, what do I do?

Lena

From: Adnan T. <adnan@eastcoastcollege.edu>
To: lena@westcoastcollege.edu
Subject: Re: you're quiet today . . .
Date: Tue, 19 Jul 94 16:18:31-0400

Balance, my friend, balance. "Live a balanced life—learn some and
think some and draw and paint and sing and dance and play and work
everyday some." —Robert Fulghum

—Adnan

He proposed to me one evening on chat, while my sister and father were in the very next room. "I have a question. Um . . . gee . . . well . . . I'm really nervous!" So a man could even stammer online! He finally confessed that he was "interested" in me. I could only type what I felt: "*blush*."

Somehow, I managed to indicate that I welcomed the idea of marrying him, so long as my parents approved, and gave him my phone number so he could call my father. At the end of our chat, he asked if he had surprised me.

"I knew what you were going to ask as soon as you said 'um,'" I wrote.

"Evil!" he cried. I laughed, and I knew he was laughing with me behind his computer screen. For both of us, it was joy as well as relief.

It was the end of summer. My mother and siblings had just returned from a trip to Syria to visit relatives. A fellow from Detroit was coming soon to court my sister, his mother having checked her out in Damascus and presumably approved. The two bickered over my sister's behavior while the rest of us hollered and prepared back-to-school shopping lists. Adnan had not called yet, and I was completely off my mother's radar. Or so I thought.

Through the din, she turned to me and narrowed her eyes. Was it true I was corresponding with a man? Adnan had mentioned our exchanges to his mother, who, it turned out, knew my aunt, who must have talked. I wished Adnan had kept quiet. My stomach clenched and I mumbled a vague affirmation. "If your father knew . . . " my mother said, before the demands of my younger siblings whirled her off.

I was in unknown territory. It was terrifying. I had only two friends who were married. One had fallen in love with her classmate at fifteen; he'd agreed to convert and marry her. My other friend's parents had arranged her marriage without consulting her, and she had gone along with it in her confusion.

I knew my parents fell somewhere in the middle regarding their plans for us, but it was hard to make out where they drew their lines. (Now I realize they must have been terrified, too. They had never married off a daughter before.) I was a quiet and sensitive girl who had survived adolescence by secluding myself in a corner of the guest room, scrawling anguished thoughts in my journal and hoping no one would notice me. I detested confrontation and avoided it at all costs. I hoped that my parents would agree to the marriage, and prayed that the experience would not be painful, whatever the outcome.

Soon afterward, Adnan called my parents and asked to visit. He made no mention of our correspondence. Relatives and friends often referred suitors to us, so it wasn't unusual for a man to call out of the blue. The day arrived; my parents greeted him first, as was custom, before I made my entrance.

I had painted an image of Adnan in my head, one that was snuffed out the moment I set eyes on him. His voice was higher-pitched, his hair lighter, and he was padded with a few more pounds. But what dragged me stumbling out of my imagination and into the real world was his physicality, the solidity of his body, the unmistakable male resonance of his voice.

My father engaged Adnan in expansive conversation while I sat on a chair with clenched fingers, struggling to muster enough guts to speak to him now that he was only a few yards away.

From: Lena H. <lena@westcoastcollege.edu>
To: adnan@eastcoastcollege.edu (Adnan T.)
Subject: Re: :)
Date: Fri, 26 Aug 1994 12:21:25-0700 (PDT)

Salaam . . .

I didn't respond to this last night. And we're both looking at each other waiting for each other to say something, so I guess I'll start, since you don't appear to be on.

So, you want to know what my reaction to you is…well, you are pretty much as I imagined. :) I was not surprised very much, so I don't have much to say, though I have to repeat what my sister said when she first heard your voice: "He's so Syrian!" I knew that, but it's weird talking with you in English, not just language-wise, but in the forms and meanings used—and then all of a sudden having to talk in Arabic and trying to remember the right words and not make any mistakes in speech or manners. I'm having trouble saying it, because I don't know what it means, if anything. Well, you *are* Syrian. It doesn't matter at all, but it's just—interesting. In ways, it's hard to believe that that man sitting across from me yesterday is you. I'm sure that would have disappeared soon if we could have talked freely and "connected" with all the stuff that we have talked about in the past. But for now, the dichotomy is there.

Let's see, what else is there to say…well, I was a lot shyer than I imagined. And I know I made a few mistakes, though I didn't know that serving coffee the way I did was one of them—hey, I bet you didn't notice, though you saw my mom trying to catch my attention, huh? I heard you laughing! :)

> I'd say the same. Your mother is a sweetheart, btw.

Oh, she *is*. And I think she likes you. And my dad is cautious, so I
don't know.

> so as far as the "mechanics" of it, i think it went pretty well and i
> am satisfied. I was nervous at the beginning, but towards the end it
> became more natural. (How nervous were you? I hope I did not
> embarrass you, did I?)

I wasn't really nervous (I never am—I usually make the other guy nervous! :)) but I was shy, and no, you didn't embarrass me. And I agree,
mechanic-wise, it went well.

> The big question of course is where does that leave the two of us.
> but i am really too tired to think.

Good question. I dunno. I haven't talked with my mother (or, she hasn't
talked with me) so I am not *quite* sure what they think. And I still
have to hear from *you* of course, to see what you think . . .

> btw, i don't know if it is "appropriate" to say this, but i will say
> it anyway: I think you're very attractive—much more than my
> expectations :-)

blush Alhamdulillah…

Your sister,
Lena

Adnan called my parents the next day and requested a second
visit (so strange, to be typing to someone at a computer screen,
in the Other World, and then hear the phone ring). This time,
he requested to speak with me alone. Years later, he would tell
me that he was jarred by the first visit, that the young woman in
front of him was much too quiet and passive to be the one he had
come to know online. He had been ready to abandon it, but my

email messages to him the night after his first visit reminded him that I was still the woman he knew. So the next day, he reached out to me again in real life, outside of the Internet, in the alien territory of my parents' guest room.

We were finally able to speak, stammering. We lunged for topics we had worn out in our email exchanges, as if they were buoys that would hold us up in this foreign sea.

Then, looking at me, he asked, "Can you see without your glasses?"

"No," I said.

"Neither can I," he said, and took his off. I did the same, and through the visual fog we caught each other's eyes for a sliver of a moment that made me tremble.

I didn't forget those eyes after he left. Brown and warm. My mother liked him too. "His face is so radiant!" she beamed. I could hope after all.

But she hadn't forgotten what had brought him. "Stop writing to him," she said. "It's not appropriate." It was hard, though, to suddenly act the part of the cloistered maiden, and I compromised by forgoing the more intimate and conversational chats (though we still continued to email) while Adnan and my parents maneuvered into formal marriage negotiations.

I had a painful role in these negotiations, precisely because I had no role at all. My parents, being older in age than all their friends, had no one to learn from; they fell back on the only courtship rituals they knew, those of the Damascene society of their upbringing. Not only was I not to communicate with Adnan outside their presence, but my father would not even speak to me regarding the suitor. Even my mother seemed too embarrassed to broach the subject more than was absolutely necessary. Forces beyond my reach would determine whether I would be able to marry the man I had come to love deeply. I faced the possibility that I might have to flip the switch off on my feelings toward Adnan at any moment. The idea was too painful for me to bear, and so, like a coward, I withdrew emotionally from the battle, leaving Adnan to wonder what he was fighting for.

I was in this state when he asked me to give him an idea of the dowry my parents would request, based on my sister's impending engagement. I replied carelessly that I would give him no hints, as it would give him an unfair advantage over other suitors (not that I had any). He was shocked at my cruelty.

"Sometimes I wonder if you and I know each other," he wrote.

I admitted to Adnan that I felt a subconscious guilt for liking him, so conditioned was I against "love marriages" by my parents' anxiety to distance me from the American dating scene. Though he didn't understand, Adnan still had faith that my heart was warmer than my words. So the days inched along while my parents inquired about Adnan's reputation in Damascus. Finally, two months after his initial visit, we—or rather, he—got the verdict.

From: Lena H. <lena@westcoastcollege.edu>
To: adnan@eastcoastcollege.edu (Adnan T.)
Subject: Re: So are we engaged or what?
Date: Mon, 24 Oct 1994 09:43:52-0700 (PDT)

Salaam!

> Lena, my sister, my friend,
> So your dad and I read the Fatiha. He said you and I can talk on the
> phone or the computer. I guess we are engaged now, are we not? :-)

Gee whiz, I wish he had told me. I really had no idea. :) (I'm serious!!)
Then again, he was on the phone for most of the evening, so we didn't
get much of a chance to talk—too many things happening . . .

> I really feel blessed that you and I will share the journey
> of life together.

:) :) :) You are sweet!

One other thing: I was in my room when you and Baba were on the
phone, and my sister came in and said, "So, Lena, quick! Yes or no?" I
said "yes," then had an unconscious jab from my standards of modesty,
and followed up with, "I guess so." "No 'I guess so's'!" she commanded, to which I complained, "Hey, I thought my silence was my
consent!" So she laughed and accepted.

Ok, now I *really* should go!

Talk to you soon, bro! :)

Your sister (still),
Lena

The Arab ladies at the mosque used to wink and say that there
was nothing that brought more happiness than being engaged. I
couldn't understand why. Being engaged was a relief of sorts, but
I still endured painful bumps on the way to married life.

Adnan called me on the phone every week. While we talked,
my sisters sniggered right outside the door. Afterward, they
would accuse me of turning my back on my family, of committing treason for the sake of a man. "Wait till it's your turn," my
mother told them.

Meanwhile, my father was having a hard time letting go of his
daughter. He haggled with Adnan's family over contract details
and wedding logistics, and grumbled, "Nobody is good enough
for my daughters. Nobody!"

I felt like a small blanket being yanked here and there by a
crowd of passionate children. Though driven by love, the experience was still painful. I tried to have faith that it would be over
soon—that in the end the pain would be worth it.

The last days before my wedding passed in a blur. While I
packed my suitcase in between exams, my mother scrambled to
prepare the wedding feast, hollowing out *kibbeh* and stuffing grape
leaves. After visiting at least a dozen stores, we finally managed to

buy my bridal gown the day before the wedding. On the wedding day, my sister summoned all she had learned about hairstyling from her friends to do my hair, and I arrived at the wedding hall in the middle of a storm, with the electricity out and the tables lit with emergency candles. But the Arabs of our mosque had not had a wedding in a long time, and the men intoned *khutbas* and joyous greetings in their hall, while in ours the women sang and danced and had the best evening they'd had in years.

The next morning, Adnan and I said good-bye to my family and drove off to the airport. He held out his hand, open, balanced on top of the gearshift, and I put mine in his and pulled it to my heart. In that moment, I finally felt at rest; we belonged at last to each other.

As my aunt would say, I had finally married the man of my destiny.

Kala Love

Suzanne Syeda Shah

*B*ismillah, Al-Rahman, Al-Rahim. *O, Allah, please don't let Ammu or Abbu catch me tonight. Allah, I promise to finish this surah—just please give me Your blessings to sneak out.*

For months I repeated the same ritual: Make a *dua* to Allah— more like a bargain—and read a different *surah* to hold up my end. Then I would crawl on my bedroom floor, reach up, and stick one leg after the other out of my narrow window and into the world. I was fourteen years old, and nothing seemed more important to me than getting to my boyfriend's house.

As soon as I became a teenager, Ammu had begun bottling my freedom, just as she did her pickled mangoes. She said, in Bengali, "If you want to go anywhere, you go with me! No more going out with friends."

At the time, I didn't understand why. Maybe they didn't want me to run away like my *apu*, my older sister. My *apu* started high school wearing a hijab, but one day she came home from school with a large, oval locket of the Virgin Mary around her neck.

Soon after, she reported my parents to child services for abuse and was placed in a foster home. After months of trying to question me, the social worker finally gave up. The judge let me stay with Ammu and Abbu, but that was the last time I saw my *apu*, until a decade later.

I would never run away. But that didn't mean I didn't long to break free every once in a while.

I made a plan. Since Abbu usually went through my room to get to his, I had to time my escape just right. One time I sat in the closet for an hour just to see if he would notice that the long body pillow stuffed under my comforter was not his sweet but stubborn daughter. He walked through the room without pause. After that, my doppelgänger slept in my bed every Friday night, while I slept in my boyfriend's.

As much as I thought I was fooling Abbu, I began to wonder if he saw the back door creak open after he locked it at night. Or if he heard my flip-flops snap a twig outside his window every Saturday morning before Fajr. Did he feel my breath missing at night, even though my bed appeared filled? Did he make *dua* for my safe return?

This was my first relationship with a boy. It was based purely on attraction. My boyfriend was a senior football player from a different high school; I was a freshman. I bragged about his dark muscles and high cheekbones to my friends at school. Every night I talked to him on the phone under my comforter to hide the sound from Ammu's bionic ears. I snuck out to his house and spent the night in his bed, not understanding that he wanted more from me than I was giving him. One night, six months after we started going out, my scrawny legs weren't strong enough to kick his six-foot-one weight off me. I lay on his cold-tiled bathroom floor, wet and torn open.

The next morning I didn't make it back to my house in time, and I faced Ammu's wrath and Abbu's disappointment. I heard

Abbu saying quietly that he knew I'd been sneaking out but had no idea I was staying out all night. After that, he didn't speak to me for six months.

For the first time in my life, I saw my father cry. But I was numb from the night before. The numbness slowly gave way to spurts of tears. I was just fourteen, without an understanding of sex, much less rape. I blamed myself for everything, for sneaking out and being in my boyfriend's house. I talked to Allah and made *dua* to ask Him to mend me by transforming me back into the girl I had been before that night. I promised Him that the next man I would be with would be my husband. I clasped my face in my brown hands, asking Him repeatedly to return me to the comfort of Ammu and Abbu—especially Abbu.

Abbu's silence lasted until one night I put my head on his feet and begged for his forgiveness.

Before I left for college at UC Berkeley, I made a new rule for myself: no talking to boys until I was married.

This vow confused my best friends. Kelly asked me in almost a whisper, "So, are you going to wear that thing around your head now?"

I responded with a smile. "Eventually, yes, I'll wear the hijab."

Tyra snapped back, "How the heck are you going to find a husband if you don't even talk to men?"

I told her, "God will bring me my husband." I wasn't worried. I didn't expect to get married until I was forty, especially not with Abbu in my life.

I'm nineteen years old, and it's a sunny April day toward the end of my second year at Berkeley. The cool breeze sweeps through the people on the streets, like wisps of hair escaping from a ponytail just to caress the face. I go to Naan 'N' Curry, a Pakistani restaurant that makes tandoori chicken like Ammu's. I am excited to go home soon, to squeeze Abbu and stuff my face all summer with Ammu's curries and rice.

Back in Los Angeles, Abbu pours water over his feet for Asr, just as here in Berkeley, the waiter brings my tandoori chicken cushioned on top of naan. Abbu climbs into his pickup truck. Steam escapes from the naan as I tear off a piece. Abbu walks into the modest two-room *masjid*. I devour the chicken tikka. "*Allahu akbar.*" Abbu's right hand folds over his left across his stomach. The curry's spices tickle my nose. Abbu's long white *thobe* glistens. The red-orange meat falls off easily as I bite down to the bone. Abbu bows down to prostrate in *sajdah* and never comes up again. Hours later, my phone rings with the news.

Allah took Abbu, my first love. Two months later, He brought me Mika'il.

Mika'il was a search result. Literally. When I came home from college the summer after Abbu died, Ammu still wouldn't let me out of the house. I wasn't ready to talk to men, but out of boredom I browsed MySpace all day, searching for black or Latino college-age Muslim men within a three-hundred-mile radius. I never looked for Bengalis, or any other *desi*. Ammu called me *kali*, which means "darkie," and made me feel I had the wrong skin, the ugly skin. I didn't want to marry into another family that looked down on my "*kali*-ness."

When Mika'il turned up in my search, we started exchanging messages. For a month, we wrote about Islam, school, and our futures. Mika'il was shy, and I was forward. I gave him my number. As soon as I heard his voice on the phone, I called my friend Issa and said, "Yeah, he is definitely not my future husband." He had a "friend" voice, like my guy friends in class.

One morning soon after that, Ammu had one of her usual mood shifts. At five in the morning, right after Fajr, she couldn't find her car keys. She became frustrated and began venting in

Bengali, "It's all your fault that he's dead. You're the one who killed him. You're Shaytan—you did this."

Then she found her keys, slammed the door, and drove off in her red Miata to the local gas station that she managed. Her words broke me. Abbu had always been the one to console me when Ammu acted crazy, but now I had no one. The first person I thought to call was Mika'il, who was attending New Mexico State at the time. Even though it was 6:00 AM there, he picked up on the first ring.

"Hello?" His voice was calm even when waking from sleep.

I couldn't say hello; the snot and tears muffled my voice.

"Are you okay?" he asked. He was really awake now.

After fifteen minutes of uncontrollable tears, I started talking, not holding back anything. I told him everything that was wrong with me. How much I missed Abbu, and how much Ammu hurt me. He listened. After I had talked for two hours without a break, he said, "You know, if I was there in L.A., I would come over and do the running man for you."

I started laughing, and he continued, "See, I haven't even done it for you yet, and you're already laughing."

Mika'il and I talked every day that whole summer, for three months straight. He had converted to Islam two months before we met, so I relearned the religion through his newly awakened eyes. I tried to teach him as much about Islam as Ammu and Abbu had taught me when I was growing up, and I set my alarm to call and wake him up for the predawn prayer. Actively worshipping Allah with him brought us closer. I still hadn't met him in person, yet it felt as if our souls were already entwined.

That fall, Mika'il came to visit me at Berkeley. When he stepped out of the car, all I saw were his eyes. Their muddy gentleness, like the earth after a summer rain, reminded me of Abbu. He was wearing old college football sweats and Air Jordans that were practically split in two. I thought, *Wow, you would think the guy would at least put on some shoes without holes before meeting his future wife.* Yet his candid and nonmaterialistic nature reminded me of Abbu, too.

We went out to eat at Naan 'N' Curry. Mika'il was sitting next to me, trying to calm his stomach postcurry, when I began my usual practice of gnawing and grinding the chicken bones between my teeth down to mere powder. He tried to mask his horror, but I kept at it. In spite of his shock, he didn't leave my side.

From then on, he visited me every weekend. I lived in a cheap apartment in a complex known as "Roachdale" with three other girls. Mika'il knew I was a germophobe but that I couldn't afford a nicer place to live, so, while visiting, he washed everybody's dishes and cleaned the bathroom and my room. He even did my laundry and folded my underwear into mini-triangles. The more Mika'il cleaned, the more I fell in love with him.

Mika'il was ready to marry me the first time we met, but I hesitated. He knew about my past, but I still questioned whether he could accept me. Rape was my only experience with sex, and now I was scared of it. I couldn't talk to Ammu or anyone for guidance. So I made *dua* to Allah.

A year later, during my senior year, I sat in the car outside the Fairfield Masjid, melting in my faded sweats from the summer heat. Mikai'il ran out of the *masjid* to say, "Right now is the only time the imam can marry us, because he's leaving town tonight for a week."

How could I get married right then? I didn't even have a hijab to enter the *masjid*. But after borrowing a *wali* and two witnesses from the *masjid*, and taking the last $20 bill in Mika'il's wallet as my dowry, I married him in the sweltering heat, adorned only with my shimmering sweat. It was impulsive, but it felt right. It was perfect, our secret.

Our first night, I undressed nervously in front of the man I loved. Mika'il saw everything—my shyness, my stretch marks, my past—but he just rested his head gently on my stomach as if he had found his home.

I had not told Ammu about my marriage to Mika'il. I wanted to tell her that I had found this amazing Muslim man who reminded me of Abbu, the man whom she had fallen in love with, but I was too scared. She would never accept an African American man as my husband, Muslim or not. I don't know if her views stemmed from the negative portrayal of black people in America, or if it was just plain old *desi* racism. I needed time to make *dua* to Allah to soften her heart.

A year after graduating from Berkeley, I brought Mika'il to L.A. to meet Ammu. By then, we'd been married secretly for two years. We pulled up to my childhood driveway, right next to where Abbu's old gray pickup truck was still parked. I could see a small pearl of sweat on Mika'il's forehead. He was nervous. I told him to wait in the car until after I had spoken to Ammu.

Ammu was in her usual place, rocking back and forth in her blue recliner and staring at the TV. The scent from the kitchen revealed my favorite meal: beef cabbage and hot basmati rice. Ammu got up and started moving toward the kitchen.

"Ammu, wait. I want to talk to you before I eat. *Mone ache* that Muslim I told you about a few months ago? *Ore nam hoche* Mika'il Ali, remember?"

"*Na!*" Ammu looked through me, as if she had no idea what I was talking about, and continued to make me a plate of food.

"Okay, Ammu. Well, Mika'il is here. And I would really like for you to meet him so you can tell me if he's the right man for me to marry. I feel like he is, but I want your opinion and approval."

She looked annoyed. "*Che kala?*"

"Yes, he's black."

"*Shaytaner bacha! Thu ammar bashai akta kala ke nea ashce? Kok-hona*, never! *Akta kala Muslim hothe pare na!*"

"Ammu, what do you mean, 'a *kala* can't be Muslim'? He *is* Muslim, and he's a good, practicing Muslim. Ammu, he's just like Abbu. Please, just meet him."

I was crying by now. She ignored my tears and kept screaming. In her mind, Mika'il was a dumb, dangerous, pants-sagging gang-banger like the ones she saw on TV. She wouldn't listen when I told her that he was in law school, had grown up in a military family, and had found Islam on his own.

She stood there, her small fingers pointing at me, right in front of a framed copy of the Prophet Muhammad's last sermon hanging on our wall, in which he said, "White has no superiority over black, nor does a black have any superiority over white; except by piety and good action."

"Suzanne, if you go marry this *kala*, I will never speak to you again. Allah will punish you. You will never be anything. You will never be a doctor; you will be cleaning people's floors like a dirty slave."

Tears blurred my vision, and my mouth was numb. "I'm going to leave now, Ammu."

"*Ja!* Shaytan!" she shouted after me.

So began my life at twenty-three as an orphan in Portland, Oregon, while Mika'il attended law school. The homeless teen-agers, the white faces, and the constant rain were all new to me. But over time, I got used to my new home. After having been long distance the whole time we had been secretly married, we felt like this was our first year of truly being husband and wife. I made eggs and *porotas* in the morning before Mika'il left for law school, went grocery shopping in the middle of the afternoon, and fucked at night. Yes, fucked. He is my husband, and in the eyes of Allah it is not only halal, but a blessing, for me to fuck him. And I enjoyed fucking him. "Lovemaking" freaks me out, so we did lovefucking instead.

I'm twenty-five now, and my Portland house smells of cardamom and chai. My home doesn't have four walls, like a box, but rather has the two muscular arms of my husband, ready to pick me up when I'm too scared to move. My husband, who, every time he lovefucks me, prays extra *namaj* to thank Allah for our union. I thought I left home for Mika'il. But every time I smell his face, I know *he* is my home.

Mika'il still looks at me and asks, "Where did you come from, tiny little thing? Woman who is my life, who runs my life? Where did you come from?"

I pout. "What do you mean?"

"Since you called me that morning, crying, I knew. I told myself that I was going to take care of you for the rest of my life."

Marriage is hard, and it's harder when you don't have a mother showing you how much turmeric to add to the dal or what to do if your husband is angry. Allah took my mother, my role model, the strongest and craziest woman I've ever met. Allah also took Abbu, my best friend, my backbone. Sometimes, lying in the dark, I fear that He will take Mika'il.

I don't know if this is my last love or just the beginning, but I do know that Allah is everlasting. In spite of all the hardships in my life, my *dua* gives me sustenance.

Brain Meets Heart

Aida Rahim

I was born in the United States but grew up in Malaysia, where Islam was part of the official curriculum in school. Malaysia is where I learned all the "Islamic rules"—specifically, those related to dressing properly and talking correctly, money and music, and gender interactions, including dating and marriage. But growing up, I cared about Islam solely for the purpose of passing exams and getting good grades.

After high school, I moved to England to continue my studies. Suddenly faced with the prospect of being a minority, both racially and religiously, I wanted an identity that I could hold on to and call my own. I decided that I would Be Muslim, instead of being Muslim merely by chance of birth. I would do this by following, to the letter, all the rules that I had learned in school in Malaysia. I thought that the more closely I adhered to those rules, the stronger my faith would be.

This was my religious conviction at twenty-four, when I met my first husband. By this time, I was living in Cambridge,

Massachusetts, and enrolled in a PhD program. I had never been on a date before, and no boy or man had ever shown any interest in me. Perhaps I was too serious and conservative—I wore hijab, dressed in long, flowy clothes, and avoided unnecessary conversation with men. Perhaps I was too independent—I had lived on my own for the past ten years and had never needed to ask permission of anyone to do anything. Perhaps my standards were too high—I wanted a fellow rule-follower and someone physically and mentally smarter and stronger than I. Or perhaps the right man just had not come my way.

So when I met a man who, after knowing me for just a couple of weeks, decided that he wanted to marry me, it was exactly as I had pictured how Muslim marriages should come about. His parents introduced us, all conversations were carried out chastely under their watchful gaze, we kept our eyes lowered modestly whenever we met, and we had absolutely no physical contact until we married.

Two years and one baby later, he left.

I had been so determined to get married that I had ignored all my doubts about my now ex-husband. I thought his religious conservatism and his zeal about following all the Islamic rules were what I needed to help strengthen my own faith. I was never really attracted to him as a person. I was attracted to his kind and sweet parents; I was attracted to the sense of duty and respect he showed them; I was attracted to his potential for professional success; I was attracted to his intention to move to Malaysia with me after my graduation. However, I never found communicating with him to be very enjoyable. Conversation was always stilted, as we did not have much in common.

But I was independent and stubborn—once I wanted something, I went all out to get it. I wanted to be married, so I got married.

Even though I did not acknowledge it at the time, even my body tried to warn me that all was not right. During the courtship, I could not sleep, would suddenly start crying, and was often stressed to the point that my menstrual cycle was disrupted. But, being a logical, emotionally disconnected person, I managed to rationalize these bad omens away.

My marriage was supposed to be the capstone of my spirituality. The divorce forced me to question the unflexible, rule-based person I had become.

Two years later, I was truly enjoying life as a single mother raising a rambunctious toddler. I had a postdoctoral research position in a lab in Singapore, doing tissue engineering. I had thought a great deal about myself and the way I had been practicing Islam. I realized that it was impossible to follow all the rules absolutely, and that there were multiple rules for any given situation anyway. By now, I usually did whatever was most convenient for me, even though I still had doubts about my choices and was often hard on myself for not following the strictest interpretation of any given rule. Still in my mind was the notion that morality was tied very strongly with following the right rules—you were a highly moral person if you chose to follow the most difficult rule.

One thing I did know was that I was definitely not looking to get married again. And then I met Javed.

We were e-introduced by a mutual friend, who had hired him to photograph her wedding in Malaysia. Javed was flying from the United States and needed a place to stay in Singapore while in transit. I was going to be away at a conference, so I offered him my house.

We met in person in Malaysia, the day before the wedding, and went to a group dinner that night with the bride and groom.

Over dinner we discussed Islamic marriage courses, which are compulsory in Malaysia for Muslim couples. Our friends had just gone to theirs and learned about their respective marital duties, family planning and birth control, and family law in Malaysia's *shariah* courts. Javed and I both agreed that such a course was unnecessary, but then he said that if it was imposed by government, supposedly for society's overall good, it should be free. I did not agree with that, though I held my tongue at dinner.

I knew that Javed didn't see things as I did, because our mutual friend told me about his Hijabman blog, and I had taken a quick look before dinner. His open and engaging personality came across online and during dinner, as did his very liberal and unconventional religious views. He was not at all impressed with rules-based Islam, finding instead that the life principles of doing good and being just rose from the pages of the Qur'an.

Since I was unsettled in my own religious convictions, I was curious to see if Javed was a person whose religious outlook and thought process I could learn from. I emailed him to explain my disagreement over the point made at dinner. It was a minor point of contention, but I was just using it as an excuse to open up a channel of communication.

I received a reply from him almost immediately.

Even though he was traveling around Malaysia by then, he took the time to think through and craft a thoughtful, lengthy response. And as we started to correspond, it was clear that not only was he interested in airing his opinions, he was also interested in me. He asked me questions about myself and my life in a way that put me at ease. We emailed almost every day, covering topics ranging from religious ideas to personality traits to future goals and dreams. Even when we vehemently disagreed with each other—the clash of my rules-based Islam with his, which challenged the status quo—he laid out his thoughts in the most respectful of ways.

And he always signed his emails, "Much love and respect, Javed." His use of the word "love" was neither offensive nor intrusive when balanced with "respect." It made me feel as though his interest was genuine—not necessarily for romantic purposes, but in me as a human being who had her own experiences and thoughts. It motivated me to be as honest as possible in our exchanges.

• • •

It had been just two weeks since our first meeting over dinner, but I was interested—interested in Javed's mind and the way he articulated his thoughts clearly, with an almost scientific process: a starting point; a fleshing-out, in which he considered, rejected, or accepted various parameters or inputs; and a conclusion. It was like reading multiple well-thought-out journal articles.

Before he returned to the United States, Javed came back to Singapore and stayed with my two-year-old daughter and me for three days. He immediately immersed himself in our lives: We went grocery shopping together, and he taught me how to select healthier food products by reading labels and picking the ones with the fewest ingredients. I was touched by his willingness to go grocery shopping with us in the first place, and by his concern for our health. We went to the playground, where he roughhoused with my daughter. It made me happy to see her laughing madly as he tossed her into the air. I also showed him around the city: We visited the marina and splashed at the water fountain, we went to the turtle farm, and we strolled around the Chinese gardens.

Overall, I was struck by the ease of our interactions. Javed was relaxed, so I relaxed, too. I never felt as if there was a stranger in our midst whom I had to cater to. My daughter's comfort with Javed indicated that, had she been old enough to express her thoughts, she would have agreed with me. My attraction to him was growing, but I had no idea whether the feeling was mutual.

During my daughter's naptime and way past her bedtime, we would sit face-to-face on the couch and pick up where our email conversations had left off. We exchanged travel stories and childhood experiences, and our email exchanges about our personality traits, including our weaknesses, expanded to include considerations about what kind of partner would best complement us.

On the second day of Javed's stay, our conversation veered

toward past relationships. He told me that he had many female acquaintances: "Often, I quickly get put into the friend category. Even if I'm interested in pursuing more than just friendship, I'm stuck in the friend box."

"Well," I replied, "I think that if you start feeling interest beyond friendship, you should just bring it up. You can talk about it, and if it goes nowhere, then that's okay," I advised.

He paused.

I got up to get a glass of water for each of us.

When I sat back down, he said, "So, Aida . . . would you consider someone like me for marriage?"

I looked straight at him and said, "*Someone* like you . . . or you?"

There was another pause. He looked slightly embarrassed but replied, "Okay, me."

"Yes," I said.

When my rational side thought about how we were expressing an interest in pursuing a relationship the day before Javed's return to the United States, it seemed a little insane. What were we committing to, after only a few weeks of emails and two days of in-person conversation? I didn't know his family, and he didn't know mine. He was going to start nursing school in the fall, while I had a child to care for and a full-time, consuming job. How were we going to build a relationship living on two different continents, separated by twelve time zones?

These challenges might have seemed insurmountable to some, but not to me. I knew then that Javed could be my partner for life, and a father to my daughter. He was too precious to let go. The worst that could happen would be that things did not work out between us. But not to try at all would have been an injustice to us both.

When the cab came at 4:00 AM on Javed's last day to take him to the airport, we parted with a long hug. It was the first time I had hugged an unrelated male. Until that moment, I had truly believed that intergender physical contact was not allowed in Islam. But when Javed hugged me, I hugged him back impulsively, surprised by how nonsexual and nonthreatening it felt.

But afterward, I was not comfortable with my decision.

When we discussed it later over email, Javed wrote: "The Qur'an says that we should 'not approach *zina*,' or illicit sexual intercourse. That is pretty open for interpretation. I know that fornication is wrong. Everything else is open to your own gut feeling (in my humble opinion). I didn't feel an ounce of regret giving you the hug and expressing my care for you through touch. Because for me that wasn't approaching illicit sex. In fact, it was not sexual at all. It was warm. It was a mutually understood expression of . . . good vibes, for lack of a better description. And yes, everyone's boundaries are different. That is why communication is so important. Different people have different boundaries, emotions, preferences, approaches, etc. To be self-aware is a hard, steep path."

His words made sense and put me at ease.

So began our long-distance relationship. We would instant message during my workday and video chat in the evening. I particularly relished our exchanges on the point of religion, triggered by Javed's favorite general question: What is your approach to religion? I felt that this was a great platform upon which to start fleshing out some of the thoughts I had been wrestling with since my divorce, my slow move away from rules-based Islam.

Javed's approach to the faith contrasted dramatically with my own. He had read a translation of the Qur'an when he was fourteen, and nothing about it even remotely resembled the Islam he was learning in Sunday school, which focused so much energy and attention on the minute details of moon-sighting and the one-eyed Dajjal. After he read the Qur'an on his own, he decided that his life would be predicated on its core messages:

Believe in God; work for good; know that deeds will be ultimately judged.

Up until this point, when something deemed "Islamic" had
not sat well with me, I had blamed my weak heart, believing my
faith was simply not strong enough to accept the truth. But at
some point during our discussions, something clicked inside me,
and I realized that there was nothing wrong with exercising my
own judgment about how to lead my life. It was such a relief to
finally give myself permission to think within my religious space.
I decided to stop believing in ultimate morality, a morality that
was tied to specific religious rules. I decided that the only ultimate truth was that God is just and merciful, and that within that
framework, there was no harm in exploring other viewpoints.

Sometimes I think of myself as a robot: I am methodical
and logical to a fault. Javed's way of communicating, speaking
straight from his heart, was helping me to open up and be more
adventurous with my emotions. I felt my relationship with God
transcend the objective rules and flood into the emotional space.

My mother was concerned when I first told her that I was interested in the photographer from my friend's wedding. Like Javed,
my ex-husband was also a Pakistani American and three years
younger than I. But that was where the similarities ended, and I
knew that when my family met Javed, they would like him.

On his next visit to Malaysia, two months after his initial trip,
we spent a week with my parents and siblings in Penang. During
his stay, they talked to him and observed his interactions with my
daughter and me. They were visibly impressed when, on his first
day there, my daughter flung herself at him, giving him a big hug
and a kiss on the cheek.

My sister let out an audible, awestruck gasp: "Wow! She refuses
to give me a kiss!"

On the last night of his visit, we all went out for dinner. Javed and I sat across the table from my mother. Javed tried all night to strike up a conversation with her, but most of his questions received only one-line replies.

When the meal was over and we were about to leave, my mother finally blurted out what had clearly been on her mind throughout the evening: "So, what are your plans?"

Without missing a beat, he looked her in the eyes and said these beautiful words: "Well, Auntie, God willing, with your permission, I'd like to marry Aida within a year."

To this day, he swears that every future Muslim mother-in-law wants to hear the following expressed:

1. God's supreme authority (only if God wills)
2. The mother's supreme authority over the couple (permission)
3. A desire to get married (the only legitimate goal)
4. Time frame (too short = unrealistic; too long = noncommittal)

With a lopsided smile on her face, my mother said, "Okay."

On a bright, sunny Malaysian June morning just ten months after we first met, Javed and I were married, surrounded by close family and friends.

After our marriage, we lived in Malaysia for a year, and then moved to Blacksburg, Virginia. The first year of marriage was one of learning for us both. Javed's calming voice tempers my impatience, his impulsive plans break me from my rigid adherence to schedules, and his happiness with his house-husband role allows me to focus on my career.

I am continually amazed that of all the people on this earth, God brought this one man to my doorstep, my perfect complement. As my husband likes to say, we plan and God laughs.

A Cairene Kind of Love

Molly Elian Carlson

W hen I first converted to Islam, I was certain I would be able to find another Spanish-speaking convert to marry. My profile on a popular Muslim matrimonial site stated my high expectations: "Spanish-speaking Muslimah looking for a Spanish-speaking Muslim to marry—must not be divorced or already have a wife."

In return, I received many angry emails about my being "picky."

"Haram, sister, haram, do you think a Spanish speaker will be a better husband? Marry an Arab; he will teach you Arabic. Marry me; I will make you so happy."

"What is wrong with a divorced man? Allah forgive you!"

And, of course, the email banishing me to the fires of hell for refusing to consider polygamy: "Allah gave men the right; it is a Sunnah and I seek to be a better Muslim. I am only following in the footsteps of our beloved Prophet, peace be upon him."

I loved to answer these emails and often engaged in lively debates, but I found very few Spanish-speaking Muslims who fit what I was looking for in a husband. Latinos were one of the groups with the highest rates of conversion to Islam, but the majority of the converts were women. Just like me.

I grew up in a Latino community in Minnesota, attending Spanish-speaking churches and spending holidays with my neighbors. Even though I wasn't ethnically Latina, I picked up the language and the culture so well that most people never knew it. I was one of the few bridges between Spanish and English speakers in the Santo Niño community, and I became an activist for their rights as immigrants. My mom was so certain that I would marry a Latino and have Spanish-speaking children that she talked about taking Spanish classes so she could communicate with my future in-laws.

During my last two years of university, I moved from Minnesota to Arizona, throwing myself into my studies and thinking that my search for love would be better now that I was in a state with more Latinos. I met my best friend, Amira, an American-born Egyptian girl, who promised to find me a good Egyptian boy to marry.

"Oh, no, no Egyptians for me, thank you. I mean, you're delightful, dear, but I've seen Egyptian men and the way they treat their wives. I've even been told *by* Egyptian women to steer clear of Egyptian men!" I told her.

I especially gave my *wali*, the Pakistani man who took the role of my father in Islam, a hard time about it. He would beg me, "*Beta*, does he have to speak Spanish? I mean, there are many good, non-Spanish brothers looking for wives. Think about them, please."

But I was unrelenting. I was certain that the only man who would understand my desire to dance through my living room to *cumbias* and *bachatas*, partake of a Sunday-morning menudo with me, and laugh with me at the telenovelas I was secretly addicted to would be a Latino.

I met some, but they never worked out. One was much too much of a mama's boy, too busy being a minority and feeling sorry for himself. Another acted like a priest who had taken vows of poverty. I'm all for giving to charity from your wealth for the sake of Allah, but expecting your wife to live on ramen noodles? Um, no thanks.

I began to feel hopeless in my quest for the perfect Latino husband, so I focused on my final semester of school. That's when Amira made a suggestion:

"Check out this guy on MySpace. He's pretty cute, *mashAllah*, and he's religious too," she said casually.

"Sure, he's cute, but he's *Egyptian*, Amira." I laughed when I saw his profile.

"Hey! You say that like it's a bad thing," she said, in mock offense.

"Sorry, dearest, but you know how I feel about Egyptians. And his name is Mohamed—you know we promised to find husbands with more original names," I said, reminding her of our pact. We had giggled about the multitudes of Ahmeds and Mohameds in the Muslim world, and had pinky-sworn to marry people with more original names.

"The least we could hold out for is an Omar or an Abdul-Rahman," I protested.

"Or a Hamza," she agreed.

"But . . . he *is* cute," I sighed, looking at his pictures again.

"He's a good guy—give him a chance. An Egyptian man isn't half bad if you train him well."

I added him to my friends list on MySpace but blew him off for months. I was certain he was a player, because no man who looked that cute could be anything but. Still, I found myself checking his profile for new pictures and admiring his good looks. I also noticed that his bulletins were always religious, never fluffy. One day, seven months after adding him, I decided to consult with him about an article I had found on Islam. We spent hours talking the first time we chatted online. I was impressed with his knowledge and his respectful reaction when I challenged his views.

Soon I had him on my instant messenger and was chatting with him while I was in class or during my night shifts at a hotel, my part-time job during college. He made a point of being available throughout my shift because I was working a dangerous time slot in a sketchy neighborhood. I was touched by his caring and found myself looking forward to talking to him each day. We talked about culture, politics, and the differences between cultural practices and real Islam. I began to deeply respect his mind and his ideas.

One day, after we'd spent all afternoon chatting, it was time for the dawn prayer for him in Cairo. He remembered that one of the things I had talked about wanting to hear was the call to prayer in a Muslim city, since mosques in America are not allowed to broadcast it outside. He took the microphone from his computer and went to the window of his room so I could hear the *adhan* being called.

As the voices of the *muezzin* rang out and "*Allahu akbar*" echoed off the buildings, I found myself in tears. He came back to the computer and heard me. "Are you crying? What's wrong? Are you okay?"

I tried to act like I wasn't. "No [sniffle]."

"What's wrong? Why are you crying?"

"I'm fine, but it means so much to me that you remembered."

"How could I forget?"

It was that moment that broke the final wall between him and my heart. I tried to deny that anything had changed, but I found myself thinking of him at random moments. While studying, I'd remember a joke he had told me the day before. When I awoke in the morning, I'd wonder if he was online yet. Little by little, he became closer to me and, against my better judgment, I fell for him.

I called Amira to tell her about my nascent feelings, thinking that she'd tease me, we'd laugh, and I'd snap out of it.

But instead, she burst into laughter.

"What's so funny?" I demanded, indignant.

"Oh, no, I can't tell you. I promised."

"You promised who what? There is no way you can say *that* and then not tell me. That's treason!"

She continued laughing, but finally admitted, "Mohamed wrote to me two months ago to say that he really liked you. He wanted me to know he was going to start talking with you more regularly, but that his intentions were honorable. And then he bound.me, by Allah, to not say anything to you about it. It was *so* hard not to tell you, but I couldn't. He loves you, I think."

"Two months ago? That was when we had just begun to talk— how could he love me? Are you serious?" I asked.

"I'm dead serious, *habibti*, but he's being good about it. I mean, he told me his intentions. I say go for it."

It was too much to consider, too quickly.

"How? It's online—it isn't even real."

"You're the one who called me to admit you had a crush on him, and now you're saying it's not real?"

"Well . . . "

"You're coming to Egypt this summer with me for my wedding; you can meet him there and see where things go. He's a good guy."

"Yes, but . . . he's Egyptian. And his name is Mohamed!" I protested weakly.

Amira laughed. "Look at me—I'm marrying an Ahmed!"

The next day, I pinned Mohamed down online.

"All right, I can't do this anymore. If you want to meet me while I'm in Egypt, I need to know what your intentions are."

"Molly, I really like you," he answered. "I think I want to marry you, but I want us to meet each other face-to-face before we make any decisions. My intentions are honorable. How do you feel about me?"

"I like you, too," I admitted. "But this needs to be serious, because I don't want to get hurt."

"I'd never hurt you."

"Good, then don't. InshAllah, we will meet when I come to Egypt and see where things go."

That day, he started calling me *habibti*.

After I graduated from college, I flew to Turkey with my mom to celebrate with a Mediterranean cruise. After my father left us, it was just her and me, and she was the closest person in the world to me. She had always been right about my life decisions thus far, so I wanted her to meet Mohamed and give me her advice. She knew a little about him, but I kept my feelings close to my heart. I was still nervous and unsure of what the future held for me in terms of my relationship with him.

Four days into the trip, we landed on the shores of Egypt, where he was waiting.

He met us directly at the door of the port of entry into the city of Alexandria. I'd like to say that rainbows erupted and symphonies played when we first made eye contact, but the truth is, I was so nervous that my teeth chattered and I couldn't stop talking, or grinning like an idiot, until about five hours into our first day together.

It was very early in the morning when we arrived, so almost nothing was open. We were a group of five altogether: the driver; our tour guide, who was a close friend of Mohamed; my mother; Mohamed; and me. Finding that none of the sightseeing locations were open yet, we stopped to have a typical Egyptian breakfast of *ful* and *ta'miyya* sandwiches at a small café.

We ate at a leisurely pace and enjoyed the morning's cool

weather. I was still so nervous that I didn't know what to do with myself. I wasn't sure if I should eat or talk, look at Mohamed or not look at him, and so confused that I often did all of those things at once. I was captivated by him but painfully shy and embarrassed, and I could tell that he felt the same way.

After we had finished breakfast, it was still too early to enter the Qaitbay Citadel, so we set off on a walk along the wharf next to it so we could talk alone. My mom and the rest of the group trailed not far behind us, though they kept a respectful distance.

Standing on the rocks with Mohamed, I decided that I wanted to get closer to the edge and look into the water, but as I inched forward, I slipped on some algae. I would have landed in the water had he not caught me. Afterward, I wasn't sure which hurt worse, my scraped foot or my bruised pride, but at least he knew exactly what he was getting into with clumsy, accident-prone me. There was no false advertising there.

Mohamed had convinced one of his best friends, a tour guide, to give us a private tour of Alexandria and Cairo, but I was too engrossed in shyly watching Mohamed to listen to what his friend said during our expedition. Later, as we descended into the catacombs of Kom el Shoqafa, I slipped for a second time on some gravel and would have fallen again if Mohamed hadn't been next to me.

As we ascended from the gloom back into the bright light of day, I heard my first call to prayer in a Muslim city, with Mohamed at my side. I had never heard anything as beautiful as the echo of the voices around us. Looking up into Mohamed's face, I felt at peace with myself, and I could picture the possibility of a future with him.

My mother approved of Mohamed and spoke repeatedly of how respectful and kind he was. After our two-day excursion in Egypt had ended and we were back on the cruise ship, she turned to me.

"You're going to marry him, aren't you?" she asked. Until that point, I hadn't even mentioned the possibility to her, but her question shocked me into complete honesty.

"Maybe."

"I would be okay with that. He's a good guy," she threw out casually, too consumed with hanging her clothes to see how bowled over I was by her announcement. I knew that she had gotten along well with him, but I hadn't expected her to be so accepting, so quickly, of the idea of her only child getting married.

For the rest of the trip, we talked about the future, and I spent each day eagerly anticipating the day I'd fly from Athens, the destination of our cruise, back to Cairo to spend the summer with Amira.

During the five weeks I was with Amira, I helped her plan her wedding, experienced more of Egypt, and fit in as many chaperoned "dates" as I could with Mohamed. He and I almost single-handedly sustained two mobile-phone companies in Cairo buying credits for our marathon conversations about our expectations surrounding life, love, and marriage.

I met his family and felt completely at home with them. His father and youngest sister took me to Al-Azhar and Khan el-Khalili. His father charmed me with his smile, and by the end of the afternoon his sister and I had become best friends. I met his mother and his older sister on another evening, and I loved them as well. Later, Mohamed told me that his mother had accepted me as a daughter from the moment she saw how much I loved Mohamed and how kind I was to everyone. She said that was all she needed to know about me.

During this time, I prayed about the choices I had to make and placed my trust in God to show me the right way. I offered a special prayer called *istikharah*:

"O God, if this decision is good for me and for my religion, then ease the path and bless it for me, and if this decision is wrong for me and for my religion, then please remove me from it, and remove it from me, and bless me with something better."

In response, I dreamed that Mohamed saved me from a life without Islam and brought me to heaven. When I woke the next morning, I knew that he was my soul mate and a marriage between us would be blessed.

At the end of June, I was sitting with Mohamed and his family, all crammed Egyptian-style into his father's ancient Mercedes-Benz, drinking cane juice. I asked, "So, it's pretty certain that we're going to get married, right?"

He nodded.

"So, why don't we get married on the Fourth of July?"

He choked midswallow, realizing that the date I had proposed was only four days away. I knew it was quick, but I rationalized that July 4 was a national holiday in America, and assuming that we settled there, we could always count on having the day off of work and an evening of fireworks to celebrate our love. He acquiesced to my request and promised to have everything ready. So, in a break from the norm, I proposed to my husband, not the other way around. Instead of having a romantic dinner, we drank cane juice with his family, and instead of a ring, we had an understanding and mutual acceptance that meant so much more. From the beginning, everyone had assumed that if we fit, there would be a marriage, so no one—not his family, not Amira, not my mother—was surprised by the announcement.

On the day of the fourth, Mohamed took me to his father's flat, where his youngest sister did my makeup and tied my hijab in a fancy way as I shook with nerves and hyperventilated. I had spent the two days before the wedding suffering from a bad case of food poisoning, and the night before praying that I would be well enough for the wedding. It wasn't until I put on my wedding dress—the prettiest abaya I could find on short notice—that I realized I was actually getting married. Forever-and-ever-amen married. I didn't doubt my decision, but I had never imagined it would happen so quickly.

Mohamed arrived, looking spectacular in a black suit, and with him came some of the family I hadn't met yet. As we posed for photographs, I took a moment to mourn the fact that my own mother was not with me. She had returned to the United States after our cruise and wouldn't be able to return for the wedding, but I felt happy knowing that she approved of my decision.

Mohamed and I smiled at each other nervously. He offered his arm to escort me, and together we stepped out of the flat to begin our new lives together. His brother's wife came behind us and began to *zagrat* loudly, the trilling sound Arab women make during celebrations, to announce our presence. Heads popped out of other flats immediately to congratulate us with wide smiles as we took the long walk down to the car. I felt like I couldn't breathe, and everything seemed surreal.

When we got to the car, I almost began to cry. Earlier in the day, Mohamed's brother had decorated it entirely, from front to back, in flowers and streamers in the style that I had admired as I watched other brides drive through the streets of Cairo. It made me feel like a true Egyptian bride.

We got into the car, which was blaring wedding music from its open windows. As we drove, my soon-to-be sister-in-law leaned from the passenger side window to *zagrat* some more, and my soon-to-be brother-in-law tapped the horn to alert people on the street that a bride and groom were passing. People yelled congratulations to us from passing cars and from the sidewalks, hooting and clapping and wishing us a thousand blessings: "*Alf mabrooooooook!*"

We arrived only three hours late for the ceremony, practically nothing by Egyptian standards. It was held beneath lit palm trees in a cafe on a bank of the Nile River. Because my *wali* was back in the States, Mohamed's best friend stood in his place. After we exchanged vows and signed our marriage contract—punctuated by many more trills from the women—Mohamed and I slipped off to stand together on a bridge and look at the river flowing below us.

"We're married," I said, as we looked at each other in amazement.

"Yeah," he answered with a huge smile. "We are."

Mohamed doesn't speak Spanish and he's never eaten a taco in his life, but he's willing to spout heavily accented and antiquated declarations of love straight out of a Castilian Spanish-Arabic dictionary from the 1920s, and to eat the *chiles rellenos* and *lengua de res* I make for him. And every once in a while, he takes me in his arms and tells me that I am his *media naranja*—the other half to his orange.

I spent so much time looking for what I thought would make me happy, but in the end, God had my soul mate waiting for me in the unlikeliest of places. I guess I was always meant for a Cairene kind of love.

It Will Be Beautiful

Yasmine Khan

When I was eight years old, I had only two goals in life: I would become a professional Frisbee player, and I would marry MacGyver. Instead, adulthood led me to a career of desk jobs, and a series of potential relationships left me wondering why I even bothered to open myself up to men other than MacGyver in the first place.

Not that there was a shortage of men. There was, for example, the man who emailed me via my blog, who was a Pakistani Pashtun, like I was; he spoke both Pashto and Hindko, the languages of my heritage, but we differed too widely in other aspects. There was the man about whom, on a flight to Spain for vacation one year, I created a pros/cons list in my notebook (as the daughter of an accountant, I would have created a spreadsheet had I had my laptop), but the cons won. There was the man who wanted to marry me, yet when I asked him to travel to my home in San Francisco so that we could finally meet in person, his response was a bewildering "I don't see why I should."

By the time I turned twenty-eight, in early 2009, I was weary of the search. That spring, I took to heart the reminder of my cousin, who is also my best friend: "Your primary commitment is not to any man. You are already in a committed relationship with *yourself*," she pointed out. Her words reminded me to step back and focus on personal dreams that had nothing to do with falling in love, getting married, or creating a family. I had thought seriously about attending graduate school for years, but now I finally applied for master's programs. While waiting to hear back on the results of my applications, I continued working—fundraising for an educational institution—which included national travel, twelve-hour workdays, and a sharp decrease in my social life.

By winter, preparations were under way for my little sister's wedding, and chaos descended as I struggled to juggle wedding planning with my professional commitments. In December, I went on a business trip to Las Vegas, the hometown of my future brother-in-law, Ali. I shamelessly mentioned Ali and his well-established family to everyone I encountered, smiling at the recognition and sheer delight that crossed their faces.

On my last night there, I curled up in an armchair in my hotel room and laughingly wrote on his Facebook wall, "Ali! Why didn't you *tell* me that all I needed for a full background check on you was to come to Las Vegas?!"

Just minutes later, I had an email notification from Facebook: One of Ali's best friends, Yasser, a stranger to me, had commented on my wall post, "Yasmine, were you at the event this evening in Vegas?"

"I try not to discuss work on Facebook," I replied immediately. "But yes, I was. P.S. Ali is my future brother-in-law!"

Yasser expressed surprise at what a small world it was, having noticed me at the event without knowing my connection to his friend. He offered some recommendations for local breakfast places, then added, "Why didn't Ali tell me he had family coming to town? I would have given you a full background report!"

Two weeks later, my family and I traveled to Portland, Oregon, where Ali's family hosted the wedding reception. Our first night in the city included an informal dinner at a local restaurant, where two dozen of us settled around a sprawling table. Yasser and I, formally introduced for the first time, ended up next to each other after a musical chairs–style shuffling of seats; he admitted months later that he had been silently praying to God for such a happy accident as soon as I walked through the door. Sitting side by side, we talked about languages, Pakistan, Bollywood films, stories about my brother-in-law, their mutual friends, Yasser's leadership role in an organization whose work I admired, his mother's death from cancer just a few months prior—and a *lot* about my job, the last thing I wanted to discuss while on vacation. I steered the conversation as much as I could toward lighter subjects, enjoying our smooth banter and repartee.

The next day was the wedding reception. There was a grand entrance, complete with music and Arabic chanting; a fountain of colorful punch; *dabka*, a feet-stamping Arab folk dance; and—my favorite part!—cake cutting with an heirloom Palestinian sword. But mostly what I remember is turning my head at one point to see Yasser, and sending him an informal wave and a casual greeting: "How goes it?" He immediately took that as a signal to approach my table, where he spent most of our conversation expressing his admiration for the organization I worked for.

"Please let me know if you need help with future events in Vegas," he said, giving me his phone number. I tapped it into my BlackBerry, then paused awkwardly. Was I supposed to reciprocate? The conversation had been mainly work related; clearly, he was interested only in my job. I gave him my phone number, too, chalking it up to professional networking. Inwardly, though,

I was intrigued and wondered if our brief exchanges could lead to something more.

The wedding ended; friends and family returned home to reminisce over photographs and shared memories. I added Yasser as a friend on Facebook and was promptly invited to click over to his profile so that I could view the photographs he had taken at my sister's wedding. In addition to the images I expected, I was greeted by an "About" section on his profile that listed him as single but that added simply, "My greatest pride is to be my daughter's father." *Huh?* I clicked through albums documenting the growth of a little baby into a little girl with a confident, dimpled smile. She seemed like a happy, outgoing child, whether alone or photographed with her father.

Even as I wondered what I was getting into, Yasser's one-line "About" section helped reassure me as to the sort of person he was. Any man who was proud to be a father, who seemed to be single-handedly raising a child—and well, at that—was worth taking a second look at. Divorce and single parenthood didn't seem to be good enough reasons to wipe a man off the list. In all my years of making lists of the qualities that I was looking for in a potential spouse, I had never considered adding, "Must never have been previously married. Must have no children." How could I have listed those as deal breakers, when I had never thought they would pertain to my relationships in the first place?

Still, my rationalizations notwithstanding—*It's not as if I'm marrying him today; I'm just opening myself up to possibilities again;* and *He's Ali's friend; therefore he must be a good person*—I couldn't help but fire off an email to my cousin the next day: "He's my age, and HE HAS A SIX-YEAR-OLD DAUGHTER!" Her response calmed me: "That's really unexpected, but maybe he'll tell you the story one of these days." I reminded myself to take it one day at a time, get to know the man, and just see where things went.

Slowly, we connected over Facebook comments, emails every

few days, and intermittent text messaging. Many of our conversations were about books, sharing recommendations and discussing novels we had both read. One night in late January, as we
wound down a Gmail Chat conversation, he said, "I have a book
of Allama Iqbal's poems in English. I can send it to you, if you
want it. Let me know, and I'll drop it in the mail."

I paused for a few minutes—sharing one's address is still such
an intimate thing, even in this digital day and age—but then sent
him my mailing address, along with a note, only half joking, "I'm
trusting that you're not some scary stalker."

The book arrived a few days later. I had to acknowledge receipt
of the gift, so I gulped, picked up the telephone, and called Yasser
for the first time. I reached him as he was picking up his daughter
and her friends from school. While he and I spoke, I could hear
little-girl voices chattering in the background, and the sound
made me smile, even as it rattled me. *What the hell am I getting myself into*? Still, our conversation flowed lightly and easily.
I laughed often and did not feel at all awkward. When I hung
up and squinted at my phone, I was shocked to find the call had
lasted an entire hour.

Our next phone conversation lasted two hours, and was about
more than just books. We talked about our families, childhoods,
and work. I was baffled. Who was this man? He was only four
months older than I, but he had already been through life experiences I was nowhere close to encountering or understanding.
What was the story of his daughter and his divorce? I could not
understand how I felt so at ease talking to him over the phone
and through emails, when I was inconsistent in communicating
with even my closest friends, who shook their heads at my "Great
Wall of Yazzo," the impenetrable fortress surrounding my heart.

Over the next several months, Yasser and I discussed shared
interests through emails and Gmail Chat, and our sporadic but
lengthy phone conversations continued. I still had questions and

concerns, but I preferred to focus on getting to know him organically. In mid-May, I attended an event in Southern California and invited Yasser to join me. Seeing him after months apart did not bring any of the disconnection I had feared between our online and in-person interactions. Wholly comfortable, we sat talking for hours in our hotel lobby before the evening program.

We spent the next day at the beach. The weather was gray, the company impeccable. We prayed on the sand, walked the piers, talked endlessly. I treated Yasser to his first gelato. Coming from the desert, he was mesmerized by the water and greenery. I was charmed by his attention to things that I often took for granted

We parted at the airport, after expressing our mutual appreciation for the shared weekend. If our farewell felt a bit stiff and formal to me, it was because we still had not addressed the proverbial elephant in the room. Half an hour later, however, my BlackBerry lit up with an email from him. *What? He just dropped me off!* Baffled, I clicked on the note:

"Salaam, Yasmine. I remember you once wrote that eligible Muslim guys are too afraid to show direct interest in you. I'm writing to let you know that I'm interested in you. I feel we have great rapport and I am very impressed by your character (among many other things about you). I'm not seeking a commitment now, but rather an opportunity for us to get to know one another more. If the feeling is not mutual, I hope we can still be friends."

I was relieved (*finally, thank God, an acknowledgment!*) and panicked (*how will this work?!*), amid a maelstrom of other emotions. I paced the airport gates, bought hot chocolate to calm my unsettled nerves, then sat in an empty corner and slowly, carefully tapped out a response just before boarding my flight:

"Thank you for the note, and for letting me know of your interest. Yes, it's refreshing to get this out in the open. You're someone I'd like to get to know better, too—and while I have to be very honest and admit that there are things about this situation, on both sides, that make me nervous about how it could be complicated, I'm open to seeing where this could go."

Yasser was relieved, and elated. He wrote back expressing his willingness to address any concerns I had. I thought it was too early to talk about my misgivings about being a second mother to his child, and my lack of knowledge about his previous relationship, so instead I admitted that geography was a big concern. I would be starting graduate school that fall, and I had no intention of leaving the Bay Area for the next two years (*if ever*, I added in my head). That was nothing to be concerned about, Yasser replied. He loved the Bay Area and its Muslim community, and would have no qualms about relocating there. He also shared what he was looking for in a potential spouse—a woman of character, one who would speak the truth, have a forgiving heart, and love and accept his daughter.

I added my own preferences: a relationship that was built on flexibility, open communication, and equal partnership. A man who would eschew stubbornness and pride—I was Pashtun, and knew all too well that my hardheaded people came preprogrammed with such qualities!—in favor of compromise and trust. A man who would respect my work in cultural competency and community building, and would understand that, for me, "community" meant not just the Muslim community or the South Asian community, but the community at large. I wrote, "My first priority is always, always my family and friends, of course—but my heart is big enough to hold the world."

Even as my friends grinned excitedly at my updates about Yasser over the next several months, I wondered if I was completely insane to be considering marrying a man who was divorced and raising a six-year-old daughter.

I knew Yasser was a good man, and felt that we had the potential to grow into a solid relationship. Still, I could not help but be paralyzed some days, questioning what the future would hold:

Would he be able to find a job in the Bay Area so that he could move there? Would his daughter accept me? How would she feel about another female's sharing Yasser's attention? Did I even feel ready to be a mother? (No. But, then again, does anyone ever feel ready?) Could I be a compassionate and capable mother? And how would my parents feel about this? Whenever I felt unsettled or unsure, I went for long walks in downtown Berkeley or along the pier at the marina.

As we got to know each other more deeply, I began asking Yasser more questions about his daughter, whom he affectionately called Lemon. I initiated conversations about her, expressing interest in her personality and the goings-on in his day-to-day life as a single parent. He answered my questions in depth, and tried to dispel concerns I had about playing a maternal role. But even though he was confident, I couldn't help but be worried.

"This relationship is not just about you and me," I said. "It's also about Lemon."

Meanwhile, though, it helped to hear his stories about her: "I am puzzled by Lemon's fashion sense: hijab and knee-length shorts." Later: "I want to see *Iron Man 2*. Lemon wants to see *Shrek Forever*. Guess who wins that debate *and* gets ice cream?"

It was clear that he adored her. Beyond the photos I had seen and the stories I had heard, though, I knew nothing about her, nor did she about me. In June 2010, she turned seven years old and I texted Yasser to say, "Happy birthday to Lemon!" but made no attempt to speak to her directly. I was wary of direct contact; he and I were still in the early stages of our relationship, and both of us felt it was too soon to involve her.

Instead, we focused on sharing the details of our respective days, and I smiled, despite my misgivings, at how huge a role fatherhood played in Yasser's life: He ironed Lemon's school uniform and made her lunch; helped her with school projects and ensured she hadn't "forgotten" to complete her homework;

mopped the floors and vacuumed the carpets every weekend, finding Lemon's dolls and books and UNO cards wedged between the sofa and the wall.

As we became closer, we discussed topics such as faith, parenting, education, money, sex, gender relations, career ambitions, and more, trying our best to balance "serious" conversations—a necessary evil, we decided—with our usual lighthearted exchanges. Yasser was forthcoming with answers to any questions I had about his previous marriage to Lemon's mother, with whom Lemon spent summers on the East Coast. Beyond our initial, in-depth conversations, though, we rarely talked about his ex-wife, choosing to focus instead on our own unfolding story.

One morning, I left Yasser a rambling voicemail in Hindko, the dialect I speak with my family, which some Pakistanis dismiss as "not a real language." I knew he wouldn't understand most of it, but he responded, "I enjoyed listening to that five times." Hindko is a deeply personal part of my heritage and family life, and I was moved nearly to tears when he approached my voicemail with such sincere curiosity, joy, and openheartedness. His request to hear me speak Hindko again removed some of the highest walls around my heart. For me, that exchange was a milestone, unexpected and sweet.

In November he came to visit, so that we could see each other for the first time since May. Spending time with him in person felt just like talking to him online or over the phone, with the added benefit of his physical presence. As we explored San Francisco together, Yasser took in the organic farmers' markets, Vespa scooters, colorful graffiti, and architecture, and smiled. "Being here makes me feel like I know you more and understand the person you are." I felt a tremendous sense of loss when he left. I had not expected how quickly I would become used to his presence. All of a sudden, my happy-go-lucky, joyful life felt lonelier with him gone.

At the beginning of December 2010, I left my job to focus on graduate school; Yasser lost his job the same week. In the midst of writing final papers to finish my semester, I tried my best to be available and supportive. "Allah has written even more beautiful things for you. I believe this," I wrote. "May you have all the strength, optimism, and patience you need. And may your next job, and next adventure, be even more fulfilling and inspiring, *inshAllah. It will be beautiful*," I repeated over and over. Soon, it became my personal mantra for our relationship. Whenever I was exasperated by our disagreements or aggravated at the geographical distance between us, I would repeat: *It will be beautiful.*

Later that month, we met again—this time with Lemon. She and I had spoken on the phone a few times after her father's November visit, so she now knew of me, although the intricacies of our association were—I thought—lost on her. I was just another friend of her father's, and she remembered me from his photographs ("You guys went to the *beach*!").

The first evening we met, she smiled at me guilelessly and exclaimed, "You look so pretty today!" I was immediately charmed. She was seven years old and tall for her age, with gorgeous, glossy hair, enough confidence to fill an entire room, and more perception than I had given her credit for. The first night, as we walked into a room together, she said casually, "People think you're my mother!"

"Which people?" I asked, stunned. "The people at the restaurant earlier? Or in the elevator?"

"Just people!" she said. I realized that she knew how she and I together must appear to outsiders. The exchange made me feel closer to this little girl who so clearly needed a mother, but it also served as a reminder to tread carefully.

• • •

We went back to the beach, this time with Lemon. She found a bamboo stick and scribbled our collective initials across the sand, complete with plus-symbols and hearts to tie all our names together. I was touched. My heart cracked open to love her at the point when she wrote, "I love you, Ya-Ya!"

During the rest of the weekend, we played UNO together, went hiking, and watched my favorite movie, *The Princess Bride*. Yasser held my hand during the movie, and I felt such over-whelming emotion, I didn't know whether to smile or burst into tears.

At the airport, I gave them both long hugs good-bye, not wanting to let go. "My hands are already homesick for yours," I wrote to him. Lemon now became a much more active part of the relationship, in a way that I found delightful. I would often leave class to find I had a voicemail from her. One night, she said, "I hope we move to California and go to the beach and hang out with you, 'cause you're *so smart*." I laughed. Another voicemail demanded, "Could you please call my dad so I can talk to you?"

Finally, one day, Yasser asked her how she would feel if he were to marry me. "You belong together," she said confidently, "because you talk to each other so much." I had constantly wor-ried about what his daughter would think of me, and whether she would be able to accept and love me. And here she was, saying we belonged together. It was a beautiful gift, and the relief of it lifted a burden I had carried for almost a year.

I turned thirty in March 2011, and our added closeness made the milestone birthday even more special than I had anticipated. "I think your wall has been reduced to a knee-high fence," Yasser wrote to me at one point. "I can see your heart." A few weeks after my birthday, my sister and brother-in-law invited me to their home for dinner. I walked in—only to find Yasser hiding behind the door and Lemon dashing in from the kitchen! "Where did you *come* from?!" I exclaimed to them both, laughing.

"Did we surprise you?" Lemon asked.

"Best surprise ever!" I assured her, returning her hug as she squeezed her arms around my waist.

She handed me a colorful drawing containing lyrics to a cartoon theme song, interspersed with original lines: "I wish you can live with me and my family," and "u r the only 1" and "I love and miss u with all my heart." I was moved. The feeling was mutual.

The entire weekend reassured me that our relationship could work. Lemon was as charmed by San Francisco as her father had been, and I smiled to see how she took the beauty and uniqueness of the city in stride while remaining curious about everything we came across. From time to time, Lemon would throw her arms around me in a tight hug and I would hug her back, resting my chin on her glossy, thick hair that I couldn't keep my hands off. This little girl needed a mother. Although I had never been one myself, I knew enough to understand that it involved patience and love, and I felt I possessed enough of both. Motherhood was not something I could prepare for, but rather something I would have to throw myself into, with a simple prayer that the end result would be good, beautiful, and blessed.

Recognizing that my heart was already large enough to envelop Lemon into my life, and seeing how much she trusted me, brought me a sense of joy I had never known. There were innumerable moments when Yasser and I would exchange glances over Lemon's head, smiling at each other. We already felt like a family.

Yasser once wrote to me, "There is no way I can envision my future without you in it. We're beautiful together."

I wrote back, "We are indeed beautiful together. We have beautiful dreams for a beautiful life, and I truly believe that, *inshAllah*, God will work with us to make them all happen." The words signified our optimism, our tenderness with each other, our collective dreams for our shared future. Our mantra—*It will be beautiful*—denoted our absolute certainty that Yasser and I were the ones for each other, and our unshakeable faith that this story would continue unfolding in a blessed way.

What I have now is a relationship that, in some ways, defies the idea of the relationship I always thought I would have and yet, in other ways, fits everything for which I had ever prayed. Even with the analytical mind I inherited from my accountant father, I cannot—as I did with previous men—distill this relationship into Excel columns and lines of pros and cons.

There are still times when I wonder how we will make this work, and what this year will bring for us. Then Lemon calls me from her father's cell phone, chattering about her day, interspersing her stories with a simple "I *miss* you" or "I love you; I wish I can see you soon" or a giggling "You're *funny*!" And that's when I remember that even the best mathematical formulas cannot align the data on a spreadsheet if the numbers do not balance. But hearts align and balance instinctively, widening infinitely to encompass the world.

This is not just a love story about a man and a woman. It is also a love story about a little girl. It is not a story I would have had the imagination to write for myself, nor a story I would have believed I'd have the openness and capacity to live. This is a story only God could have written. And it is already beautiful.

Glossary

Abaya: "cloak"; long overgarment; robelike dress for women

Adhan: call to prayer

Alhamdulillah: "Praise be to God," an expression of gratitude

Allahu akbar: "God is greater"

Allahu alim: "God is the knower of all"; used colloquially as "God knows best"

Al-Talaq: decree of divorce

Asr: late-afternoon ritual prayer

As-salaam-alaikum (or "salaam"): "Peace be upon you"; used colloquially as a greeting or hello

Astaghfirullah: "I seek forgiveness from God"; used colloquially as "God forbid"

Ayah(s): verse(s) of the Qur'an

Baraka: spiritual blessing

Beta: term for daughter/son; also used as a term of endearment

Bismillahi rahmani rahim (*bismillah*): "In the Name of God, the Compassionate, the Merciful"

Burqa: a loose full-body and head covering for women

Chador: a full-body-length semicircle of fabric that is split open down the front, with an opening at the top worn by women

Choli: blouse

Dajjal: the Antichrist

Dawah: "issuing a summons" or "making an invitation"; usually denotes the proselytization of Islam

Dawood basha: Lebanese meatballs

Deen: "way of life" or "faith"

Desi: "one from our country"; usually refers to people from India, Pakistan, and Bangladesh

Dhikr: remembrance of God

Dua: personal supplication to God

Eid (Eid-al-Fitr): Muslim holiday that marks the end of Ramadan, the month of fasting

Fajr: predawn ritual prayer

Farangi: Westerner, foreigner

Gori/a: white person

Habibti (hababa): "sweetheart"; term of endearment

Hadith: saying of the Prophet Muhammad

Halal: religiously permissible

Halaqa: religious-study circle

Haram: religiously proscribed

Hijab: headscarf

Hijrah: migration

Iddat: three-month waiting period for women after the decree of divorce

Iftar: meal to break fast

Imam: minister; person who leads prayer

InshAllah: God willing

Isha: nighttime ritual prayer

Istikharah: special prayer for guidance

Jaanu (jaan, maman jaan): "darling"; term of endearment

Jamah: congregation

Jilbab: long, loose outer coat or garment for women

Jumma: Friday congregational prayer

Kali/a: dark-skinned or black

Katb kitab: marriage ceremony

Khimar: head scarf

Khutbas: religious sermon

Kibbeh: an Arab dish made of bulgur or rice and chopped meat

Kom el Shoqafa: historical archaeological catacombs in Alexandria, Egypt

Korma: South Asian dish, usually considered a type of curry

Kufi: skullcap

Kurta: tunic

Maghrib: evening ritual prayer

mashAllah: "whatever God wills"; expresses appreciation, joy, praise, or thankfulness for an event or person just mentioned

Masjid: mosque

Mehndi: henna

Muezzin: one who performs the call to prayer

Mumin: believer

Musallah: prayer space

Mutah: fixed-term marriage contract

Namaz/j: Urdu and Bengali for one of the five daily ritual prayers

Naseeha: wisdom or advice

Nikah: Islamic legal marriage contract

Niqab(i): face veil, or a woman who wears one

Raita: South Asian condiment made from yogurt and herbs

Rakat: one complete cycle of the ritual prayer

Ramadan: sacred month of fasting

Ras: syrup

Rishta: marriage proposal

Sajdah: prostration during ritual prayer

Salafi: a follower of an Islamic movement; in contemporary times, "Salafiyyah" has been associated with literalist approaches to Islamic theology

Salat: one of the five ritual daily prayer or additional prayers

Sayyid: a descendant of the Prophet Muhammad, peace be upon him

Shahada: declaration of faith

Shaikha: female religious teacher

Shalwar kamiz: traditional long tunic and pants worn in the Indian subcontinent by men and women

Shami: Syrian

Shami kebobs: Indian or Pakistani kebo

Shariah: "way" or "path"; code of conduct or body of Islamic law

Shaytan: Satan

Shi'a: follower of Shiite Islam

Subhan'Allah: "Glory be to God"; expression of gratitude or praise upon seeing or hearing something beautiful

Sunna: actions of the Prophet Muhammad

Sunni: follower of Sunni Islam, the largest branch of Islam

Surah: chapter of the Qur'an

Surah al-Fatiha: the opening chapter of the Qur'an

Tahajjud: night prayer

Tawaf: circumambulating around the kabah

Taqwa: God consciousness

Tasbih: prayer beads

Thobe(s): ankle-length garment, usually with long sleeves, like a robe; worn by men in the Middle East and East Africa

Ummah: "community" or "nation"; often refers to worldwide community of Muslims

Umrah: religious pilgrimage to Mecca at any time of the year aside from Hajj, the annual pilgrimage

Wali: legal guardian or representative

Wudu: ablution before prayer

Zabiha: ritually slaughtered meat

Zina: sexual intercourse outside of marriage

Contributors

TOLU ADIBA (pen name) is an American Muslim who from time to time peeks outside of the closet. She currently resides on the East Coast.

TANZILA "TAZ" AHMED is a writer, community organizer, and policy researcher based in Northern California. She founded South Asian American Voting Youth (SAAVY) and is a contributing blogger at SepiaMutiny.com, where she writes about pop, music, politics, and anything tied to a *desi* identity. Her writing has been featured in TheNation.com, Left Turn magazine, Angry Asian Man, MTV Iggy, Taqwacore Webzine, WireTap magazine, AlterNet, and PopandPolitics.com and has been published in the books *Mirror on America* and *Storming the Polls*. She also has two self-published chapbooks of poetry, *Secret Confessions* and *Diamond in the Rough*. She is currently working on a memoir about her journey to find purpose, love, poetry, and familial revolutionary history.

HUDA AL-MARASHI is an Iraqi American at work on a memoir about the impact of dual-identity on her marriage. Excerpts from this memoir are forthcoming in the anthologies *Becoming* and *In Her Place*. Her poem *TV Terror* is part of a touring exhibit commemorating the Mutanabbi Street Bombing in Baghdad. She holds a B.A. from Santa Clara University and a M.Ed. from

Framingham State College. She is a 2012 Creative Workforce Fellow, and she lives in Ohio with her husband and three children.

INSIYA ANSARI (pen name) is a writer who was raised in the San Francisco Bay Area.

MOLLY ELIAN CARLSON converted to Islam in 2005 and then converted to marriage in 2007, to the man of her dreams, literally. She was born in Minnesota but has lived in many other places, including Cairo, Egypt. She, her husband, and the Egyptian street cat she took in moved back to Minnesota in 2009 and live there currently. She loves to read and to write, and hopes to one day publish that novel that has been sitting in the back of her head for years.

PATRICIA M. G. DUNN received her MFA from Sarah Lawrence College, where she currently teaches creative writing. She was managing editor of *Muslim Wakeup!*, America's most popular Muslim online magazine, with over two hundred thousand monthly readers, from 2003 to 2008. Her fiction has appeared in *Global City Review*, the *Christian Science Monitor*, the *Village Voice*, the *Nation*, and *L.A.Weekly* and on Salon.com and Women's eNews, among other publications. Her work is anthologized in *Stories of Illness and Healing: Women Write Their Bodies*, published by Kent State University Press.

NOUR GAMAL (pen name) is a global nomad who was raised across the eastern United States and the Arabian Gulf. After failing to realize the Egyptian American dream of becoming an engineer or a doctor, she earned a BA in Middle Eastern studies and an LLM in human rights law instead. She is employed as a part-time freelance translator and a full-time bleeding heart and lives with her *farangi* husband and their four adorable computers in the UK.

ASIILA IMANI converted to Islam over thirty years ago and has followed the Jafari *madhab* for the last twenty. She has a BA in communications and sociology and did some graduate work in linguistics. She is a strong proponent of polygyny, viewing it as extended family ideally for the benefit of women. She writes about and counsels women on this topic. Asiila is a doula and home-birth midwife. She homeschooled her sons, twenty-seven and fifteen, and teaches language arts to other homeschooled children. She is currently studying the healing arts of homeopathy and reflexology.

LENA HASSAN (pen name) has been happily married to her husband for sixteen years, thanks to God and the veil of cyberspace. They have three children and currently live in Damascus, Syria, though the Internet allows her to keep a perpetual foot in her home country of America. Lena has worked as a software engineer, served as an administrative volunteer for an Islamic school in the United States, homeschooled her children, and edited an online literary journal. She is an aspiring fiction writer and recently published her first short story in a national magazine.

LEILA N. KHAN (pen name) lives and works in Northern California. She enjoys Italian films, classical music, and spending time in her kitchen. Her favorite places in the world are Strasbourg, Dubrovnik, and Maui.

YASMINE M. KHAN was born in Berkeley and has lived all over Northern California and in Barazai, Pakistan. She is a writer and photographer whose favorite things include gelato, high fives, and practicing terrible cartwheels with Lemon. She dreams not so secretly of traveling the world, learning how to swim, and making the perfect homemade strawberry shortcake. Her professional background lies in cultural competency training and fund development for nonprofit organizations and institutions of higher education. Yasmine studied human development at the University of California, Davis, and educational leadership at Mills College. She lives in the San Francisco Bay Area.

S.E. JIHAD LEVINE (Safiyyah) is a Muslim prison chaplain and is on the executive committee of the Pennsylvania Prison Chaplains Association in the United States. Safiyyah is also a freelance writer and has been published in magazines, journals, anthologies, and online venues. She is currently writing a series of booklets for the benefit of incarcerated Muslims, and enjoys indoor and outdoor gardening, photography, digital art, and jewelry making. She is also a principal and teacher at the Sunbury Islamic Center weekend school and is dedicated to *masjid* interfaith activities. She maintains a website at www.Shaalom2Salaam.com.

J. SAMIA MAIR is the author of two children's books, *Amira's Totally Chocolate World* and *The Perfect Gift*. She is a staff writer for *SISTERS* magazine and has been published in magazines, books, anthologies, scientific journals, and elsewhere. Prior to her current writing, she was on the faculty of the Johns Hopkins Bloomberg School of Public Health, where her research focused on reducing violence in and protecting the health of vulnerable populations. She also practiced law for over eight years, including several years in the appeals unit of the Philadelphia district attorney's office. She lives in the United States with her husband and two daughters, whom she homeschools.

MELODY MOEZZI is an Iranian American writer, speaker, author, attorney, and activist. Her first book, *War on Error: Real Stories of American Muslims*, earned her a 2007 Georgia Author of the Year Award. Melody is also a United Nations Global Expert with the UN Alliance of Civilizations and a member of the British

Council's Our Shared Future Opinion Leaders Network. She is a commentator on NPR's *All Things Considered* and a blogger for the *Huffington Post* and *Ms.* magazine. Her writings have appeared in publications around the world, including the *Washington Post*, the *Guardian*, the *Christian Science Monitor*, CNN.com, Al Arabiya, and the *Gulf Times*. She is also a regular blogger and columnist for *Bipolar* magazine.

NIJLA BASEEMA MU'MIN is a writer, filmmaker, and photographer from the San Francisco Bay Area. She is a 2007 graduate of UC Berkeley, and also attended Howard University's MFA film program. She was the recipient of the 2009 Paul Robeson Award for Best Feature Screenplay. At UC Berkeley, she served as a student teacher in June Jordan's Poetry for the People program. Her writing has appeared in the *Berkeley Poetry Review*, *Poets for Living Waters*, the *Diverse Voices Quarterly*, *Kweli Journal*, *Mythium: Journal of Contemporary Literature*, and the GirlChild Press anthology *Woman's Work: The Short Stories*. She is an MFA student in writing and film directing at the California Institute of the Arts.

ZAHRA NOORBAKHSH is a writer, actor, and stand-up comedian whose one-woman shows, "All Atheists Are Muslim" and "Hijab and Hammerpants," have appeared at the New York International Fringe Theater Festival, the San Francisco Theater Festival, and the Solo Performance Workshop Festival, to widespread critical acclaim. She graduated from UC Berkeley in 2006, with a degree in theater and performance studies. Though she began as a stand-up comic, Zahra's love of storytelling drew her into the world of theater and, ultimately, the art of short-story writing.

CHINYERE OBIMBA is in her final year at Harvard Medical School and is applying for residency in family medicine. She hopes to work with underserved populations, practice obstetrics, and participate in intervention planning for health promotion programs. Among her role models she counts her parents, Enyichukwu and Khalilah, who continue to show her what love and marriage are all about. She considers her younger brother, Chukwuemeka, who has autism, one of her life's inspirations. When she's not being a medical student, she enjoys dancing samba, listening to and singing Brazilian music, and writing. She also aspires someday to be a wife, a mother of three or four children, and the proud owner of a talking bird.

AIDA RAHIM is an engineer by training and a crime-TV aficionado in practice. She currently lives in the middle of southwest Virginia. She wasn't expecting to like this small town, but she wasn't expecting to meet and marry a small, hairy Pakistani man in Malaysia, either. She's pretty athletic and can probably beat you in most racket sports. She's also been getting excited about the barefoot-running movement.

AISHA C. SAEED was born and raised in South Florida. She is a teacher, attorney, and writer. She recently completed her first two novels. In her free time, Aisha enjoys traveling, reading, and blogging at www.aishaiqbal.blogspot.com. She lives in Atlanta, Georgia, with her husband and son.

DEONNA KELLI SAYED is a coffee-drinking, ghost-hunting American Muslim of global proportions. She has lived and traveled throughout the Muslim world, and her work has appeared in lifestyle magazines such as *Women This Month Bahrain* and *FACT* magazine. In 2006, Deonna helped establish Elham, the premier grassroots creative-arts group in the Persian Gulf. She is currently the editor of Ghostvillage.com and the author of *Paranormal Obsession: America's Fascination with Ghosts & Hauntings, Spooks & Spirits*, which is a cultural studies discussion regarding the role of paranormal-reality TV in a post-9/11 American society. Deonna's writing, regardless of the subject, ultimately examines the intersections of identity and culture. Visit her website, www.deonnakellisayed.com.

SUZANNE SYEDA SHAH is a Muslim poet and writer and a human activist. She was born in Saudi Arabia to Bengali parents and immigrated with her family to Los Angeles when she was four years old. After she completed her bachelor's degree in Islam and modernity at UC Berkeley, her passion for community service and the need to improve the health care system led her to pursue a career in medicine. She currently resides in California with her husband, Mika'il.

NAJVA SOL is an Iranian American writer, photographer, and multimedia artist. She received her BA in creative writing from the New School in New York City. Najva is cofounder of Lowbrow Society for the Arts, where she curates fabulous art extravaganzas. Her writing has been published in *Look Look* magazine, *amNewYork*, *Bitch* magazine, and more. Her photos and performances have been featured in the National Queer Arts Festival (2010 and 2011), numerous galleries, the Commonwealth Club, and the *Nuyorican*. Lowbrow Society has appeared in Nerve. com, *NewYork Press*, the *San Francisco Bay Guardian*, and *Time Out New York*. When not making art, Najva is active in various nonprofits that deal with some combination of art presenting, queer empowerment, and social justice.

ANGELA COLLINS TELLES lives in São Paulo, Brazil. Before her relocation, she served as the director of a private Islamic school in Orange County. She has appeared on CNN, *Inside Edition*, the *Today* show, Fox News, and Al Jazeera and has been featured in *People* magazine. Angela and her husband, Marcelo, are the proud parents of two sons, Gabriel and Ryan.

About the Editors

AYESHA MATTU is a writer and international development consultant. Her work has appeared in the International Museum of Women, *Religion Dispatches*, and the award winning blog, *Rickshaw Diaries*. She was selected a Muslim Leader of Tomorrow by the UN Alliance of Civilizations and the ASMA Society in 2009. Ayesha is working on a memoir about losing faith and finding love from which "The Opening" is excerpted. She lives with her husband and son in Northern California.

NURA MAZNAVI is a civil rights attorney. She has worked with migrant workers in Sri Lanka, on behalf of prisoners in California, and headed a national legal advocacy organization's program to end racial and religious profiling. Nura is working on a screenplay and several short stories. Nura's third love—after food and traveling—is California, where she was raised and lives currently.

Acknowledgments

This project began in the Name of God, the Merciful, the Compassionate. Our gratitude to Him, and prayers that this effort will be filled with *baraka*.

This book would not have been possible without the support and encouragement of our families and friends.

Almost five years ago we came to our friend and mentor Safir Ahmed with the seed for this book. Over countless weekends in his gorgeous Noe Valley apartment he generously devoted his time and expertise to making it a reality.

Randy Nasson has consistently talked us down from the ledge and from self-destructing. He spent years helping brainstorm ideas, believing in us when we were ready to give up, and providing the time and space to work without which this book would not exist. And, he came up with the brilliant title.

If not for our fairy godparents, David Sterry and Arielle Eckstut, this book would have languished as a book proposal. David and Arielle, winning the San Francisco LitQuake Pitchapalooza in 2010 was a much-needed boost to our confidence, but the real prize was the consultation with you, and the enthusiasm, insight, and connections you so generously shared.

Laura Mazer, thank you for believing in this project and your willingness to take a risk on unknown writers and an untested market. Your editorial vision for all the book could be pushed us to reach the full potential of ourselves and this collection.

Soft Skull Press epitomizes the best in independent publishers. Thank you for respecting our intentions and context, from the title and content to the cover design.

Rebecca Spence, thank you for sharing your craft and teaching us to become editors. You went above and beyond the call of duty because of your passion for this project.

We procrastinated for as long as possible on our individual stories, and they were only written because of Kathleen McClung's memoir class at the San Francisco Writing Salon. Kathleen, your gentle shaping of our stories gave us the courage to write.

To the wonderful ladies of our memoir class, Ayesha's virtual writing group, and Christine Sowder, thank you for reading countless versions of our stories and for providing invaluable, constructive feedback.

Thank you to all those who charted this course before us and so willingly shared their wisdom with wit and warmth to help us on our own journey to publication and beyond: Wajahat Ali, Reza Aslan, Tamim Ansary, Zahir Janmohamed, Fatima Ashraf, Zahra Suratwala, and Kathy LeMay.

Sharing our personal stories has not only been challenging for us, but also in some ways for our parents. We recognize that in telling our stories we are also telling part of yours. Your love, encouragement, and support allowed us to honestly share our lives.

Our siblings—Rabia and Aamna Mattu, Hasna, Khalid, and Riyad Maznavi—thank you for helping us keep it real with a healthy dose of laughter and perspective.

Thank you to our support networks: Our *halaqa* for keeping us spiritually grounded; David Evans for calmly and willingly stepping into the whirlwind; Sawssan Ahmed and Arshad Ali for hours of IM therapy; Kathie Tsoukalas, Salma Malik, and Erin Sharkey Carter for their unconditional love; and Marcy Michaud Franck for her friendship, astute memory, and incredible editing and graphic design feedback.

Finally, our deepest gratitude to the hundreds of women who trusted us and shared their lives and loves. Your honesty and courage moved and inspired us. We are proud to stand beside you.

Questions for Discussion

1. What are some common cultural understandings of Muslim women/men? How do these stories complicate these cultural understandings?

2. Culture and religion are intertwined. What are some ways that the women in this anthology balance their faith and American identity with their search for love?

3. What did you find especially surprising or compelling in these stories or about these women?

4. Whose story did you identify with most strongly, and why?

5. Discuss the idea of being honest with your parents (or children) about sex and other relationship issues. How do some of the authors handle this and how did you do so in your life?

6. How did your religious upbringing contribute to who you are today?

7. If you believe in a religion that has a sacred scripture, do you know what every word means and adhere to every command? If not, why not?

8. Some of the authors discuss juggling family expectations and the search for love. How is their experience similar or dissimilar to yours? Did familial expectations, race/ethnicity, religion, or socioeconomic factors play a role in your search for a partner?

9. Are there any passages in the book you would like to share (or have already shared) with your friends or family?

10. In the introduction, the editors explained why they collected these stories. Do you think the editors were successful in their aims? Why or why not?